CITIZENS
of
CONVENIENCE

EARLY AMERICAN

HISTORIES

Douglas Bradburn, John C. Coombs,

and S. Max Edelson, Editors

Winner of the Walker Cowen Memorial Prize

for an outstanding work of scholarship

in eighteenth-century studies

CITIZENS *of* CONVENIENCE

The Imperial Origins of American Nationhood

on the U.S.-Canadian Border

LAWRENCE B. A. HATTER

UNIVERSITY OF VIRGINIA PRESS

Charlottesville and London

University of Virginia Press
© 2017 by the Rector and Visitors of the University of Virginia
All rights reserved
Printed in the United States of America on acid-free paper

First published 2017
First paperback edition published 2025

ISBN 978-0-8139-3954-4 (cloth)
ISBN 978-0-8139-5363-2 (paper)
ISBN 978-0-8139-3955-1 (e-book)

1 3 5 7 9 8 6 4 2

Library of Congress Cataloging-in-Publication Data
is available from the Library of Congress

Cover art: Detail from *Trigonometrical Survey of the Falls of Niagara*, drafted by W. S. Haines from an 1841 survey by E. R. Blackwell, engraved by Endicott. From James Hall, *Geology of New York, Part IV,* Albany: Carroll and Cook, 1843.

For Beth

CONTENTS

Acknowledgments / ix

Introduction / 1

1. "You Damn Yankee What Brought You Here?" / 15

2. "It Shall at All Times Be Free to His Majesty's Subjects" / 47

3. "To Guard the National Interest against the Machinations of Its Enemies" / 78

4. "The Equivocal Attributes of American Citizen and British Subject" / 104

5. "We Ought to Have the Trade within Our Awen Country" / 135

6. "When the American Stripes Alone Protect the Western Hemisphere" / 163

7. "British Subjects Are Always Black Sheep" / 192

Epilogue: "The Gallant Champions of British Influence" / 203

Notes / 209

Selected Bibliography / 245

Index / 259

ACKNOWLEDGMENTS

My earliest memory of writing is of having strived to complete a story of a few sentences and wondering how anyone ever managed to come up with enough things to say to write an entire book! What I have learned in the thirty years since then is that no one does it alone. This book, like all others, is a collaborative product, born of casual chats over coffee or gin and the far more formal process of peer review. I am profoundly grateful to all those who have helped to make this book possible.

Jeff Pasley first introduced me to the early American West when I began my graduate studies. What follows, then, is his fault. Jeff also introduced me to Peter Onuf, who, ironically, needs no introduction to anyone who has read the acknowledgments of so many young scholars. His uncanny ability to draw out the broader significance of his students' work is the stuff of legend. Peter is the most generous of mentors, sharing his energy and insights with both his own graduate students and junior scholars far beyond Charlottesville. I will always consider myself lucky to have been his student.

The University of Virginia is a wonderful place to study early American history. The origins of this book lie in the generous responses of the Early American and Transatlantic seminarians to far too many draft dissertation chapters and aspiring articles. In particular, I wish to thank Patrick Griffin (now of Notre Dame), Max Edelson, Christa Dierkshiede, Adam Jortner, Whitney Martinko, Armin Mattes, Brian Murphy, Martin Öhman, John Ragosta, Dana Stefanelli, and Russell Stoermer. Although not fortunate enough to be early Americanists, I was also supported by the friendship of Brent Jones, Chris Loomis, Logan Sawyer, Scott Spencer, and the odious James Wilson.

This book was made possible by the generous support of a number of different institutions. Fellowships from Harvard University's Baker Library, the Bentley Historical Library and the William L. Clements Library at the University of Michigan, and the Gilder Lehrman Institute of American History in New York allowed me to consult valuable manuscript collections. The Canadian government and the International Council for Canadian Studies funded research in Montreal, Ottawa, and Toronto. The Bankard Fund for Political Economy, the Corcoran Department of History, and the

Graduate School of Arts and Sciences all supported my graduate studies at Virginia. The generosity of the Thomas Jefferson Foundation allowed me to write my dissertation in the bucolic setting of the International Center for Jefferson Studies at Monticello. At Washington State University, the award of a New Faculty Seed Grant, funding from the College of Arts and Sciences, and the many contributions of Ray Sun and Steve Kale from the History Department's Pettyjohn and Converse Funds helped me to complete my manuscript and the production of this book in a timely manner.

Correspondence, comments, and conversations with a wide range of wonderful colleagues and friends have shaped this book in many different ways. Martin and Whitney have remained dear friends and trusted advisers since we left Charlottesville. I have been fortunate to work with generous and supportive colleagues at both the University of Nevada and Washington State University. Catherine Cangany, Peter Kopp, James E. Lewis, Jr., Dael Norwood, Bill Rowley, and Susan Gaunt Sterns have all helped me along the way, whether they realized it or not. In addition, I presented an earlier version of chapter 4 to the Pacific Northwest Early Americanist group organized by Richard Johnson of the University of Washington. Emily Anderson and Clif Stratton both read the entire thing. I am proud to say that I have finally made good on publishing the third book from our writing group. I thank them for their comradeship. I also owe a debt to Dick Holway, Anna Kariel, and Morgan Myers at the University of Virginia Press and to my copyeditor, Margaret Hogan, for helping to guide my manuscript through the arcane process of publication. The generous advice of the Press's two anonymous reviewers greatly improved this book. Thank you, whoever you are!

It is a long way from Sussex to the Palouse, and my parents helped to make that journey possible by instilling in me an abiding interest in learning and a deep respect of knowledge. They kindled my ambition without weighing me down with expectation. I also wish to thank my parents-in-law for their support and understanding as I dragged their daughter from coast to coast. During my frequent visits to Detroit during the early stages of my research, Fred and Janet Gibson provided a home away from home in Motown.

This book is dedicated to my wife, Beth, who has lived with the highs and lows of my scholarly travails for all of our lives together. It is impossible to think of this book without remembering the ways that it is intertwined with the birth of our three children and our family's migration across North America from Columbia to Charlottesville to Reno and (finally) to Pullman. She is the rock on which we have built our lives and, without question, the reason why things have always turned out for the best.

CITIZENS
of
CONVENIENCE

INTRODUCTION

The London newspapers revealed the long-awaited peace preliminaries between Great Britain and the United States of America to the British public on the morning of January 29, 1783. Londoners awoke to learn that their former countrymen across the Atlantic Ocean were now foreigners. After eight years of war, George III's formal recognition that thirteen of Britain's former American colonies were "free Sovereign and independent States" came as little surprise. But Britons were shocked to read about the extensive territory embraced by the United States. The press reported that the new boundary separating Britain's remaining North American colonies and the American Republic, running "from the north west Angle of Nova Scotia" to the "River Missisippi," had granted the vast region of the trans-Appalachian West to the United States.[1]

Merchants in London mobilized to oppose the new border. Two days after the peace terms were announced, the committee of merchants trading to the province of Quebec met in the New York Coffee House to draw up a petition opposing the treaty. It must have been difficult for the merchants to imagine how the British peace commissioner, Richard Oswald, could have framed a boundary settlement more damaging to their trade in furs and peltries with the Native peoples of the Great Lakes and the trans-Appalachian West. The proposed running of the line transferred control of nearly every fort, trading post, portage, and river to the United States. The merchants explained to Prime Minister William Petty, Lord Shelburne, that if Oswald did not renegotiate the proposed boundary, "the whole Trade with the Indians must be entirely cut off from the province of Quebec."[2]

Shelburne did not think that the border would make any difference to the merchants because he was convinced that the British Empire and the American Republic would trade freely with one another. In a meeting held a few days after the merchants had drafted their petition, the prime minister assured them that the two countries would enjoy a perfect reciprocity in commercial affairs.[3] The merchants heard the same story from Oswald. The diplomat explained to them that there was "nothing in the Treaty to hinder an Englishman passing and transporting Goods *over all or any part*

1

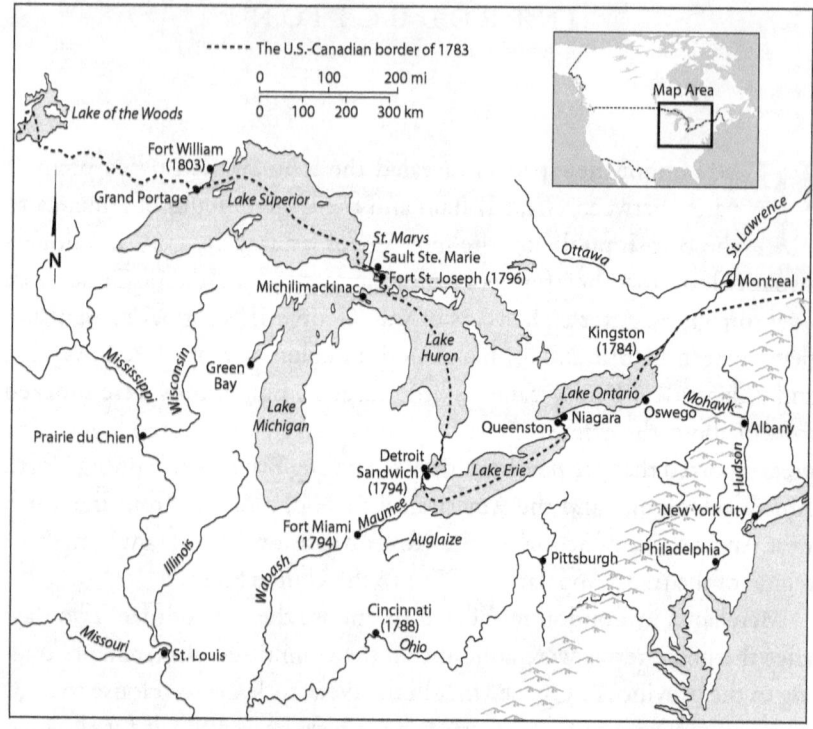

The Montreal fur trade and the border of 1783. (Map by Bill Nelson)

of America." Oswald predicted that Indian hunters would cross the border "with as little difficulty as one may go out of Mid[d]lesex into Essex."[4] Traveling between Quebec and the neighboring American states would be no different than leaving one English county for another. In other words, Oswald anticipated that there would be no barriers to free movement between the United States and the British Empire. Moreover, the minister produced a copy of the first plan of a treaty, from October 1782, in which "it was stated that an Englishman in America should be considered in all matters of Commerce, as an American. And an American in Engd., the same as an Englishman."[5] Independence might now mean that Americans and Britons lived under different jurisdictions, but for Shelburne and Oswald, they were essentially still one people.

With the benefit of two centuries of hindsight, it is all too easy to dismiss Shelburne and Oswald as sore losers who refused to face the new reality of American independence. But they were not simply engaging in wishful thinking when they looked to a future in which Britons and Americans would remain closely intertwined. The American Republic emerged from a civil war within the British Empire that remained incomplete in 1783. While the conflict equally divided Britain's twenty-six North American colonies between those that remained loyal and those that broke away to form the United States, there was no such clear division among the peoples of the former British Empire.[6] British Americans from the thirteen rebellious colonies fought both for and against independence. As historian Maya Jasanoff has shown, there was no demographic determinism that could predict who would become a loyalist or a patriot during the American Revolution. Rather, individual circumstances shaped volatile political loyalties among people who were often reluctant to pick sides.[7] This ambiguity persisted after the war as the peoples of the American Republic and the British Empire continued to intermingle through migration, travel, and trade. The fact that Great Britain and the United States fought a second civil war in 1812 helps us to realize that the predictions that Shelburne and Oswald made thirty years earlier were not all that far from the mark.[8] The American people were not present at the Founding.

This book tells the story of how the northern border helped to make the American people. The idea that a distinct American people represented a sovereign nation was central to the United States' claim to nationhood. Thomas Jefferson invoked this sovereign right on behalf of the American nation to dissolve the political bands connecting them to the British people in the Declaration of Independence. The idea of an American people was essential to the self-enacting sovereignty of the United States in 1776, but it was a useful fiction rather than a political reality.[9] The sociologist John Torpey argues that the ability of nation-states to monopolize the "means of movement" is an essential part of establishing nations as a distinct membership group. The facility of nation-states to control movement across territorial boundaries ultimately depends on the capacity of their agents to identify their own nationals and the nationals of other nation-states as mutually exclusive groups.[10] If people can freely cross the territorial boundaries of the nation-state, it becomes increasingly hard to determine who is a member of the nation. The northern border was a critical site of state formation during the first forty years of the American Republic because it was a place where U.S. agents could regulate people's movement to distinguish between American nationals and the nationals of other states in the eighteenth-century Atlantic World. In this way, the American national state preceded the American nation.

This is also the story of how citizens of convenience forced the border into being. Like eighteenth-century merchant ships flying flags of convenience to help them navigate foreign waters, citizens of convenience switched between nationalities to aid their free movement across national borders. This is not a book about the cultural meaning of citizenship nor is it a study of nations as imagined communities.[11] Rather, it views citizenship as a form of nationality, a legal status denoting membership of a national state. Whatever the difference between the philosophical underpinnings of citizenship and subjecthood, they are both forms of nationality that identify an individual as part of an exclusive membership community, be it a republic or a monarchy. For people who found ways to move among different nationalities, citizenship was a strategy that allowed them to avoid the exclusivist demands of emerging nation-states. We tend to think of citizenship as an inherently empowering thing. We focus on the rights of citizenship as a liberating force in American history. Indeed, the story of American freedom is the tale of the expansion of citizenship to include groups who have suffered from ascriptive inequality, whether defined by race, class, religion, gender, sexuality, or something else.[12] While the creation of an American nation in the late eighteenth and early nineteenth centuries unquestionably involved the exclusion of subaltern groups, such as American Indians and enslaved peoples, from membership in the national community, citizenship also constrained the political behavior of those individuals who did enjoy the full rights of citizenship by demanding their monogamous allegiance to the state. Such ideas were not fully formed during the Age of Atlantic Revolutions when the nation-state remained a protean concept.[13] Consequently, it is a mistake to assume that it was inevitable that the United States would assume the form and dimensions that it did during the course of the nineteenth and twentieth centuries.

Citizens of Convenience moves beyond narrow national histories of the Founding of the American Republic by investigating the intersection of nationhood, empire, and commerce. Independence was not born of some isolationist or autarkic impulse to separate the American nation from the irredeemably corrupt Old World. Rather, scholars now recognize that the Founders saw the American Revolution as a way for the United States to join the European Republic, the protean system of international law that evolved from the Treaty of Westphalia (1648), which bound together the sovereign nations of Europe.[14] The United States aspired for Europeans to recognize it as a nation among equals. At the same time, American policymakers were concerned with protecting their vast imperial domain in the West from European rivals. Commerce was one of the most important ways in which the newly independent United States would engage with the world. The American Revolution promised to free the former residents of Britain's North American colonies from the mercantilist restrictions of the Navigation Acts, which had prevented them from legally trading with other European powers. But Thomas Jefferson's and James Madison's approach to commerce was driven by a pragmatic commitment to imperial expansion in the North American West as well as an ideological interest in reforming the geopolitics of the Atlantic World.[15] Commerce might have the power to reform the international state system by promoting peace among nations, but, if managed correctly, it was also a powerful force for empire.

In the same way that North America was imperfectly integrated into the system of treaties that underpinned the European Republic as a law-bound community of nations, commercial diplomacy among European powers often distinguished among the more liberal customs observed between European nations and the exclusionary systems applied to European colonies overseas.[16] Commercial treaties between European powers frequently granted foreign merchants the privilege of residing and trading in one another's European domains while prohibiting foreigners from trading with their North American colonies. For example, the commercial treaty agreed between Great Britain and France at Utrecht in 1713 promised that their respective subjects would enjoy the "reciprocal and entirely perfect liberty of navigation and commerce," but only in the "kingdoms, states, dominions, and provinces of their Royal Majesties in Europe."[17] The treaty made no provision at all for trade between British and French colonies in North America and the Caribbean. Even when European powers did grant commercial concessions in North America to their rivals, these privileges were limited and not reciprocal. Spain offered British merchants unprecedented legal access to Spanish American ports in 1713 when it granted the *Asiento de negros*—the contract to supply African slaves to Spanish America—to Great Britain for thirty years. The Treaty of Utrecht offered Spanish merchants no equivalent commercial privileges in British America, and Spanish ministers constantly looked for ways to deny a permit for the British

South Sea Company to send their annual ship to the trade fairs at Portobello and Veracruz, which was also meant to be guaranteed by the agreement.[18] A line of separation divided the commercial systems of the Atlantic World between the more liberal trade policy that governed trade among European nations and the mercantilist policies excluding foreigners from the colonial trade of European empires in the Americas.[19]

The creation of restricted trade zones in the Americas was an important part of empire-building in the early modern Atlantic World, which marked a significant break with traditional commercial practices in Africa, Asia, and Europe.[20] What historian Elizabeth Mancke has termed "diasporic polities"—networks of alien peoples who lived and traded in foreign communities under privileges granted by local authorities—formed the basis of long-distance trade since the very beginning of urban life.[21] The efforts of the Iberian powers to exclude their European powers from trading with their expansive imperial claims challenged ancient commercial practices. In his 1608 treatise *The Freedom of the Seas,* the Dutch jurist Hugo Grotius denounced the Portuguese attempts to prevent foreign merchants from trading with the East Indies as an act of "violence to Nature herself." He argued that it was an "unimpeachable axiom of the Law of Nations ... [that] every nation is free to travel to every other nation, and to trade with it."[22] Despite the appeals that England, France, and the United Provinces might make to the customary practices of granting privileges of free movement and residence to foreign merchants, they also contributed to the emergence of restricted trade zones in the Americas by ensuring that trading rights became part of commercial diplomacy transacted between states, rather than arrangements agreed upon by merchants and local authorities.[23] By the beginning of the eighteenth century, European empires had developed a system of commercial regulation in the Americas that distinguished the colonization of the Atlantic World, with the exception of West Africa, from traditional practices employed elsewhere around the globe.

Rather than advocating the wholesale dismantling of the European mercantilist system that governed their colonial trade in the Atlantic World, American policymakers, notably Thomas Jefferson and James Madison, embraced these new forms of commercial regulation. Like their European rivals, they distinguished between national and colonial trade in the United States. Jefferson and Madison looked to extend the European system of liberal national trade to include the Atlantic port cities of the United States while restricting the access of foreign merchants to the American imperial domain in the West. The presence of cosmopolitan communities of foreign merchants in the Atlantic port cities helped to forge bonds of union between the established eastern states and American colonists west of the Appalachians by providing them with access to a marketplace in which the colonists could sell their agricultural produce and purchase manufactured goods. These same merchant communities in the West, however, threatened rebellion and resistance to the American imperial project by connecting Native peoples and colonists to the commercial and diplomatic networks of rival European empires.[24]

The cosmopolitanism that made merchants useful conduits of international trade raised questions about which master they truly served, for their self-interest led them to London, the great metropole of global trade in the eighteenth and nineteenth centuries. While this risk might be tolerable in New York or Philadelphia, Jefferson and Madison considered it extremely dangerous in the West, where the volatile allegiance of colonists and the determination of Native peoples to defend their homelands invited the intervention of the British Empire to the north and the Spanish Empire to the west and south. The different attitude that American policymakers entertained toward the commercial regulation of trade east and west of the Appalachian Mountains is less evidence of ideological inconsistency in applying the principles of free trade than it is of their pragmatic approach to promoting American imperial expansion, which the Founders believed was essential to the survival of the republic.

Citizens of Convenience argues that the merchants and traders involved in Montreal's fur trade played a critical role in defining the northern border of the American Republic and, therefore, determining the course of the American Empire. The fur trade converging on the St. Lawrence River formed a transnational network of commerce and kinship, which linked the Atlantic entrepôt of Montreal with an ever-expanding western hinterland south of the U.S.-Canadian border.[25] The Montreal fur trade accounted for the annual movement of hundreds of canoes and boats, thousands of people, and property worth hundreds of thousands of pounds between the territories of the British Empire and the American Republic.[26] It is difficult to think of another group of people who would move such large volumes of capital, goods, and labor across the border with such regularity. The activities of Montreal merchants also offer a continuous perspective on border conditions across the forty-year course of this study. Many of the same Montreal firms remained in business between 1783 and 1820, most notably through their involvement in the North West Company. Consequently, the merchants' perspective on the border helps us to assess change over time. The survival of the trade owed much to its ability to exploit new commercial territory. While this study does emphasize the importance of certain critical junctions of movement at places such as the Detroit River Valley and the Mackinac Straits, Montreal merchants solidified their trade through St. Louis and the Missouri River Valley, as well as expanding their commercial operations into the Columbia River Valley in the Pacific Northwest. Consequently, an examination of the Montreal fur trade allows us to follow the northern border west during the early nineteenth century.

This book focuses primarily on merchants of English, Irish, and Scottish descent who arrived in the province of Quebec in the decades following the British conquest of New France during the Seven Years' War. Merchants from across the British Atlantic World migrated to the St. Lawrence River Valley and the Great Lakes region after 1760, drawn by the commercial promise of the Montreal fur trade. These British merchants of Montreal both competed and collaborated with long-established Francophone merchants and traders in the "creole corridor," a network of French towns that extended from Quebec to New Orleans.[27] While British merchants engaged in the fur trade operated from London, Montreal, Detroit, and elsewhere in the Atlantic World, they most frequently referred to themselves as "Canada merchants" (not Canadian merchants) when lobbying government.

The Montreal fur trade does not just provide a useful viewpoint for understanding how the boundary changed over time; it was also integral to the story of how the border was made. As members of a transatlantic political organization, Canada merchants lobbied both British and American policymakers to advance their commercial interests in the American West. The merchants exploited their commercial and geographical knowledge of the North American interior to influence policymaking and diplomatic negotiations. Traders also influenced conditions on the ground. The commercial intercourse between Montreal and the Native homelands in the U.S. territories raised security fears about the northern border among American policymakers, particularly after Thomas Jefferson's election as president in 1800. Jefferson's and Madison's pragmatic approach to commerce and empire meant that while they often encouraged international trade through the nation's Atlantic port cities, they increasingly endorsed the local innovations of U.S. agents on the border who tried to restrict the privileges of foreign merchants in America's imperial domain. Empowered by the common state practice of rewarding its agents with a share of fees and seized goods, U.S. customs officials and Indian agents became interpreters of the Jay Treaty. These local state entrepreneurs discovered new ways to control movement across the border without violating the letter of the United States' commercial agreements with the British Empire. In this way, the actions of individuals associated with the Montreal fur trade provoked responses from U.S. agents that helped to define the local operation of the border differently for British subjects and American citizens.

Finally, this book argues that imperial expansion played an integral role in defining the American people as a distinct nation. While contemporary Americans might feel squeamish about calling the United States an empire, the Founders felt no such discomfort. For them, the United States was participating in a historic imperial tradition that dated back to classical antiquity.[28] While the Founders believed their republican form of empire was something new, U.S. imperialism was at its heart about conquest and colonization. Like its European counterparts, American Empire meant appropriating and occupying Native homelands *and* rival foreign colonies through the application of military and diplomatic force. It also involved the colonization of occupied lands through a territorial system that transformed the socioeconomic structure of established communities of European colonists and Native peoples through the promotion of market-oriented agriculture.[29]

Knowing that the American Republic was destined to become a global superpower in the twentieth century, it can be difficult to avoid viewing the contemporary dimensions of the United States as preordained. Naturalizing the northern border means that the occupation of foreign towns such as Detroit, St. Louis, and New Orleans by U.S. forces appears to be a homecoming of sorts. These cities seem quintessentially American, albeit with an exotic Cajun twist in the case of the Big Easy. Nothing could be further from the truth for the British, French, and Spanish residents of towns that had never been part of the United States. The arrival of American imperial agents in Detroit in 1796, for example, looked little different to locals than when British authorities had arrived thirty years before to replace the French regime. Recovering the foreign character of American imperialism to western residents helps to remind us that the United States did not just encounter people from other sovereignties in the maritime Atlantic World; it happened in the North American interior too. Indeed, François Furstenburg has shown us that the trans-Appalachian West was very much part of the Atlantic World in the eighteenth century.[30]

The success of American Empire depended on the ability of the American national state to exercise control over all the people residing within the sovereign domain of the United States. To establish authority over both its own nationals and a variety of aliens within the bounds of the American Republic, U.S. agents needed to be able to categorize citizenship and verify individual claims to nationality. In other words, the success of American imperial expansion depended, to a significant degree, on U.S. officials being able to tell who was a member of the national community and who was not. Making this distinction was not straightforward. As the political theorist Elizabeth F. Cohen has explained, citizenship is best understood as a continuum of different combinations of rights enjoyed by different groups, rather than as a normative category. As such, all democratic states contain "semi-citizens" who enjoy some rights of citizenship, such as residence or movement, without being nationals.[31] This was certainly true for merchants engaged in international trade in the eighteenth century. Citizens of convenience occupied an ambiguous position somewhere on the broad spectrum of U.S. citizenship. And so did American Indians. The experience of merchants and traders helps to reveal the ways in which the process of defining the American people was tied up with subordinating Native peoples within its borders. As the recent work of Leonard J. Sadosky and Eliga H. Gould has shown, the United States isolated Indians from the commercial and political networks of the Atlantic World during the early nineteenth century, creating the conditions for statelessness among Native peoples.[32] While Indians did not become U.S. citizens until 1924, American imperialism undermined Native sovereignty by classifying Indians as neither nationals, enjoying rights of American citizenship, nor foreign nationals, forming part of another sovereign national community. By helping to codify the spectrum of citizenship, empire served as the midwife of the American people.

This book explores the northern border and its connection to American Empire and nationhood by examining the interactions among three different groups of actors: Canada merchants and traders, imperial agents, and policymakers and diplomats. It employs historian Peter Kastor's concept of "local diplomacy" to study the everyday interactions of life on the border and the less frequent formal negotiations of high diplomacy.[33] Canada merchants engaged in geopolitics at both levels. They mobilized a transatlantic lobbying machine to represent their interests in London and Philadelphia (and later Washington, D.C.), and in provincial and territorial capitals. Merchants gained access to prime ministers and presidents from time to time, but their traders and other employees engaged with imperial agents far more frequently through everyday interactions with customs officers, Indian agents, and other officials on the border. The complaints and petitions registered by merchants offer important insights into these complex interactions. The memorials not only explain how merchants and traders tried to shape border policy, but the responses that these petitions provoked from British and American officials point to a widening trail of sources produced by imperial agents, policymakers, and diplomats.

Three key diplomatic settlements structure this book: the Treaty of Paris (1783), the Treaty of Amity, Commerce, and Navigation (better known as the Jay Treaty, 1794), and the Treaty of Ghent (1814) and the accompanying British-American commercial convention of 1815. These agreements not only shaped the interactions among merchants, imperial agents, and policymakers and diplomats, but they each framed the problem of citizens of convenience in distinctly different ways. The Treaty of Paris was an inconclusive peace settlement that left unanswered many important questions about the relationship between the peoples of the British Empire and the American Republic. It was unclear to people on the ground where the northern border was located or how it would function because British and American diplomats failed to agree about the conditions of trade between the United States and the British Empire, and British soldiers continued to garrison the western posts on what was meant to be American soil.

The Jay Treaty confirmed the location of the northern border by securing the withdrawal of British forces from the western posts. But it did so by ensuring that an open boundary would facilitate the free movement of American citizens, British subjects, and Native peoples between the territories of the British Empire and the American Republic. The Jay Treaty granted commercial and residential privileges to British merchants in the United States that mirrored the rights enjoyed by European merchants in cosmopolitan trading centers around the globe. Still, by allowing the residents of the western posts to choose their nationality, the treaty exempted them from the regular system of naturalization, creating the conditions for citizens of convenience to switch back and forth between American citizenship and British subjecthood.

Citizens of convenience developed their strategy of evading government regulation as part of an entrepreneurial competition with U.S. border officials and Indian agents between 1796 and the outbreak of the War of 1812. Believing that the Jay Treaty functioned as a charter of rights, these merchants and traders claimed that U.S. efforts to regulate border crossings and the fur trade violated their privileges under international law. The entrepreneurial conflict assumed more aggressive proportions when the Jefferson administration took office in 1801. As opponents of the Jay Treaty, and of allowing foreign merchants to infiltrate the United States' colonial trade in the West, Jefferson and Madison embraced many of the local innovations of U.S. customs agents in the Great Lakes, who looked to assume greater regulatory power over cross-border movements of the Montreal fur trade.

The entrepreneurial innovations of American customs collectors on the northern border dovetailed with the Embargo and Nonintercourse Acts sponsored by the Jefferson and Madison administrations between 1807 and 1811. These measures imposed commercial restrictions on U.S. foreign trade in an effort to pressure the belligerent powers of Europe (though, increasingly, the British Empire) to respect the neutral maritime trading rights of the United States. The Royal Navy's impressments of sailors from U.S. merchant vessels and efforts to starve Napoleonic France into submission each threatened the American imperial project by denying American colonists in the West access to the Atlantic marketplace. The Embargo and Nonintercourse Acts applied to the United States' maritime trade in the Atlantic World and cross-border commerce with Britain's Canadian provinces. The escalation of the entrepreneurial innovation of customs collectors into open economic warfare was deeply troubling for merchants and traders, who increasingly lost confidence in the protections that they believed the Jay Treaty was meant to provide for the Montreal fur trade.

The Embargo and Nonintercourse Acts also allowed the United States to buy time to prepare for war. Congress declared war on the British Empire on June 18, 1812. Believing that the actions of the Royal Navy in the Atlantic World and the scheming of the Montreal fur trade in the West both imperiled the American imperial project, President James Madison initiated a conflict that would be fought largely along the northern border of the

American Republic. Although militarily indecisive, the War of 1812 abrogated the Jay Treaty, ensuring that British diplomats would have to renegotiate the commercial and residential privileges essential to the survival of the Montreal fur trade.[34]

The Treaty of Ghent and the British-American commercial convention of 1815 redefined the ways in which the northern border would function after the War of 1812. American diplomats articulated expansive claims over non-citizens residing within the boundaries of the United States to oppose British efforts to create a sovereign Indian state in the trans-Appalachian West. U.S. diplomats also steadfastly refused to renew the commercial and residential rights that British subjects and Native peoples had exercised under the now defunct Jay Treaty. In doing so, the American ministers in Ghent and London created the geopolitical conditions that would allow U.S. agents to use the northern border as a tool to distinguish between American citizens and foreign nationals.

I

"YOU DAMN YANKEE WHAT BROUGHT YOU HERE?"

. . . .
. . .

The British garrison of Fort Niagara received some uninvited guests on the morning of August 1, 1783. The fort's commander, Brigadier Allan Maclean, expressed his "great surprise" at the arrival of "three Batteaux's... from Schnectady Loaded with Rum to trade at the Upper posts."[1] The traders, who had successfully slipped past Major John Ross, the commander of Fort Oswego, presented Maclean with papers and certificates from U.S. general Philip Schuyler, New York governor George Clinton, and the mayor of Albany requesting safe passage to Detroit and Michilimackinac.

Maclean was at a loss as to what to do with the New Yorkers. He explained to the traders "how improper it was in them; to come to trade here so soon, Even before the Definitive treaty of Peace was signed, or before the commercial Treaty had been ratified and concluded." Maclean was loath to turn them away, because he was "afraid it might be looked upon as an act of violence in me." Instead, he allowed the traders to remain at Niagara and ordered Ross at Oswego to stop all boats arriving from Schenectady while he awaited urgent instructions from General Sir Frederick Haldimand, the governor of Quebec.[2]

The British commandant was not alone in his desire to wish away the New Yorkers. The Americans' presence angered the king's Indian allies at Niagara, who felt betrayed by their exclusion from the British-American peace negotiations in Paris. The British commandant reported an ugly confrontation between "five or six Indians half drunk" and the Montreal merchant Isaac Todd, who had only recently returned from London where he been a member of the contingent of Canada merchants who met with Lord Shelburne and Richard Oswald. Mistaking Todd for a New Yorker, the Indians "told him in broken English 'You damn Yankee what brought you here.'" Luckily, a British Indian agent intervened to save the startled Todd from the disastrous consequences of this case of mistaken identity. Still, Maclean noted that "our Indian friends look at these People very crooked indeed."[3]

Portrait of Isaac Todd, Donald Hill, c. 1922. A native of Ireland, Todd partnered with James McGill in the Montreal fur trade for over twenty years. (McCord Museum, Montreal, M1595)

The incident at Niagara helps to recover the pervasive uncertainty on the imagined border at the end of the American War of Independence. Fixing the boundaries of the new American nation was not simply a matter of surveying the physical geography of the trans-Appalachian West. The ambiguity of the border had less to do with the geographical ignorance and geopolitical arrogance of diplomats in Paris than it did with unresolved questions about the relationship between the American Republic and the British Empire. The presence of Maclean and his brother officers at Oswego, Detroit, Michilimackinac, and other western posts revealed the tension between the border as it was located by the preliminary peace settlement and the geopolitical realities on the ground. Moreover, as Isaac Todd discovered almost to his peril, the boundary between American and British nationals was difficult to distinguish.

Maclean may have taken comfort from knowing that the confusion he faced at Niagara was likely only a temporary period of uncertainty which further negotiations would help to resolve. As he pointed out to the Schenectady traders, British and American diplomats would soon negotiate a definitive peace treaty and a commercial agreement that would resolve many of the unanswered questions about the relationship between the peoples of the British Empire and the United States. Moreover, the anger of Indians at Niagara paid testament to the ongoing hostilities between the king's Native allies and the United States. The decision of the Paris negotiators to exclude Indians from the diplomatic process meant that American and Native diplomats would need to conclude their own peace in North America. Haldimand exploited the inconclusive character of the peace to order the New York traders to return to Schenectady. He also refused the request of George Washington's agent, Major General Friedrich Wilhelm von Steuben, to prepare for the transfer of the western posts.[4] While the peace process remained incomplete in 1783, British and American ministers were due to renew their negotiations in Paris in the spring, and the American Congress began taking steps to negotiate peace with the hostile Indian nations of the trans-Appalachian West in May.[5] Surely it was simply a matter of time before the final pieces of the border settlement fell into place.

It was not. Agreement proved elusive in both Paris and North America. In Paris, the initial optimism of British and American diplomats that they could easily reconstitute their transatlantic trade along lines of commercial reciprocity and mutual interest proved ill-founded. While the idea of full commercial reciprocity among nations was an important tenet of the United States' republican foreign policy, the principle proved divisive among British politicians, many of whom cherished the mercantilist Navigation Acts governing the imperial economy as the bulwark of national greatness. In more concrete terms, a deal could not be done that would clarify the operation of the boundary between the United States and British North America because the British and American diplomats were at loggerheads over trade between the United States and Britain's West Indian colonies. It was one thing to welcome the United States into the European system of liberal national trade by offering Americans the status of most favored trading nation; it was quite another to allow the United States free access to Britain's valuable Caribbean colonies.

In the trans-Appalachian West, negotiations between the United States and the Indian nations of the Ohio and Illinois countries failed to clarify American claims to sovereignty in the region. The United States insisted on negotiating with the Iroquois and western Indian nations as victors because American policymakers were determined to undermine the sovereignty of Native peoples. Most clearly demonstrated by the American peace commissioners literally holding hostage leaders of the Iroquois and western nations to extract land concessions as the price of peace, the refusal of the United States to deal with Indians on the basis of reciprocity was also part of proving American nationhood. By dictating peace terms, the United States acquired Native homelands that American colonists could transform into farms, villages, and towns that would substantiate American imperial claims in the trans-Appalachian West. Perhaps more importantly in the minds of American policymakers, the unequal terms of these treaties also elevated the status of American nationhood by diminishing the sovereignty of the Indian nations residing within the territorial boundaries of the United States. As it turned out, the Indians were not defeated peoples, and the tiny U.S. Army could not back up the diplomatic bullying of American policymakers with armed force. By the end of 1786, a pan-Indian confederacy formed by the Mohawk Joseph Brant and western war captains organized collective armed resistance to American imperial ambitions north of the Ohio River that revealed the geopolitical weakness of the United States.[6]

Despite all the indications that negotiations would help to resolve uncertainty on the border, the confusing situation at Niagara became the norm. British soldiers garrisoned what were supposed to be American forts. The Montreal fur trade continued much as it had done for the past twenty years. But for thousands of merchants, traders, and hunters, the uncertainty surrounding the northern border of the American Republic remained deeply unsettling. At its heart, Montreal's fur trade was a commercial venture. Yet its success depended on networks of kinship and friendship, patronage and dependence, which bound together diverse polyglot peoples from across the Atlantic World and the North American continent. This world might survive while British agents controlled the means of movement along the boundary, but, given the shifting geopolitical tides of empire, how long would this last?

Montreal merchants founded the Beaver Club in 1785. The commercial promise of the St. Lawrence River had lured enterprising merchants from around the British Atlantic World to Montreal after the fall of New France in 1760. Irish traveler Isaac Weld recorded that "winter in Canada is the season of general amusement. The clear frosty weather no sooner commences, than all thoughts about business are laid aside." The Beaver Club served as a center of the social life of Montreal, a town renowned for the "constant and friendly intercourse" among its residents, which gave the impression that "the town were inhabited but by one large family."[7]

At first glance, the Beaver Club seems to look little different than the numerous mercantile organizations and gentlemen's clubs found in any of the great commercial cities of the eighteenth-century Atlantic World. While the club did not maintain its own premises (it usually met in the Montreal Hotel), it provided its members with a venue to discuss politics, transact business, and entertain ship captains and visiting merchants with lavish dining and an excellent wine cellar.[8]

On closer inspection, however, a guest from London or Philadelphia would notice that the Beaver Club and its members differed from their counterparts in other cities. All of the club's members had wintered in Indian Country. Each member wore a gold medal, hanging by a sky-blue ribbon, on his chest. The medal was inscribed with the Beaver Club's motto—"Fortitude in Distress"—on the front, while the reverse recorded its owner's membership number in order of the year in which he first wintered in Indian Country, beginning with Charles Chaboillez in 1751. At dinner, guests would note that a toast to the Catholic "Mother of All Saints" preceded the loyal toast to the Protestant King George III. Guests would feast on exotic fare, such as roast beaver and pemmican, served on the club's specially commissioned silver plate, alongside the familiar madeira and port served in the club's own crystal. After dinner, members smoked tobacco in Indian calumets and sang traditional French river songs, such as "A la clare fontaine," before grabbing whatever furniture or accouterments came to hand to use as paddles in an imaginary canoe.[9]

The traditions of the Beaver Club reflected the French, Indian, and Brit-

James McGill's Beaver Club medal, c. 1785, front and back. The medal records the date of James McGill's first winter in Indian Country in 1766. Worn on a sky-blue ribbon, the medal would have adorned McGill's chest at Beaver Club dinners. (McCord Museum, Montreal, M1149)

ish worlds in which its members lived.[10] The silver and crystal adorning the club's well-kept table demonstrated the refined tastes of Montreal merchants, who had a voracious appetite for British consumer goods. At the same time, the club's members combined their performance of European gentility with their shared experiences as North American adventurers. The after-dinner entertainment recalled the apprenticeship that merchants served as clerks or junior partners wintering in the hunting grounds of the Great Lakes and trans-Appalachian West. For young men, many of whom had only recently arrived in North America, the first winter in Indian Country was an introduction to a foreign world. Wintering was not merely a lesson in privation or a test of masculinity; rather, it was an important introduction to French and Indian culture and rituals, which governed Montreal's fur trade during the eighteenth and early nineteenth centuries. Membership in the Beaver Club reflected an individual's success in straddling these different cultures, so it was only appropriate that the club's rituals embraced overlapping French, Indian, and British traditions.

The Treaty of Paris threatened to tear these worlds apart. As Canada merchants in London warned Lord Shelburne in January 1783, the proposed international border dividing the American Republic from the British Empire "cuts off all the Trading Posts and almost all the Indian Nations; the Trade with whom was the grand object of the commercial Intercourse between Great Britain and the province of Quebec."[11] London was the metropole of imperial trade, and Montreal merchants depended on their business connections in the British capital to extend them credit, supply them with manufactured Indian trade goods, and provide them with a market for their furs. Eight representatives of London merchant houses trading with Quebec signed petitions to the British government protesting the provisional treaty in early 1783, alongside the Montreal merchants Isaac Todd and Charles Patterson.[12] Alexander Ellice was among the most prominent London signatories. Born in Scotland in 1743, Ellice began his career as a merchant in Schenectady, New York, in the 1760s. In partnership with James Phyn and John Porteous, Ellice pursued the fur trade of Detroit and Michilimackinac before the Continental Congress's nonimportation policies forced the merchants to shift their business to Montreal, where Isaac Todd served as his agent. By 1783, Alexander Ellice was traveling between the London office of Phyn, Ellice & Company and the Montreal branch run by his brother Robert Ellice and his nephew John Forsyth. While Phyn, Ellice & Company expanded its trade to British colonies from Newfoundland to the West Indies, the company maintained its interest in the Montreal fur trade. With the death of Robert Ellice in 1790, his nephews John Forsyth and John Richardson took over control of the Montreal office under the new name of Forsyth, Richardson & Company.[13] Richardson would prove one of the most aggressive advocates of Montreal's fur trade until after the War of 1812. In London, Phyn and Ellice (Phyn, Ellices & Inglis after 1787) filled their correspondents' orders for Indian trade goods and sold their furs at annual auctions. While London served as the main fur exchange, most of the lots bought at auction ended up on the European market. The final destination of the furs depended on their type, but Russia, France, and the German and Italian states were important re-export markets for the Montreal fur trade.[14]

Montreal was the commercial capital of the fur trade in the Great Lakes in 1783. While the Hudson River Valley had traditionally been the center of the English fur trade in the late seventeenth and early eighteenth centuries, the fall of New France in 1760 opened up commercial competition between Albany and Montreal within the British Empire. By 1776, Montreal merchants had largely defeated their New York rivals for control of the fur trade, aided by the expansion of Quebec's provincial boundaries to include the Ohio River Valley in 1774, and by the disruption that the Continental Congress's policies of nonimportation and nonintercourse wrought on the merchants of Albany and Schenectady, who also depended on London connections to maintain their trade.[15]

Montreal and its suburbs numbered around eighteen thousand residents in 1790. An English visitor in 1785 thought the town's location beautiful and its climate mild and healthy when compared with Quebec, though he maligned both the muddy, unpaved streets and the inelegant stone houses that lined them.[16] Isaac Weld recorded that "by the far greater number of the inhabitants of Montreal are of French extraction; all the eminent merchants, however, and principal people in the town, are either English, Scotch, Irish, or their descendants." The *Canadiens* seldom spoke any English, Weld noted, while the British residents of the town were "for the most part, well acquainted with the French language."[17] Ethnic divisions, however, were less important than the division between the bourgeois merchant class and the landed *seigneurs*, which did not neatly divide along British and French lines.[18] In 1783, at least twenty-five merchant houses were involved in the fur trade.[19] Montreal was part of the French river world.[20] While the 1763 Treaty of Paris ending the Seven Years' War marked the end of French rule on the North American mainland, French Canadien communities remained. A "creole corridor" of French-speaking communities extended from Montreal to Detroit to St. Louis and, finally, to New Orleans.[21] French merchants built the Montreal fur trade in partnership with Native peoples in the Great Lakes during the seventeenth century. In particular, French traders had learned that marrying into Native kinship networks was an effective way of opening up commercial opportunities in the heart of the continent.[22] Many of the British merchants who arrived in Montreal followed the same practice by marrying into commercial Canadien families. The Glasgow-born James McGill married the widow Marie-Charlotte Desrivières in 1776. His stepson, François-Amable Desrivières, apprenticed as a clerk for the house of Isaac Todd, James McGill & Company before becoming a junior partner in 1792 and a senior partner in 1810.[23] Canadien merchants welcomed these new connections because they found it increasingly difficult to maintain their old commercial relationships with the French port cities of La Rochelle and Bordeaux now that Quebec was part of the British Empire. Intermarriage between the British and Canadien merchant families of Montreal helped to reinvigorate the French river world.[24]

Miniature of James McGill, William Berczy, c. 1805–11. The Glasgow-born McGill married Marie-Charlotte Desrivières in 1776. He remained an influential figure in the Montreal fur trade until shortly before his death in 1813. (McCord Museum, Montreal, M1150)

Marriage between British and Canadien merchant families created new transatlantic kinship networks, connecting the wintering grounds of the Great Lakes with the schoolrooms of the British Isles. Many of the merchants who settled in Montreal after the conquest of New France were drawn from the periphery of the British archipelago. McGill's partner, Isaac Todd, was from Ireland. The prominent merchant Simon McTavish, who married the daughter of the influential Charles Chaboillez, was from the Scottish highlands.[25] Montreal merchants often recruited family members from Europe to apprentice in the fur trade. McGill worked with his brothers Andrew and John, while Todd traded with his nephew Andrew Todd. Simon McTavish created a family dynasty. McTavish employed a swathe of cousins by blood and marriage, including John Fraser, with whom McTavish partnered to create the London firm of McTavish, Fraser & Company. McTavish's sister Anne supplied him with no fewer than three nephews, including the heir to his business empire, William McGillivray.[26] Family ties reinforced commercial relationships among British and Canadien merchants.

Montreal served as the critical interchange between the Atlantic and North American economies. Merchants like Isaac Todd and James McGill imported Indian trade goods and liquor, which they then arranged to be transported to the upper country posts of Niagara, Detroit, and Michilimackinac. In 1783, Montreal merchants dispatched Indian trade merchandise worth over £225,000 into the "upper country" above the Lachine Rapids on the St. Lawrence River.[27] The following year, the town's merchant houses received furs worth over £236,000 from the Great Lakes and Ohio River Valley.[28] Some of the poorer quality furs were sold in the local auctions held at Gillis's Coffee House, but Montreal merchants baled most furs and shipped them across the Atlantic to the London market. Montreal merchants helped to manage a massive logistical exercise. In 1783, they employed almost 2,500 men, 126 canoes, and 321 boats to carry trade goods, and over 100,000 gallons of rum and wine into Indian country, while the fur returns of 1784 included 227,568 deer skins and 128,620 beaver pelts.[29] The Montreal fur trade relied on the annual movement of large numbers of people, goods, and furs.

The strenuous labor of carting goods from Montreal to Lachine and paddling the canoes and boats down the St. Lawrence River fell to *voyageurs*. Traders and clerks usually enlisted these Canadien servants from the parishes surrounding Montreal and Trois Rivières to provide the muscle needed to paddle for eighteen hours a day and carry their canoes and contents across miles of portages. The *voyageur* world, distinct from that of the literate bourgeois traders and clerks, was shaped by their Canadien peasant roots, their acquisition of Native culture, and their shared sense of masculinity expressed through arduous labor. At Lachine, traders and clerks assigned the *voyageurs* to different canoes, with crews varying from four to eighteen paddlers, who sang songs to maintain their stroke.[30]

It would only take the *voyageurs* about a day of paddling to reach the border proposed in the Treaty of Paris. In their representation to the Shelburne ministry, the Canada merchants explained with painstaking detail how the running of the boundary sliced through the riverine network of Montreal's fur trade. The border entered the St. Lawrence River fifty miles above Montreal at "a Place call'd St. Ridges." By following the center of the river in its southwestern course, the boundary separated the province of Quebec from Fort Oswegatchie in New York before entering Lake Ontario at the Bay of Quinte, denying British merchants access to the important logistical center at Carleton Island. While canoes could continue their journey across the lakes, the shallow-keel boats that plied the St. Lawrence River would deposit their cargoes at Carleton Island to be loaded aboard ships bound for the Niagara peninsula. The border continued westward through Lake Ontario, cutting off Fort Oswego and access to Albany, Schenectady, and New York City.[31]

The ships from Carleton Island unloaded their cargoes at Niagara. In 1783, extensive colonization of the Niagara peninsula was in its infancy, where a hastily constructed town of over eight hundred loyalists had sprung up around the ancient military fort.[32] The town, renamed Newark, served as the provincial capital of Upper Canada in the 1790s. When Isaac Weld visited in 1797, he discovered a boomtown. Newark had only seventy houses, but Weld commented that "few places in North America can boast of a more rapid rise than little Niagara, nearly every one of its houses having been built within the last five years: it is still advancing most rapidly in size."[33] There were around eighteen merchants in business at Niagara in 1783. Robert Hamilton and Richard Cartwright formed their partnership to prosecute the fur trade in 1780. Hamilton was born in East Lothian, Scotland, in 1751. He got his start in the fur trade with Phyn and Ellice in London before serving an apprenticeship in Montreal and at Carleton Island. After 1783, his partner, Richard Cartwright, moved to Cataraqui (renamed Kingston in 1784), while Hamilton remained in Niagara. By operating at both ends of Lake Ontario, the pair managed to control much of the forwarding trade of Montreal's fur trade, arranging the transportation of goods and furs across the lake. From 1791, Hamilton and Cartwright were part of a monopoly operating the government portage on the Niagara peninsula, across which passed almost a third of the private goods heading west and around 40 percent of furs destined for Montreal.[34] At the southern end of the Niagara peninsula, the goods portaged around the falls were again loaded aboard ships at Fort Erie to make the westward voyage across Lake Erie to the Detroit River Valley.

At the western edge of Lake Erie, the vessels from Fort Erie entered the narrow straits of the Detroit River. The border continued to carve an imaginary center line through the river, separating the town of Detroit from the farms lining the British shore. Founded by Antoine de La Mothe Cadillac in 1701, Detroit was the most important trading town in the Great Lakes in 1783. Over two thousand people lived within the town's wooden walls and on the narrow farms that stretched back from both shores of the river between Lake Erie and Lake Huron.[35] There were more than twenty merchant houses engaged in the fur trade operating in Detroit in the 1780s.[36] The town stood at the nexus of an extensive trade network whose commercial territory embraced parts of present-day northern Ohio, Indiana, and southern Michigan. Detroit controlled a system of waterways that included Lake Erie, Lake Huron, and the Cuyahoga and Sandusky Rivers, as well as tributaries of the Miami, Scioto, Wabash, and Maumee Rivers. Detroit's geographic advantages were only part of the story of its prominence in Montreal's fur trade. Over several generations, French-Native kinship networks had transformed Detroit into a center of "indigenous urbanity." Bound together through marriage and godparentage, these French and Indian *coureurs de ville*—members of a network of urban entrepreneurs—concentrated their power at Detroit while projecting the town's influence outward to Native villages in the Ohio and Illinois countries.[37]

As with their patrons in Montreal, the British merchants who made Detroit their home after 1760 married into the world of the *coureurs de ville*. Ulster-born merchant John Askin arrived in New York sometime during the Seven Years' War. He was among the first British merchants to venture westward after Pontiac's War, establishing a merchant house at Michilimackinac in 1764 before moving his business south to Detroit in 1780.[38] Askin married Manette, an Odawa, "à la façon du pays" (in the fashion of the country), who bore him three children, including his namesake, John Askin, Jr. Askin's and his children's kinship ties with the Odawa continued to open up commercial opportunities throughout his life. In June 1772, Askin married Marie Archange Barthe in Detroit.[39] The Barthes were one of the town's oldest Canadien families, and Askin and his brother-in-law Jean Baptiste Barthe conducted business together at Michilimackinac and Sault Ste. Marie in the late 1770s.[40] Other British merchants at Detroit also married into local Canadien families: the Scottish-born George Meldrum married Angélique Chapoton, while his longtime business partner William Park married Thérèse Gouin.[41] The merchant class of Detroit became multi-ethnic within a generation, connecting its members to the transatlantic marketplace dominated by the British Empire and the Native-Canadien commercial networks in the heart of the North American continent.

While cooperation between British and French communities was essential to the success of the Montreal fur trade after 1760, it is important not to downplay ethnic divisions and cut-throat competition. The 1780s witnessed a growing ethnic divide within British North America. The American Revolution altered the demography of the province of Quebec with several waves of loyalist immigration. Around six thousand loyalists arrived in Quebec in the immediate aftermath of the war, with a further eight thousand claiming land by 1791.[42] With most of the new arrivals forming communities in the western part of the province, including the Detroit River Valley, the British Parliament divided Quebec into the two new colonies of Upper Canada and Lower Canada in 1791. Upper Canada, which included Niagara and Detroit, was inhabited largely by Anglophone loyalists; Lower Canada maintained a Francophone majority in established towns such as Quebec and Montreal and in the parishes of the St. Lawrence River Valley. This political division reflected increasing ethnic polarization in British North America, particularly after the radicalization of the French Revolution in 1792 and 1793.[43] The 1790s also witnessed the division of the Montreal merchant community with the formation of the New North West Company (better known as the XY Company), which engaged in bitter competition with Simon McTavish's North West Company.[44] Despite these divisions, merchants proved surprisingly united when it came to protecting the Montreal fur trade from imperial efforts to restrict free movement across the border.

Detroit served as a logistical base of operations for traders destined for the wintering grounds of the Ohio and Illinois countries. As a so-called forwarding merchant, Askin would equip traders with the goods he received from his patrons in Montreal. In 1783, the Detroiter was in partnership with his future son-in-law Robert Hamilton and Richard Cartwright. John Askin and Company's account with Todd, McGill & Company shows that the firm asked its patrons to import over six thousand pounds of goods from Phyn and Ellice in London in preparation for the 1783 season.[45] The inventory of the merchandise has not survived, but another from 1788 does indicate the sorts of goods used in the fur trade. Phyn, Ellice & Inglis dispatched firearms, lead balls and gunpowder, and a large quantity of textiles, ranging from Irish linens to various colored strouds (woolen blankets manufactured in the English counties of Gloucestershire and Yorkshire specifically for the fur trade).[46] Askin acquired these goods on credit from Todd and McGill, and it would usually take two years before forwarding merchants would see a return on their investment with the sale of their furs in London. He transported his furs to Montreal, which Todd and McGill then consigned to Phyn and Ellice. The furs ended up on the London auction block in February and March 1784, where they sold for close to £12,500.[47] By the 1780s and 1790s, however, Detroit merchants had diversified their involvement in the Montreal fur trade. Askin and the partnership of George Meldrum and William Park operated a number of vessels on the Great Lakes to transport goods and furs, while they also constructed a windmill to supply flour to Montreal's North West Company.[48] The growth of these ancillary services strengthened Detroit's position as a key logistical center for both the southwest and northwest fur trades.

The traders that departed Detroit spread out to wintering grounds throughout the Ohio and Illinois countries. Although mostly Canadien, a growing number of British traders had formed the kinship ties and acquired the necessary skills to trade for furs with Native hunters. Askin contracted traders who worked at various locations during the 1780s. He supplied the Lachine-born trader Louis Lorimer, who, with the help of his Shawnee wife's connections, operated a storehouse near the Glaize, a collection of Native towns and trading posts clustered around the Auglaize and Maumee Rivers.[49] Francis Vigo, an Italian-born former Spanish soldier, supplied Askin with furs from around Vincennes, while Gabriel Hunot, of an old Montreal family, traded on behalf of the Detroit Miami Company on the Huron River.[50]

The relationship between traders and hunters played an important role in the social and political lives of Native peoples because gift exchange in American Indian culture was imbued with obligations. Trade, conceived as an exchange of gifts, was a medium for creating peace and conditional friendship. At the diplomatic level, the exchange of furs and goods was intertwined with political and military alliances between the British Empire and the Indian nations and villages of the Ohio and Illinois countries. The fur trade played an important role in Indian politics by creating obligations and constructing social relationships. Savvy politicians distributed European trade goods among kinspeople and villagers to consolidate power within their communities, as well as a means of extending their influence over neighboring villages and nations.[51] Status and leadership often depended on the ability of individuals to supply others with goods. At a more fundamental level, European trade goods made life easier. Metal knives and axes were sharper and more durable, while brass kettles were easier to cook with than earthenware.[52] A range of motivations, then, fed into the willing participation of Native hunters in Montreal's fur trade, from conducting diplomatic relations with representatives of the British Crown to acquiring metal cookware to make it easier to prepare a meal.

Indians from a variety of different nations appear in the trading accounts of the Miami Company, an organization formed by six of Detroit's leading merchant houses in the mid-1780s. A Miami Company trader operating at Roche du Bout, the Wolf Rapids, and the Shawnee Towns in the Maumee River Valley recorded the accounts of individual hunters in the winter of 1786–87, which included Shawnees, Miamis, and Delawares. The accounts also reveal prominent Indian "chiefs" among the unknown trader's customers. The Miami war captains Le Gris and The Deer both traded with the Miami Company, as did the Shawnee leader Captain Johnny.[53] It is no coincidence that these war captains would also play a key role in opposing American imperialism in alliance with the British Empire during the 1780s and 1790s. These individual accounts testify to the political role that the fur trade played in diplomacy between the Crown and the king's Indian allies, and within Indian nations and villages in the Great Lakes region.

The proposed border did not just threaten to cut off Montreal from Detroit and its extensive commercial networks south of the Great Lakes; it also threatened to sever trade routes to the Mississippi River and the wintering grounds northwest of Lake Superior. From Detroit, the boundary line continued through the middle of Lake Huron and the Mackinac Straits (the waterway dividing the upper and lower peninsulas of Michigan), separating Michilimackinac and Sault Ste. Marie from the British Empire. Fort Michilimackinac commanded the Mackinac Straits at the strategic crossroads of Lakes Huron, Michigan, and Superior. Michilimackinac had been home to a multiethnic society of British and Canadien merchants and traders, and Odawas, Ojibwas, Menominees, Sacs, and other Native peoples until 1781, when British forces removed the fort from the lower Michigan peninsula to Mackinac Island.[54] In 1783, the island hosted a seasonal community of merchants, traders, and hunters. It served as an important logistical center for the fur trade of the upper Mississippi River Valley and the Northwest. Traders from Michilimackinac traveled to Prairie du Chien, via Green Bay and the Fox and Wisconsin Rivers, and St. Louis, via the future site of Chicago and the Des Plaines and Illinois Rivers. They would also journey north from Michilimackinac, through the St. Marys River, into Lake Superior.

The boundary divided Lake Superior and, by a matter of a few miles, threatened to deny British merchants and traders access to Grand Portage on the lake's northwest shore. In 1783, Grand Portage was the only practical means by which traders could carry goods through the Pigeon River to the wintering grounds of the inland lakes and rivers leading to the Lake of the Woods. The northwest region was an area of considerable growth in Montreal's fur trade. In the winter of 1783–84, Montreal merchants resurrected the North West Company, a collective agreement among the leading fur houses, to conduct trade for five years.[55] According to the company's official history, Montreal merchants decided to cooperate in the northwest trade for the first time in 1779 because unchecked competition among traders had proved violent and ruinous to their commerce.[56] From 1783, the North West Company would remain in business until its merger with the Hudson's Bay Company in 1821. From Grand Portage, the proposed border ran due west to the Mississippi River, the international boundary separating the United States from the Spanish colony of Louisiana.

The running of the proposed boundary for thousands of miles from the St. Regis River in the East to the Mississippi River in the West threatened to destroy Montreal's fur trade. This trade was intertwined with family networks and a multiethnic cultural world, which connected diverse peoples from the banks of the Mississippi River to the shores of Loch Ness. This is not to suggest that the destruction of the Montreal fur trade would have represented the loss of Eden. The fur trade was not some kind of utopian world in which ethnic and racial boundaries and cutthroat competition did not exist. A handful of merchants amassed great fortunes, but many more found themselves saddled with crippling debts. The trade depended on the back-breaking labor of thousands of *voyageurs;* it eroded Native cultural practices and over time promoted the dependence of American Indians on European manufactures. The trade also led to the destruction of game stocks through overhunting. Nevertheless, the outcome of negotiations in Europe and North America would help to determine the future of a trade that involved the lives and livelihoods of thousands of British, Canadien, and American Indian people.

In February 1783, Prime Minister Lord Shelburne asked John Pownall, an experienced imperial administrator, to explore what legal changes the government would need to pursue to bring British statutes into line with the peace preliminaries with the United States. Independence had voided the "fundamental Constitution" of laws and statutes regulating trade between Great Britain and the former American colonies, but Pownall anticipated that these regulations could easily be adapted to frame a new commercial system, incorporating the independent American states. Pownall believed that "it would be an Injury to Common Sense to suppose, that, the Subjects of the United States are to continue in the predicament of Aliens." The policymaker predicted that "Mutual Convenience and reciprocal Advantage" would supply the firm "Basis of an Union" that would reconstitute the relationship between the British Empire and the American Republic by securing "by consent what was before established under the Authority of Law."[57] The war may have torn the British Empire apart, but shared interests would bring Great Britain and her former colonies back together in much the same way as before independence.

The year 1783 was a contingent moment in British-American relations. While negotiating independence had been a difficult and painful process, British and American ministers believed that the hard business was behind them once they had agreed to the preliminary peace articles in November 1782. Overshadowed by the "cold war" of the later 1780s and early 1790s, the diplomats parted with the genuine expectation that they would meet again the following spring to negotiate a more expansive framework for British-American relations.[58] The preliminary articles, then, were just the first step in a longer peace process. The agreement of November 30, 1782, provided a broad outline for the future of British-American relations by recognizing the political independence of the United States from Great Britain and drawing a border to divide the provinces of British North America from the states and territories of the American Union. While much remained undecided, the British and American negotiators believed that their shared interests would lead to a quick agreement in 1783 which would reopen trade between the two countries.

Reciprocity was central to new thinking about geopolitics in the post-revolutionary Atlantic World. For the Founders, reciprocity promised to bring republican principles of equality and mutuality to international affairs. Free trade would promote a new system of alliances among nations. Commerce would act as a civilizing vehicle of mutual association, rendering obsolete dynastic and territorial competition for resources and markets. Peace would replace conflict. John Adams distilled these principles into his Model Treaty of 1776, which he intended as a blueprint for American diplomacy.[59] Reciprocity, then, encapsulated the global potential of the American Revolution to perfect human society. Republican principles could promote friendship and association between states as they did among citizens.[60] Congress charged the American ministers in Paris with negotiating treaties of trade and amity with any European state willing to agree to reciprocal terms. British-American negotiations held a particular importance because they promised to herald a revolution in international politics. If Europe's commercial hegemon would agree to commercial reciprocity, others would surely follow. Above all, reciprocity was essential to validating American claims to nationhood. Being treated as an equal by other European nations was a way for the United States to gain the recognition of its peers as a member of the international community of nations.

For British policymakers, reciprocity was intertwined with their thinking about the future of empire in the British Atlantic World. In many ways, British free-trade advocates shared the American Founders' understanding of the power of commerce to unite nations through mutual interest. Shelburne and diplomat Richard Oswald both hoped that reciprocity would lay the foundations for a future "federal union" between Great Britain and the United States.[61] Indeed, Shelburne had agreed to cede the vast trans-Appalachian West to the United States because he expected that British manufacturers and merchants would supply American colonists in the Ohio and Illinois countries. By advocating a de-centered union of equals that would accommodate the dual sovereignties of Great Britain and the United States, Shelburne and Oswald were essentially envisioning a form of republican empire as the basis for British-American reconciliation.[62] Commercial reciprocity was merely the first step toward a more intimate union between the American and British body politics in which the boundaries between American citizen and British subject would remain ill-defined. British-American reciprocity would embrace a porous border that would unite, rather than divide, the peoples of the American Republic and the British Empire.

But Shelburne and Oswald would not get to negotiate with the United States. Just three weeks after John Pownall penned his optimistic predictions about the future of British-American relations, Shelburne resigned from office. The prime minister's attempts to amend Britain's venerable Navigation Acts provoked a strong backlash from politicians who believed that Shelburne's policy of reciprocity threatened the imminent destruction of the British Empire. The Navigation Acts, the first of which was passed by Oliver Cromwell's Parliament in 1651, embodied the broad mercantilist principles that the trade between the metropole and its colonies should be restricted to English (and, after 1707, British) subjects. By providing a market for metropolitan manufactured goods and supplying the mother country with products that it had traditionally had to acquire from foreign countries, mercantilist trade policies improved the balance of trade between Great Britain and its European rivals. In short, mercantilism promoted national power through a policy of beggar thy neighbor.[63] William Eden, who helped to lead the opposition to the government in the House of Commons, argued that abandoning the Navigation Acts would mean the loss of Britain's colonial trade and, consequently, the fatal weakening of the Royal Navy, as the merchant marine would no longer serve as a nursery for British seamen.[64] These arguments gained traction among the British political classes with the publication of John Baker-Holroyd's *Observations on the Commerce of the United States* in the spring of 1783. Lord Sheffield (Baker-Holroyd's courtesy title) argued that American independence was a self-evident truth, but it was a fact in which Britons ought to rejoice. Independence had saved the British taxpayer from the expense of colonial administration, while the strength of Britain's manufactures and financial institutions ensured that its merchants alone possessed the "solid power of supplying the wants of America." He supported the idea of welcoming the Americans into the European trading system by offering the United States the status of most favored nation, a position that the American Republic would share with most of Britain's European trading partners. Nonetheless, Sheffield argued that the British government had no need to court the Americans by opening access to Britain's colonial markets.[65] The United States could not escape the web of British credit and the lure of its manufactures.

Shelburne's resignation by itself did not determine the outcome of the British and American negotiations in 1783. The conflict among British politicians over the future of the empire's commercial relations with the United States remained undecided, despite the fall of the government. Indeed, the American merchant Henry Laurens was optimistic about the new ministry headed by William Cavendish-Bentinck, the duke of Portland. Despised by George III, the new foreign secretary, Charles James Fox, was considered a friend of America. Laurens wrote Benjamin Franklin about a conference he had had in which "Mr. Fox discoverd a disposition to proceed to business with us with Liberality & effect."[66] Moreover, Fox appointed Franklin's old friend David Hartley to replace Richard Oswald as Britain's chief negotiator. Hartley was a fervent supporter of British-American reconciliation. He had opposed the American war and worked as an advocate for peace and reunion in both Paris and London.[67] Fox himself expected the negotiations to run smoothly, instructing Hartley to dispense with any "reserve" in his discussion with the Americans, but to speak plainly to the British government's "earnest desire to renew the Intercourse & Commerce so beneficial to both Countries."[68] There was no reason to tread lightly when both parties shared a common interest in a liberal commercial agreement.

Hartley crossed the English Channel to renew Britain's negotiations with the United States armed with a series of proposals, penned by the Canada merchants, to frame an open commercial border. First, British subjects and American citizens should both enjoy free access to the lakes, rivers, and portages that formed the border. Second, British troops should continue to garrison the western posts for three years because the merchants did not believe that the United States was currently capable of protecting the lives and property of traders. Third, the Indian trade should be open to all parties without any "Tax or Impost" on goods or furs "passing or repassing through the Country."[69] The merchants delivered the regulations to Fox in person, relaying to him the former assurances they had received from Oswald that "there will be no difficulty in obtaining the consent of the American Commissrs. to there proposals." Fox sent the regulations to Hartley with his endorsement, describing them as "important and desirable" and urging the diplomat to "do the utmost in your power" to secure their adoption by the United States.[70] The change in ministry had not changed the Canada merchants' expectations that they would enjoy free commercial access to the United States.

The early meetings between Hartley and John Adams, Benjamin Franklin, and John Jay seemed to bode well for a quick agreement. While Hartley waited for his commission to arrive from London so that the diplomats could begin their formal negotiations, he and the American commissioners drew up an article that would allow British subjects and American citizens to enjoy free access to "all Rivers, harbours, Lakes, Ports and Places" belonging to the United States and Great Britain.[71] The draft article made no distinction between the British archipelago in Europe and its overseas colonies. Fox rejected the proposed article. Hartley and the foreign secretary recognized that "the American principle of equal reciprocity, & the restrictive principle of the british acts of navigation must come to issue," but they both hoped to postpone the moment of reckoning.[72]

While a quick deal on a comprehensive commercial treaty proved elusive, the American commissioners were ready to agree to include many of the regulations authored by the Canada merchants in the definitive peace treaty. Hartley proposed that British subjects and American citizens should enjoy free access to the portages, rivers, and lakes that formed the border; that British soldiers should continue to garrison the western posts for three years; and that neither the United States nor the British Empire should levy taxes or raise duties on any commercial articles crossing the border to allow both citizens and subjects the freedom to pursue the fur trade. In addition to the Canada merchants' suggestions, Hartley also asked the American commissioners to guarantee the "peaceable Enjoyment of all civil Rights" by British merchants and traders operating within the United States.[73] Hartley reported to Fox that his proposals exceeded both his instructions and "what the Quebec Merchants seem to expect," but he thought it "well worth the trial to rescue their property & trade from the desponding state mentioned in their Memorial."[74] The privileges that Hartley was trying to gain for British merchants in the fur trade of the United States were relatively commonplace for foreign merchants operating in European cities and trading communities in the Ottoman and Mughal Empires, but in the context of foreign merchants operating in the colonial trade of a foreign empire, they were quite an audacious request, particularly given Fox's present refusal to allow American merchants equal access to the carrying trade of Britain's Caribbean colonies.

Hopeful of gaining reciprocal commercial privileges for U.S. merchants to the British West Indies, Adams, Franklin, and Jay gave Hartley almost everything he asked for. They agreed that British subjects and American citizens would share equal access to portages, lakes, and rivers under regulations to be settled in the future commercial treaty. They would also allow British subjects to remain in the trans-Appalachian West under the protection of the American government for a period of two years after a notice of removal was issued. The American ministers were even open to British troops garrisoning the western posts until Congress ordered their evacuation. While the ministers were not opposed to exempting customs duties on the border, they suggested that it should form part of a future commercial treaty.[75] Hartley believed that he and the American ministers had a provisional agreement in hand for the definitive peace treaty in late June that would create an open border between the United States and Britain's North American colonies.

The U.S. commissioners provided Hartley with a proposal for the definitive peace treaty in August that promised even greater freedom of movement and commerce for British subjects and American citizens. The nationals of both countries would enjoy free and open access to the Mississippi River, the St. Lawrence River, and the portages, lakes, and rivers along the border without being subject to any discriminatory taxes or duties. The U.S. government would guarantee the civil rights of British merchants on American soil, and it would allow them to continue to live in the United States for two years after U.S. officials issued them with a notice of eviction. British troops could continue to garrison the western posts until asked to leave by Congress.[76] This was more than Hartley had asked for in his proposed articles two months earlier.

But the deal was never done. The Navigation Acts' defenders in Whitehall and Westminster gradually consolidated their control over British policy during the spring and summer of 1783. Henry Laurens warned the American commissioners about the shifting political climate in London. He noted that "'reciprocity' . . . has undergone a certain Degree of Refinement; the definition of that term appears now to be, Possession of advantages on one side, and Restrictions on the other."[77] The British home secretary, Lord Frederick North, asked William Knox, an experienced colonial administrator, to draw up commercial regulations to open trade with the United States. Knox was a critic of Fox's conciliatory policy and an ally of Lord Sheffield. A strong supporter of the Navigation Acts, Knox was determined to exclude American merchants from the valuable trade with Britain's colonies in the West Indies. His recommendations formed the basis of a new order-in-council of July 2, which opened the British West Indies to American produce but continued to exclude American ships. Ensuring that U.S. merchant vessels would have access to the carrying trade of the British West Indies was one of the chief objectives of the American commissioners. The new order-in-council almost guaranteed that the negotiations in Paris would fail to produce a commercial agreement between the United States and the British Empire.

To Hartley's deep embarrassment, the American ministers had to tell him about the order-in-council. He scolded Fox about his ill-treatment at the hands of his masters in Whitehall, which, by leaving him uninformed about changes in government policy, had only added to the "jealousy or surprize" of the American ministers and lessened the chances of a broad settlement that might one day lead to "a family compact between our two nations."[78]

In the end, the British and American commissioners in Paris failed to agree to any new terms beyond those of the preliminary peace treaty. Fox sent Hartley a proposal for the definitive treaty that merely repeated the terms of the provisional treaty that Oswald and the American ministers had agreed to in November 1782. Sidelined by Lord North and William Knox in American affairs and with Congress having opened the U.S. Atlantic ports to British merchants, Fox had more pressing concerns. In particular, he explained that finalizing peace with France depended on a quick conclusion of Hartley's negotiations with the American ministers.[79] Adams, Franklin, and Jay agreed to sign.[80] An exasperated Franklin wrote Laurens that "after making and sending over many Propositions of ours & of Mr. Hartley's and long Delays of Answers, it is come finally to this, that the Ministers propose our signing as a Definitive Treaty the Preliminary Articles, with no Alteration or Addition, except a Paragraph or Preamble."[81] After almost five months of negotiations, and over nine months since the peace preliminaries had sketched out the new boundary, British and American officials were no closer to agreeing on how the border would function.

The American commissioners believed that the weakness of American nationhood was responsible for the failure of their negotiations. In a report sent to Elias Boudinot, the president of Congress, Adams, Franklin, and Jay explained that they found it "hard to decide" whether "the Strife of the two opposite and nearly equal Parties in the [British] Cabinet" or "the exaggerated Accounts of Divisions among our People, and Want of Authority in

Congress" was responsible for the lengthy and fruitless negotiations. The diplomats believed that they might yet secure "extensive Concessions" from Great Britain "were it certain that the United States, could be brought to act as a Nation." They were convinced that the British government was reluctant to enter into a commercial agreement with the United States because it did not believe that the Confederation Congress was capable of enforcing treaties on the states. Above all, the ministers counseled, "the prospect of Disunion in our Council, or want of Power and Energy in our Executive Department" meant that the British government had no incentive to offer commercial concessions to the United States because the national government was not capable of enforcing commercial retaliation against British merchants. Without this fear, the ministers reasoned, Great Britain "lose their principal Motive to Liberality."[82] If literal reciprocity inferred a mutually satisfying relationship between equals, then American policymakers would need to prove that the United States could act like a unified national state if it ever expected to strike a deal with Great Britain.

Hartley, however, was not yet willing to accept defeat in his mission to effect reconciliation between the peoples of the United States and the British Empire. He continued to write to Franklin after he returned to England, passing on encouraging rumors that the new ministry of William Pitt meant to renew negotiations. When the new government sent Hartley to Paris to exchange ratifications of the peace treaty with the American commissioners in 1784, the aging diplomat was convinced that he was really being sent on a secret mission to broker a commercial treaty.[83] The British foreign secretary, Francis Osborne, the marquess of Carmarthen, recalled Hartley in May, but he refused to come home. Hartley ignored his second recall in August, and he only left Paris in September when Carmarthen informed him that his powers to negotiate on behalf of the British government would expire. Even so, Hartley tried to reassure Franklin of "the ready & friendly disposition of the Court of London to receive any proposals from the United States."[84] While Franklin might have believed his old friend in 1783, Hartley's parting words must have struck him as hopelessly naive in September 1784. British and American negotiators would not conclude a commercial agreement until a decade later.

Rumors of the peace reached Niagara in May 1783. Governor Frederick Haldimand received official notification of the preliminary articles on the evening of April 25. Horrified and humiliated by the proposed cession of the trans-Appalachian West to the United States, he hoped to keep news of the peace from reaching the ears of the king's Indian allies for as long as possible.[85] The struggle for independence had sparked a bitter civil war in the trans-Appalachian West. The war spread confusion and division, rather than promoting unity among Native peoples.[86] Oneidas, who had mostly allied themselves with the American patriots, carried the news of the peace to Niagara to share with their fellow Iroquois, who had fought for the king. They also carried a promise that the United States would soon visit vengeance on the king's Indian allies and treacherous agents. Brigadier Allan Maclean's report of a council he held with the Mohawk Captain Aaron Hill and others on the morning of May 18 confirmed Haldimand's fears. Hill told Maclean that he and his allies viewed British conduct toward them "as treacherous and cruel." The Indians were incredulous that "our King could pretend to cede to American what was not his own to give." But, Hill continued, "if it was really true that the English had basely betrayed them by pretending to give up their Country to the Americans without their consent, or consulting them, it was an act of cruelty and injustice that Christians *only* were capable of doing."[87]

The Oneidas' gleeful description of the preliminary peace suggested that their Iroquois brethren had suffered a double betrayal at the hands of the British government. Not only had the British and American negotiators in Paris left the king's Indian allies out of the treaty, but they had also torn up the Treaty of Fort Stanwix, which Sir William Johnson had negotiated with the Six Nations in 1768 to establish a line of settlement that would protect Native lands north of the Ohio River from Euro-American colonization. If the Oneidas were to be believed, the king, their father, had given away Iroquoia to the Americans. Hill reminded Maclean that "the Indians were a few People subject to no power upon earth—That they were the faithful Allies of the King of England, but not his subjects." The king's ministers simply did not have the right to "grant away to the States of America, their rights of properties without a manifest breach of all Justice and Equity."[88] Maclean assured Hill that the Oneidas had deceived him. The British officer promised that he and "all the King's Troops" would stand side by side with their Indian allies in defense of their lands.[89]

While the peace preliminaries sketched out an international border to divide the British Empire from the American Republic, they left undecided the boundary between Native homelands and Euro-American settlement in the trans-Appalachian West. Put simply, the Paris treaty did not determine who possessed the land in the territory ceded by the British Crown. What sovereign rights had Great Britain ceded to the United States? This was a difficult question to answer, not simply because British and American diplomats had ignored the rights of Native peoples, but also because of Euro-American fictions of sovereignty. As historian Francis Jennings has explained, it is almost impossible to provide a uniform explanation of the relationship between the Crown and Native peoples. First, it was a contested and constantly shifting process of negotiation. Second, different groups of Crown officials and Native leaders construed their relationship in different ways. Sovereignty was a moving target. That being said, it broadly encompassed a system of alliances that embodied a form of clientage; it was a relationship that triangulated among dependence, independence, and interdependence. Jennings suggests the term "ambigupendence" to encapsulate the superficial contradiction between the dependence and independence of Native peoples within the British Empire.[90]

Whatever the conceptual difficulties, Hill recognized that negotiations with the United States would help determine the realities of American sovereignty on the ground. By excluding the Native peoples from the Paris negotiations, the British and American governments ensured that the United States and American Indians would have to make their own peace in North America. Technically, the United States remained at war with the king's Indian allies in 1783.

Hill requested that Sir John Johnson, the British superintendent of Indian affairs, and the American general Philip Schuyler arrange a conference at Niagara or Oswego to discover what terms the United States would offer. Hill and his allies were particularly anxious to learn "whither or not they are to be allowed to keep Peaceable possession of their own Country unmolested."[91] The Mohawk worried that the United States would demand the right of soil—in effect, property ownership—over their lands.

As the work of historian Alan Taylor has shown, the negotiations between the United States and the king's Indian allies pivoted on the relationship between two different kinds of border: the international border described in the preliminary peace, which delineated the separate sovereign domains of the British Empire and the American Republic, and the boundary of settlement outlined in the Fort Stanwix treaty of 1768 that divided Native homelands from zones of Euro-American colonization.[92] The former imagined the fixed, bordered lands of national and imperial states; the latter promised a porous borderlands in which Native peoples could maintain their autonomy in a space between empire and republic.[93] The survival of Native homelands also promised to protect hunting grounds in the Ohio and Illinois countries from American colonization. The outcome of these negotiations, then, would have profound consequences for the border crossings and transnational community that underpinned the Montreal fur trade.

British officials in North America were determined not to leave the outcome of these negotiations to chance. The security of British North America depended on Native alliances.[94] While Great Britain had little to fear from the American military, Governor Haldimand and Sir John Johnson, the superintendent of Indian affairs, worried that American diplomats would exploit Native resentment toward the Treaty of Paris to forge an anti-British pact. British officials envisioned a bloody reenactment of Pontiac's War, when a pan-Indian movement under the titular leadership of the Odawa chief Pontiac launched coordinated attacks against the western posts in the 1760s.[95] Native peoples could still shift the balance of power in the trans-Appalachian West in the 1780s. The British Indian Department worked to reassure their Indian allies of the Crown's fidelity to their alliance by supporting the Fort Stanwix boundary of settlement and the protection of Native lands. Haldimand dispatched Johnson to Niagara "to quiet the apprehensions of the Indians, by convincing them that it is not the Intention of Government to abandon them to the Resentment of the Americans."[96] Johnson sought to dodge accusations of the king's betrayal of his allies by readily adopting the Six Nation's argument that the Fort Stanwix line protected Native homelands in Ohio during the council he held at Niagara in late July.[97]

The Six Nations proposed to Johnson that they assemble a council at Sandusky to organize a general confederacy of Indians to protect their homelands. Johnson agreed to support the ambitious scheme, which would unite thirty-five nations. In late August 1783, the Mohawk leader Joseph Brant and forty representatives from the Six Nations joined with Delawares and Wyandots from Upper Sandusky, Hurons from Detroit, Shawnees from Scioto, Mingoes from upper Ohio, Odawas from around Saginaw Bay, Ojibwas from Lake Huron, and a large delegation of Creeks and Cherokees to discuss how best to resist American claims north of the Ohio River.[98] Brant, or Thayendanegea, was a powerful figure in the extended British Atlantic World. A Mohawk leader, captain in the British Indian Department, and brother-in-law of the late Sir William Johnson, Brant commanded respect from warriors in the Ohio country and grabbed the attention of London society when he visited in 1775 to present a personal appeal to George III in support of Mohawk land claims.[99] With the aid of British Indian agents Alexander McKee and Matthew Elliott, the confederacy pledged to uphold the Fort Stanwix boundary with the United States by agreeing that no nation ought to dispose of land without general consent.[100]

While Native peoples organized their collective resistance to the colonization of their homelands by the United States, American policymakers debated peace and their imperial schemes for the Ohio country. The land sales in the vast territory of the trans-Appalachian West promised a path to solvency for the heavily debt-laden United States. Moreover, such sales also provided a means to mobilize individual colonists as agents of American imperialism. By monopolizing the right to extinguish Native land claims, the United States would raise money to pay off wartime debts and secure the interest of individual property holders as the guarantors of their land titles. The question was, how best to bring western lands to market at the highest price? The answer depended in large part on the character of U.S.–Indian relations. As the United States remained at war with Britain's Indian allies, General Henry Knox advocated continuing the conflict against the Ohio Indians. George Washington, an experienced surveyor and land speculator of longstanding, adapted Knox's plan to extend bounties to veterans of the Continental Army. Knox and Washington both intended to dispossess the Native peoples of their lands by force and remove them westward.[101] General Philip Schuyler, a New Yorker, suggested an alternative plan: to make peace with the Native peoples of the trans-Appalachian West and then encircle their ever-shrinking lands with American colonists. Washington endorsed Schuyler's plan, which Congress adopted in October 1783.[102] The confederacy organized at Sandusky had dedicated itself to maintaining the Fort Stanwix boundary as the basis for a peace settlement with the United States, while Congress had committed its agents to demanding large land cessions from the Iroquois and western nations as the price for peace.

Over the next eighteen months, American commissioners cajoled and bullied different Indian nations into a series of piecemeal land cessions north of the Ohio River. Beginning with the negotiations with the Iroquois at Fort Stanwix in October 1784, U.S. representatives used the military muscle of one hundred New Jersey militiamen to effectively hold hostage Captain Aaron Hill and Cornplanter, a Seneca. The Americans demanded that the Iroquois recognize congressional authority over Indian affairs, and exacted a series of land cessions, including territory along the Niagara River, which would isolate the Six Nations from the British-held province of Quebec. Representatives of the United States repeated this formula with the Wyandot, Delaware, Odawa, and Ojibwe nations at the Treaty of Fort McIntosh in January 1785, and the Shawnee at the Treaty of Fort Finney in January 1786.[103] On paper, at least, these dictated treaties ended the war west of the Appalachian Mountains and opened the way for Congress to enact its plan of encircling Native peoples with colonists.

In reality, the United States had no means of enforcing these treaties, and the bullying tactics of dictating peace helped to galvanize Indian resistance to American imperialism. While U.S. policymakers reasoned that they had defeated the king's Indian allies by association, there were more Indian warriors in the field at the end of the war than ever before. Joseph Brant led an ambush on a detachment of George Rogers Clark's soldiers near the Ohio River in 1781. Loyalists and Native warriors defeated Kentucky militiamen, killing a younger son of American icon Daniel Boone, at the Battle of Blue Licks in 1782.[104] Congress could ill afford to supplement its meager force in the West. By bullying a handful of Native leaders into piecemeal concessions during a vulnerable moment when their alliance with Great Britain seemed to hold out little prospect of protection, the American commissioners hoped to divide and conquer Brant's protean confederacy.

In the short term, the signatories of the dictated treaties returned home to the unveiled contempt and, in some cases, physical violence of their fellow villagers. But Native peoples soon turned their anger outward toward the United States. Violence in the West, which had been largely restricted to Mingo and Cherokee scalping parties in 1785, expanded in size and scope. By the summer of 1786, Shawnee, Potawatomi, Ojibwe, and Odawa raiding parties stalked the fledgling American colonies in Kentucky and the Ohio River Valley. American soldiers reported that around 450 warriors from numerous nations appeared menacingly at Vincennes on July 31 before dispersing. Around the same time, the western nations indicated that they wished to make common cause with the Six Nations, speaking at a council held at Buffalo Creek.[105] The confederacy lived and was growing in strength.

Kentuckians launched their own campaigns in the fall of 1786 to attack Native villages in the Wabash and Great Miami River Valleys. Eight hundred militiamen led by Colonel Benjamin Logan attacked the Shawnee village of Mackachack in October, killing a dozen warriors and taking prisoner around thirty women and children. The Kentuckians sacked the village and then divided their forces to pillage and burn Wakatomica, Pekowi, McKee's Town, and Blue Jacket's Town. Logan's force did not merely burn buildings; more seriously, his soldiers destroyed around twelve thousand bushels of corn that the Shawnees needed to sustain them through the winter.[106] Native resistance succeeded in defending villages on the Wabash, forcing George Rogers Clark's expedition to return to Vincennes. It was clear at the end of 1786 that the West remained at war.

In November 1786, the confederacy gathered at Huron Village at the mouth of the Detroit River to organize their collective resistance to American imperialism. Appealing to the right of soil vested in Native peoples by the Great Spirit, the Six Nations spoke forcefully in favor of unanimity as the only means by which the individual nations of the confederacy could hope to preserve their homelands from American encroachment.[107] The confederacy prepared a message to send to Congress on December 18, which invalidated the dictated treaties. The Indians argued that only a general treaty was capable of granting territory to the United States. Consequently, "when a division of territory is agreed to by some particular nations without the concurrence of the whole of our confederacy, we look upon it as illegal and of no effect." The confederacy asked Congress to send commissioners to negotiate a new treaty in the spring. In the meantime, they warned, no surveyors or "others that march on lands" should cross the Ohio River.[108]

The United States and the Native peoples of the trans-Appalachian West remained at war more than three years after the Oneidas had first brought news of the British-American peace preliminaries to Niagara. The disputed character of the northern border and the weakness of the American national state ensured the failure of diplomacy in the Ohio country in the 1780s. Native peoples contested the character of American sovereignty in the trans-Appalachian West by asserting the boundary of settlement established by the Fort Stanwix treaty of 1768. The United States claimed a right of conquest over Native homelands but lacked the fiscal-military power to coerce the Indian confederacy into accepting the confines of the new international border. It still remained unclear at the turn of 1787 whether the trans-Appalachian West would remain a porous borderlands in which Native homelands would thrive on the fringes of the British Empire and the American Republic, or would be divided between the bordered lands of British Canada and the United States.

The ratification of the Treaty of Paris by Great Britain and the United States in 1784 did not resolve the ambiguity about how the new border would function. Merchants continued to fret about what this uncertainty would mean for their trade. The Montreal merchant Benjamin Frobisher lamented the fact that the treaty relied on imaginary geographical features in locating the border. He complained to Adam Mabane, the de facto leader of Quebec's provincial council, that "there is no such Thing as a *Long Lake* as expressed in the Treaty," which the diplomats had used to locate the running of the border from Lake Superior to the Mississippi River. Frobisher explained how he and his fellow merchants were "at a loss to know from the Tenor of the Treaty where the Line is intended to be drawn," and "anxiously wish to be informed about it." The "Ambiguous Sence" of the treaty meant that Canada merchants worried that they might lose access to Grand Portage on Lake Superior, a critical junction in the northwest Indian trade. Frobisher urged Mabane to commission a provincial survey to "ascertain and fix unalterably, the Line in that Quarter."[109]

But resolving the ambiguity of the northern border was not simply a matter of correcting geographical errors. It would also require diplomats and policymakers to define the relationships among the peoples of the British Empire, the American Republic, and the Indian nations of the Great Lakes region. Above all, resolving uncertainty about the boundary would mean either the United States would have to reshape geopolitical realities on the ground or amend its claims of sovereignty north of the Ohio River.

Where the Paris diplomats had envisioned the boundary as the meeting place between two sovereign states, in reality the British Empire was the only presence along much of the water-bound border, allowing Crown agents to monopolize the means of movement at key installations from Fort Oswegatchie on the St. Lawrence River in New York to Fort Michilimackinac at the junction of Lakes Huron, Michigan, and Superior. While Great Britain had agreed in the peace preliminaries to evacuate its garrisons from the western posts "with all convenient speed," holding the forts was an efficacious policy that pleased important constituencies in the British Empire. The king's Indian allies received important gifts and supplies from the posts, as well as looking on them as an important symbol of the Crown's fidelity to their alliance. Canada merchants had argued as much with the Shelburne ministry in February 1783, while Brigadier Maclean warned Haldimand the following May that "I would be no means answer for what they [Six Nations] may do, when they see us evacuate these Posts."[110] Governor Haldimand decided not to evacuate the posts without explicit orders to do so from London. In the meantime, he and his successors continued to issue Indian trade licenses to Canada merchants trading in the Ohio and Illinois countries.

The presence of these British garrisons on what was meant to be U.S. soil did not just question the reality of the northern border but offered a more fundamental challenge to American nationhood. It was not simply that the boundary was misplaced, that locating it further south or east would create a border that reflected local conditions. Rather, the British occupation of the western posts disputed whether the United States was capable of asserting de facto sovereignty in the trans-Appalachian West. In other words, it was unclear in the 1780s whether the American Union was capable of enforcing a border regime wherever the line was drawn. Hundreds of British soldiers remained on American soil after 1783 because they could. The weak American national state did not possess the military force necessary to expel the troops of a foreign power. Indeed, the borders between the individual American states were more heavily policed in the 1780s than the international boundary with the British Empire. Virginian customs agents collected duties on goods carried across the Potomac River from Maryland, but there were no American officials to regulate border crossings at places like Detroit or Michilimackinac.[111] It was difficult for Americans policymakers to claim that the United States was a nation in equal standing with the other nations of the world when it was more difficult for Marylanders to cross the Potomac River into Virginia than it was for Britons to pass into the United States.

2

"IT SHALL AT ALL TIMES BE FREE TO HIS MAJESTY'S SUBJECTS"

At daybreak on the morning of November 4, 1791, the confederates launched their attack on the slumbering American forces camped on both banks of the Wabash River. The attacking army was a multiethnic body, with representatives of numerous nations from the Great Lakes and the Ohio River Valley under the command of Blue Jacket, Little Turtle, and Buckongahelas, the leading war captains of the Shawnees, Miamis, and Delawares. The confederates began their assault with a chilling cry before concentrating their musket fire on the militiamen, who made up the majority of U.S. general Arthur St. Clair's army. The militia broke. Desperate to escape, they forded the icy waters of the Wabash, pushing their way through the ranks of soldiers on the neighboring riverbank. The militiamen could not escape, however, for the confederates had encircled St. Clair's army. Forced to abandon his wounded, as well as eight pieces of artillery and the army's baggage and equipment, St. Clair began a hasty retreat to seek refuge in Fort Jefferson. In the space of three hours, the American forces suffered almost one thousand killed and wounded. The confederate's losses did not exceed thirty-five.[1]

The future of American Empire hung in the balance in the 1790s. The confederates' victory at the Battle of the Wabash handed the United States the heaviest defeat it would ever suffer at the hands of American Indians. Moreover, it followed barely a year after the confederacy had handily vanquished the invading army of U.S. general Josiah Harmar. The U.S. Constitution was meant to have created a more energetic national government when its provisions went into action in 1789.[2] Two years later, the American fiscal-military state had failed to conquer the confederacy of Indian nations who joined to oppose the colonization of their homelands north of the Ohio River. The sale of land in the Northwest Territory was meant to provide a source of revenue for the U.S. government. Instead, the region increasingly resembled a fiscal black hole. It was by no means clear to U.S.

policymakers and politicians whether it was wise to throw good money after bad by continuing to finance military failure in the Northwest Territory.

News of St. Clair's defeat raised the hopes of Canada merchants that a new border settlement could be reached between the British Empire and the American Republic. The Niagara merchant Robert Hamilton encouraged John Graves Simcoe, the lieutenant-governor of the province of Upper Canada, to urge the United States to accept British mediation of their conflict with the confederacy. Recognizing the American government's perilous situation, Hamilton reasoned that "surely peace to the Americans must be a desirable object: the difficulty they experience in raising men, and the expence they incurred in this expedition were very considerable." Moreover, the merchant had recently spoken of peace with Joseph Brant and had received the Mohawk chief's assurances that the confederates would welcome the Crown's help with ending their conflict with the United States. Hamilton, like his patrons in Montreal, saw British mediation of the conflict in Ohio as a means to remedy the deficiency of the border of 1783. He expected the Ohio River to form a boundary between the United States and Indian homelands, in concert with a new border dividing the British Empire from the American Republic along the contours of the Appalachian Mountains. Appealing to Simcoe's ambitions for imperial rejuvenation, Hamilton predicted that a new settlement along these lines would ensure that "the American farmer will continue for centuries yet to come to labor for the English Mechanic, and the English Merchant and Mariner will share at least the Business of transport from one country to the other."[3] A new border, then, would bring peace and prosperity, and in the wake of St. Clair's costly defeat, it was theirs for the taking.

Canada merchants believed their fortunes were intertwined with that of the confederacy. Almost a decade after the Treaty of Paris first sketched out the U.S.-Canadian border, the American Indian victories against Harmar and St. Clair promised a new peace settlement in the Great Lakes region. With the support of British officials in North America and imperial policymakers in Whitehall, the merchants hoped that British mediation of the conflict would either redraw the border or otherwise secure them commercial privileges south of the Great Lakes. Increasingly, British officials proposed, and merchants accepted, the project to create an Indian state north of the Ohio River, which would divide the British Empire from the American Republic. While this scheme might not formally have adjusted the border between the two countries, an independent Indian state, under the "protection" of the British Empire, would have allowed the merchants and traders of Montreal's fur trade to conduct business as usual with their Indian partners.

As it turned out, the merchants were wrong. The U.S. victory over the confederacy at the Battle of Fallen Timbers in August 1794 meant that the British government would play no role in brokering peace between the American Republic and the Indian confederates. Indeed, the refusal of the British commander at Fort Miami to provide refuge for fleeing confederates helped U.S. general Anthony Wayne dictate peace terms and exact hefty land cessions from the demoralized western Indian nations at Greenville in 1795. The Battle of Fallen Timbers and the Treaty of Greenville were clear victories for American Empire.

The British Empire and the United States did agree to a new border settlement. But it was reached in London. And it was an American initiative. President George Washington sent U.S. Supreme Court chief justice John Jay on a special mission to London in 1794. The radicalization of the French Revolution and the outbreak of war in Europe had put increased urgency on resolving the impasse over Great Britain's occupation of the western posts while also introducing the new problem of the Royal Navy's seizure of American merchant vessels in the Caribbean and English Channel. Jay might not have managed to broker a deal with the British government to guarantee American maritime trading rights, but the Treaty of Amity, Commerce, and Navigation—better known as the Jay Treaty—which he and the British foreign secretary, William, Baron Grenville, signed in November 1794 prevented the outbreak of war and expanded commerce between Great Britain and the United States. Moreover, the treaty's second article secured the withdrawal of the British garrisons from the western posts by June 1, 1796.[4]

The 1790s proved an ambivalent decade for U.S. imperialism. Historians usually view the Battle of Fallen Timbers, the Treaty of Greenville, the Treaty of San Lorenzo, and the Jay Treaty as complementary developments that contributed to a major turning point in the history of American Empire north of the Ohio River.[5] The Treaty of San Lorenzo—also known as Pinckney's Treaty—negotiated between the United States and Spain in 1795, secured the access of American citizens to the commercial navigation of the Mississippi River and the right to deposit goods in New Orleans. The

Jay Treaty also opened limited direct trade between the United States and the British West Indies.[6] This provision clearly benefited port cities and their economic hinterlands in the eastern states, but securing access for American producers and consumers to foreign markets was part of the broader U.S. imperial scheme.[7] While it is true that the treaties of the mid-1790s confirmed the location of the border as it was described in the Treaty of Paris, the Jay Treaty codified how the boundary would function in ways that prevented either the British Empire or the American Republic from controlling the means of movement. The Jay Treaty ensured that British subjects, American citizens, and American Indians could freely cross the border for the purpose of trade.

The inability of U.S. border agents to monopolize control of people entering and leaving the United States had important implications for American nationhood. An open border denied the United States an important tool to identify the American people as a distinct nation. If peoples of various nationalities could come and go as they pleased, how could government agents determine who was an actual member of the American body politic and who was not?

The Jay Treaty also created the conditions for citizens of convenience to erase the line between British and American nationals. While the Jay Treaty granted British merchants and traders residential and commercial privileges in the United States that were customary in cosmopolitan trading centers in Europe and Asia, it likewise allowed western residents to claim subjecthood or citizenship without following the usual process of naturalization. As such, the Jay Treaty does not fit neatly alongside the Battle of Fallen Timbers and the Treaty of Greenville as an instrument of U.S. imperialism. The Jay Treaty may have confirmed the border of 1783, but the privileges that it granted to western peoples made this a moot point.

John Graves Simcoe arrived in Montreal in early December 1791. After a frigid passage across the North Atlantic from England, he was keen to take up his appointment as lieutenant-governor of the new colony of Upper Canada, which the British Parliament had formed from the western districts of Quebec earlier that year. This appointment would be no sinecure: Simcoe had commanded the loyalist Queen's Rangers regiment during the American War of Independence, and his heart burned with patriotic zeal to be "instrumental to the *Re-union of the Empire,* by sowing the seeds of a vigorous Colony."⁸ Montreal merchants spied an opportunity to enlist a powerful ally in their efforts to convince the British government to reach a new border settlement with the United States. James McGill, John Richardson, and Joseph Frobisher met with Simcoe to explain how "the Surrender of the Posts" would spell financial disaster for Upper Canada. They also explained how "the impolicy and want of local information" during the 1783 Paris negotiations had placed the new colony in such a precarious situation by inducing "the Negotiator of the Treaty with America to lay at her feet the most valuable branch of trade in this Country."⁹ The merchants bid Simcoe farewell feeling confident that they had convinced the lieutenant-governor that the border of 1783 threatened his ambitions for Upper Canada.

For the first time in years, Montreal merchants had good reason to believe that the British and American governments might soon agree to a new border settlement. The failure of the Paris negotiations to agree to any additions to the provisional treaty of 1782 were followed by a cold war in British-American relations. With the ideas of the political economist Lord Sheffield in the ascendency, the government of William Pitt had little interest in coming to a commercial agreement with the American Republic. At the same time, the United States found the power of British credit and manufacturing irresistible. Stories of internal rebellion and western separatism convinced many British policymakers and colonial officials that the United States would not last long. News of the tax revolt in western Massachusetts led by the patriot veteran Daniel Shays encouraged Guy Carleton, Lord Dorchester, the governor-general of British North America, to request permission from London to send aid to the rebels. While state government forces had suppressed Shays' Rebellion by June 1787, Dorchester was convinced that the popular rising was indicative of grassroots opposition to the republican government of the United States among his neighbors to the south. He reported to the British home secretary, Thomas Townshend, Baron Sydney, in April 1787 that "there is not a gentleman in the states from New Hampshire to Georgia, who does not view the present Government with contempt, who is not convinced of its efficacy, and who is not desirous of changing it for monarchy." Dorchester advised Sydney to consider which of George III's younger sons might be a suitable candidate for the American throne.¹⁰

The failure of Shays' Rebellion did not put an end to speculation about the disunion of the United States. Representatives from separatist movements from Vermont to Kentucky sent agents to solicit support from Dorchester in the late 1780s. The Vermont Republic had jealously guarded its independence from both the British Empire and the United States during the War of Independence, but after a commercial accord in 1787, an increasingly liberal trade flourished between Quebec and Vermont.[11] Rumors that the United States was preparing to abandon its right of navigation on the Mississippi River for commercial concessions in Spanish America prompted colonists in Kentucky to approach both British and Spanish colonial officials in the mid-1780s. "A gentleman of Kentucky" wrote to Dorchester in 1789 to offer his prediction that "the politics of the Western country are verging fast to a crisis, and must speedily evacuate in an appeal to the patronage of Spain or Britain."[12] Another Kentuckian told Dorchester that if he supplied the rebels with arms and ammunition and promised them the free navigation of the Great Lakes, Kentucky would declare its independence from the United States.[13] It seemed to many British colonial officials that the United States was on the verge of disunion in the late 1780s. The British government had such little regard for the American Republic that it excluded American merchants from the system of free ports that it established in the British West Indies in 1787 by restricting their use to traders from other European colonies.[14] Moreover, the publication of a government report by Lord Sheffield's protégé Robert Jenkinson in 1791 appeared to confirm Sheffield's prediction that independence had done little to change the pattern of British-American trade.[15] There was little urgency, then, for the British government to negotiate with the United States.

The creation of an American national state also lessened the likelihood of a new border settlement in the late 1780s. George Washington and Lord Dorchester shared the same understanding of Shays' Rebellion. The uprising portended the disunion of the United States. Washington wrote James Madison of the rebellion in November 1786: "How melancholy is the reflection, that in so short a space, we should have made such large strides towards fulfilling the prediction of our transatlantic foe! 'leave them to themselves, and their government will soon dissolve.'" While Dorchester positioned Britain's North American provinces to take advantage of the dissolution of the United States, Washington hoped that a more energetic national state would preserve the American Union. He wrote his fellow Virginian of his belief that only "a liberal, and energetic Constitution, well guarded and closely watched, to prevent incroachments, might restore us to that degree of respectability and consequence, to which we had a fair claim, and the brightest prospect of attaining."[16] By the second half of the 1780s, most American politicians agreed that the survival of the American Republic depended on creating an energetic national state. As historian Max Edling has persuasively argued, both Federalists and Antifederalists saw the U.S. Constitution of 1787 as a means of creating a national government in the mode of contemporary European states, that is, a government capable of making war.[17] While there was a broad consensus over the need to create a fiscal-military state in the 1780s, Federalists and Antifederalists disagreed over the means to achieve this end. More specifically, Antifederalists and, to a lesser extent, Federalists gave voice to a deep-seated suspicion of centralized power in American political culture. The fear of government tyranny ensured that the power of the new American state would be disproportionately felt in the West. The U.S. government garrisoned its regular troops at forts in the trans-Appalachian West in part to create an inconspicuous state that would not alarm the more numerous citizens living in the eastern states.

American policymakers intended for the newly empowered national state to play a leading role in realizing their imperial ambitions in the West. The U.S. Army would not simply garrison western forts but would conquer Native homelands by force. Moreover, the passage of the Northwest Ordinance by the Confederation Congress in 1787 ensured that the new national government would continue to direct the colonization of the Northwest Territory once the army had wrested the territory from American Indians. The earlier Territorial Government Ordinance of 1784 had left the formation of governments in the trans-Appalachian West largely in the hands of colonists. The chaotic violence between Indians and colonists north of the Ohio River in the 1780s convinced American policymakers that the national government would have to play a more active role by establishing a temporary colonial rule over the Northwest Territory.[18] Only by securing the lives and property of colonists could the United States hope to raise revenue from land sales and attach the interests of industrious, market-oriented western landholders to the survival of the American Republic. Consequently, the Northwest Ordinance established a stadial system of government that, while it began with the colonial rule of a governor and officers appointed by the president, provided a pathway to statehood and equal membership in the American Union.[19] Together, the U.S. Constitution and the Northwest Ordinance lessened the likelihood that the United States would negotiate a new border with the British Empire because these documents renewed the American Republic's imperial ambitions north of the Ohio River.

But the new federal government of the United States did not prove any more successful in conquering Native homelands than its predecessor. Combining cost-cutting with paternalism, the new secretary of war Henry Knox recommended that the United States follow the example of the French and British colonial regimes by recognizing the Native right of soil and by using diplomacy and gift-giving to purchase land north of the Ohio River.[20] Congress agreed, and eventually representatives of the Iroquois, Wyandot, Delaware, Odawa, Ojibwe, and Potawatomie nations met with Governor Arthur St. Clair at Fort Harmar in January 1789. St. Clair, however, had little patience for paternalism. He maintained the U.S. claim of a right of conquest over the Native homelands north of the Ohio River. He also demanded that the gathered diplomats confirm the boundaries of the despised dictated treaties of the 1780s, though the governor was prepared to offer some payment for the land. While St. Clair succeeded in cajoling the Indians to accept his terms, the two treaties signed on January 9, 1789, were worthless as instruments of empire. The treaties were condemned by those who did not attend. War parties from the Wabash continued to raid across the Ohio River, provoking an unauthorized counteroffensive by Kentuckians in August 1789. Desperate to maintain U.S. authority in the West, Congress empowered Washington to call out the state militia. Washington ordered St. Clair west to negotiate with the Wabash Indians, granting him the power to mobilize the Virginia and Pennsylvania militias if he should fail. St. Clair arrived at Vincennes in January 1790 but could find no one willing to talk seriously about peace. In May he advised Washington that military force would be necessary to end the war in the West.[21]

The Treaties of Fort Harmar divided the Iroquois, but Shawnee war captain Blue Jacket helped to reinvigorate the confederacy in its fight against U.S. imperialism. Blue Jacket knew better than most that there could be no accommodation with the United States. He had experienced the racial hatred of American colonists toward Indians during his brief captivity in Kentucky in 1788. He was an influential powerbroker, who drew successfully on his connections with both the Montreal fur trade and other western nations. Blue Jacket had family and friendship ties with the trading community at Miamitown. The Shawnee war captain could also rely on fielding around six hundred Mingo, Delaware, and Cherokee warriors, but he particularly reached out to the Miami-speaking nations of the Wabash River Valley—Miamis, Weas, Piankeshaws, and Eel Rivers. By 1790, the three most influential Miami leaders—Le Gris, his brother The Deer, and his brother-in-law Little Turtle—all favored the confederacy. Other nations remained uncommitted. The Iroquois who signed the Fort Harmar treaty did not respond to the Shawnee wampum belts calling for renewing the confederacy, nor did the powerful Odawas, Potawatomis, and Ojibwes of the Great Lakes.[22] The failure of the Shawnees and Miamis to organize a pan-Indian congress in August 1790 reveals the contested nature of the confederacy.

In September 1790, General Josiah Harmar led an expedition of nearly 1,500 men north from Fort Washington (present-day Cincinnati) to attack the Indian towns at the head of the Maumee River. With only three hundred regular soldiers, Harmar relied on poorly trained and equipped militia from Pennsylvania and Kentucky. Moreover, the belligerent expedition was further undermined when a diversionary attack from Vincennes failed to materialize. Harmar's force did level over three hundred houses before arriving at Miamitown, at the portage between the Maumee and Wabash Rivers, but shadowing Shawnees and Miamis had already partially burned the town to deny it to the Americans. Unable to bring the warriors to battle, Harmar divided his force into two detachments, which the Indian confederates defeated in two separate engagements in October. With the loss of over one hundred men, Harmar retreated to Fort Washington the following month.[23]

Harmar's defeat raised the hopes of Canada merchants that the British government could secure a new border settlement with the United States as part of a mediated peace between the American Republic and British Indian allies. While American policymakers and colonists on the Ohio River might doubt his sincerity, Governor-General Lord Dorchester was genuinely troubled by the ongoing war between the United States and the Native peoples of the Ohio and Illinois countries. War threatened the security of Canada. British officials on both sides of the Atlantic feared that they would be powerless to stop the British Empire being drawn into the escalating conflict.[24] Moreover, the nature of the Crown's alliance with the western Indian nations also demanded that the king's agents help broker peace; this was a role expected of a "father" in the diplomatic culture of the middle ground.[25] For a multitude of reasons, then, Dorchester took steps to mediate peace in February 1791. He instructed Sir John Johnson, the superintendent of the

Indian Department, to seek out peace terms from the western nations, which the governor-general intended to convey to the American government by his agent Colonel George Beckwith.[26] Whitehall approved of Dorchester's scheme, and the new foreign secretary, Lord Grenville, planned to discuss it further during the governor-general's scheduled return to England in the fall of 1791.[27] In the wake of Harmar's defeat at the hands of the confederates, British officials realized that any realistic hope for a sustainable peace would have to include a new border settlement protecting Native homelands and recognizing the autonomy of the western Indian nations. St. Clair's crushing defeat the following year only added further encouragement that the United States would have to sue for peace. The opportunity to mediate peace, then, was also a chance for the British government to rectify the mistakes of the border settlement of 1783.

The Montreal merchants intended to make sure that this chance did not go begging. Beginning with their audience with Simcoe, the merchants launched a transatlantic campaign to educate the British government on the geography of North America in the hope that their expert knowledge would secure a border favorable to the Montreal fur trade. Desperate to avoid a repetition of the mistakes that Richard Oswald had made in the "baneful" Treaty of Paris, Montreal merchants prepared a memorial for Simcoe to forward to Whitehall outlining six potential sites for a new border. The best possible outcome for the Montreal fur trade—and by their reasoning the British Empire, too—was to obtain the traditional boundaries of the province of Quebec, most recently framed by the Quebec Act of 1774. This would mean that the United States would have to cede all of its territory north of the Ohio River to the British Crown. While the merchants recognized that this was a long shot, they still believed that the British government could get them a better deal than the current border. They suggested a series of alternative boundaries, moving progressively westward from the Cuyahoga River in present-day northeast Ohio to the Maumee River and then to the Illinois River, leading, eventually, to the British Empire only gaining control over the upper Michigan peninsula. Each westward shift of the border sacrificed a larger share of Montreal's fur trade.[28] McGill, Richardson, and Frobisher wanted to make it clear to Simcoe and the imperial authorities that it was worth haggling with the Americans over the precise location of the border because it would have a significant impact on British commerce and power in North America.

The Montreal merchants made sure that their voice was heard in the U.S. and British capitals. Simcoe dispatched his agent Charles Stevenson to deliver the merchants' petition to George Hammond, who had recently arrived in Philadelphia to take up his post as the first British minister plenipotentiary to the United States. Leaving nothing to chance, James McGill spoke with Stevenson about the border when he passed through New York City in March 1792.[29] While McGill was in the United States, his partner Isaac Todd, along with the Detroit merchant William Robertson and other "Canada gentlemen," lobbied British government officials in Whitehall. Robertson urged Prime Minister William Pitt to bring an end to the "barbarous & destructive war" by securing a new "frontier between the Indians & Americans." He wrote fellow Detroit merchant John Askin that the Genesee River boundary was making the rounds in Whitehall. Despite the "dreadful slaughter of the American army," Robertson remained skeptical that the United States would agree to a permanent cession of the territory.[30] By spring 1792, the merchants' transatlantic information campaign had succeeded in bringing their border proposals to the attention of British officials in Canada, the United States, and the metropole.

The merchants were pushing against an open door. In Whitehall, Lord Dorchester and Home Secretary Henry Dundas were already finalizing their plans to secure U.S. recognition of an Indian state between the British Empire and the American Republic. It was now British policy to secure "exclusively to the Indians a certain portion of territory lying between, and extending the whole length of the lines of their respective frontiers, within which both parties should stipulate not to suffer their subjects to retain or acquire lands whatever."[31] The new Indian state would protect the homelands of the king's Indian allies from American imperial expansion while allowing Montreal merchants and traders to maintain and extend their trading networks in the Ohio and Illinois countries. Together, British officials hoped, the new border settlement and the Indian state would guarantee Canadian security by preventing American colonization in the vicinity of the provinces and by strengthening the Crown's alliance with the Native peoples south of the Great Lakes.

The schemes hatched in Whitehall depended on the Washington administration's cooperation, and hopes for a new settlement were dealt a serious blow when the U.S. government dismissed British minister George Hammond's suggestion that Britain could help mediate peace with the Indians.³² President Washington and his cabinet saw the offer as a challenge to American imperial ambitions.³³ If the United States accepted Britain's intercession on behalf of the western nations, it would have to abandon its claim to exercise sovereignty over Native peoples as dependents of the American state and its imperial schemes for the colonization of the Northwest Territory. Besides, the Washington administration had already gambled on continuing the war. Secretary of War Henry Knox asked Congress to raise an army of five thousand men in December 1791. Meanwhile, the United States hoped to buy time for their military preparations by sending out piecemeal peace missions. The American government, in the words of scholar John Sugden, had "no recipe for peace."³⁴

The news from Philadelphia was disappointing, but British officials still believed that they might convince the American government to accept their offer of mediation. Moreover, U.S. treasury secretary Alexander Hamilton had suggested to George Hammond that the United States might be open to granting British subjects free access to the Indian trade of the Ohio and Illinois countries in future border negotiations.³⁵ Montreal merchants wanted to relocate the border to protect their access to the Indian trade south of the Great Lakes, but they found consolation in the prospect of a free-trade zone in the trans-Appalachian West. The Montreal merchants wrote Simcoe again in April 1792 to insist that the permanent possession of the western posts was the only means of securing "Military or Commercial Protection for these Provinces," imploring the British government to dispute "the ground by Negotiation Inch by Inch." Despite urging a hard line in future negotiations with the American government, the merchants also floated the idea of proposing "neutrality or reciprocity of Trade with the Indians inhabiting *within the limits of each.*" They reassured Simcoe that an open commercial border would not pose a security risk to Upper Canada: "The mutual reciprocity of Trade with Indians would be much in our favor because there would then remain within our confined limits not one tenth part of the Trade, (the North West Excepted) that would be on the other side."³⁶ A border that functioned in efficacious ways could overcome the disadvantages of its location.

The British government remained committed to the creation of an Indian state. George Hammond realized that there was simply no point in continuing to approach the Washington administration with a direct offer to mediate peace. Rather, the British minister hoped that the U.S. government would be more open to foreign intervention for peace if the request came from the confederates. He wrote Simcoe in July to suggest that the lieutenant-governor solicit a "spontaneous" request for the Crown's help in negotiating peace from the confederacy at the forthcoming council to be held at the Glaize.[37] Simcoe instructed Indian agent Alexander McKee to attend the council to secure a request for mediation from the confederates. In doing so, however, the lieutenant-governor cautioned the Indian agent "that this solicitation should be the result of their own spontaneous Reflections." The Americans were already suspicious about Britain's involvement with the confederacy; the success of the plan would depend on McKee's avoiding the appearance of "Collusion or any active Interference to inspire them with such a sentiment."[38] With coaching from the British Indian Department, Simcoe hoped that the confederates would be able to convince the United States to accept British mediation.

The British government would get its "spontaneous" request for mediation, but the outcome of the council owed more to the influence of the Shawnees Blue Jacket and Red Pole than it did to the machinations of Simcoe and McKee. The confederates were not dupes: they knew an Indian state would help to secure their homelands and geopolitical autonomy. The Shawnees looked to exploit the credibility that they had gained from the stunning victory over American forces at the Battle of the Wabash to rally the confederacy around the Ohio River boundary that they had negotiated with Sir William Johnson in 1768. During the course of 1792, Blue Jacket played the same unifying role that Tenskwatawa and Tecumseh would play on the eve of the War of 1812, traveling throughout the Great Lakes and Mississippi River Valley to solicit support for unified Native opposition to American imperialism.[39]

In the late summer of 1792, Shawnee diplomacy succeeded in gathering representatives from numerous nations at the confederacy's new headquarters at the Glaize. Despite this encouraging sign, the outcome of the council was uncertain. Not everyone was in favor of pursuing an uncompromising line with the Americans. The Mohawk Joseph Brant favored moderation, while the influential Odawa leader Equshaway advocated peace. Red Pole opened by attacking those who wanted to negotiate with the United States. The Shawnee focused his attack on Red Jacket and the Senecas, who had traveled to Philadelphia the previous spring as guests of the Washington administration. Red Jacket responded in favor of pan-Indian unity, but he continued to support negotiating with the U.S. government. Red Pole countered that bartering with the Americans was pointless: the Shawnees wanted their lands, not payments and pensions from the United States. The council was a triumph for Shawnee diplomacy. The confederates renewed their commitment to fixing the Ohio River as the boundary between their lands and those of the American Republic. Moreover, they agreed to give peace one last chance, by meeting with the American diplomats at Lower Sandusky the following spring.[40] Simcoe and McKee got what they wanted too. A deputation of confederates requested the aid of their British "Father" at the negotiations "to see justice done to us, as it must be through his power & mediation."[41] Not everyone was pleased with the outcome of the council, however. Joseph Brant, who had arrived at the Glaize too late to argue in favor of compromise, feared that the United States would never agree to the aggressive demands of the confederates for the Ohio River boundary.[42] But it was Blue Jacket and Red Pole, rather than Brant—whose own connections with the American government made him suspect—who were the driving force behind pan-Indian unity in 1792.

The Washington administration agreed to send peace commissioners to meet with the confederates at Lower Sandusky, but it was unlikely that a deal could be done so long as neither party was willing to compromise over the Ohio River boundary. Henry Knox authorized the peace commissioners to offer fifty thousand dollars' worth of goods and an annuity of ten thousand dollars to the confederates if they would agree to uphold the territorial cessions made by the piecemeal treaties of the 1780s. Washington's cabinet also authorized the commissioners to renounce some land claims, so long as the U.S. government had not already granted or sold them. While the American government was prepared to make these small concessions, it was not willing to abandon American colonists north of the Ohio River. Red Jacket and the Senecas tried to strike a note of optimism on the willingness of the confederates to compromise, but the U.S. government looked on the negotiations as an opportunity to buy time for General Anthony Wayne to complete his preparations for a new military campaign to conquer the Ohio and Illinois countries.[43]

The American government would not agree to a formal British presence at Lower Sandusky, but Simcoe was determined to exert control over the proceedings. He refused to allow the American commissioners to purchase supplies for the council in Upper Canada because he saw this gesture as part of an insidious plot to lure the confederates away from their alliance with the Crown. As "Father," the British government believed that it should foot the bill for provisions and presents.[44] Simcoe also succeeded in getting the United States to agree to the attendance of Alexander McKee and fellow Indian agent John Butler at the council as interpreters, not as Crown representatives. McKee and Butler would help the confederates make their case for the Ohio River boundary by presenting government documents from Sir William Johnson's time, outlining the negotiations of the 1768 Treaty of Fort Stanwix. Although pleased by this coup, Simcoe cautioned the pair not to raise the suspicions of the Americans commissioners that the British government was actively trying to influence the outcome of the council, which, of course, it was. Rather, the agents should try to shape the peace settlement through private conferences with key figures and expressions of "silence" in council.[45]

Simcoe needed McKee and Butler to attend the council because he was afraid that the divisions between neutral and militant factions within the confederacy would come to the surface once the negotiations began at Lower Sandusky. Despite Blue Jacket's and Red Pole's securing the confederacy's support for the Ohio River boundary the previous fall, Joseph Brant continued to favor compromise with the American government, and he was willing to offer the more westerly line of the Muskingham River. Disunion, rather than unity, characterized the confederacy in the summer of 1793. It was proving impossible to reach unanimity within a single nation, let alone to establish consensus across ethnic and linguistic divides.[46] While Simcoe privately believed that the American commissioners were more likely to accept the Muskingham River boundary, he instructed McKee to push for the Ohio River at a council held in May in advance of the Lower Sandusky negotiations because he thought that this boundary was more likely to maintain unity among the confederates. Without unity, the confederacy could not hope to secure a peace settlement with the United States.[47] Unity demanded that Brant's voice be silenced. Rumors, allegedly spread by the Shawnees, painted Brant as an avaricious traitor who was in the pay of the American government. Despite his efforts to face down these accusations, Brant continued to feel marginalized. He and the Six Nations were not invited to private councils held by the Shawnees, Delawares, and Miamis.[48] Whether McKee was behind the attacks on Brant is unclear, though Brant certainly thought so. What was clear by July 1793 was that the confederates would only negotiate with the American commissioners on the basis of the Ohio River boundary.

The American commissioners spent an awkward six weeks as the personal guests of John Graves Simcoe at Niagara. The Washington administration had chosen moderate figures to negotiate peace: Beverly Randolph, General Benjamin Lincoln, and Timothy Pickering. The commissioners gladly boarded a vessel bound for the mouth of the Detroit River in late June to await word from the confederates that they were ready to convene the council at Lower Sandusky.[49] While awaiting passage at Fort Erie, the paths of the commissioners crossed those of a confederate deputation sent to Niagara to ascertain whether the American representatives were empowered to negotiate a new boundary. The two parties returned to Niagara where the confederates, led by the unlikely figure of Joseph Brant, met with the American commissioners in Simcoe's presence. Brant asked the commissioners whether they could negotiate a new border, but he did not explain that the confederates saw the Ohio River as a *sine qua non*. The Americans replied that they were empowered to negotiate a new border, and with Brant's assurances that a lasting peace was possible so long as the commissioners dealt with the Native peoples as one, the two parties made their way westward.[50]

The American commissioners waited at the mouth of the Detroit River, at British Indian agent Matthew Elliott's house, for the confederate's formal invitation to proceed to Lower Sandusky to begin negotiations. The invitation never arrived. The militant elements of the confederacy were furious to learn that Brant had made no mention of the Ohio River boundary in his speech to the American commissioners. With the aid of British Indian agents, the militant confederates wrote out an ultimatum to send to the Americans, which Brant and the Six Nations refused to sign. A new delegation led by the Delaware war captain Buckongahelas presented the confederates' demand for the Ohio boundary to the American commissioners at the end of July. The U.S. commissioners explained that this was impossible: the government could not evict lawful colonists from their lands north of the Ohio River. They did, however, express their willingness to negotiate land purchases from the confederacy, which Buckongahelas and the deputies conveyed to the confederate council.[51] Militant and moderate factions fought over how to respond to the Americans. Randolph, Lincoln, and Pickering received an uncompromising reply on August 16: The confederates rejected the Americans' offer to purchase their lands. They suggested, instead, that the U.S. government should hand over this money and the funds it had squandered on failed military campaigns to their own colonists to induce them to quit the Ohio Valley. If the United States would not agree to the Ohio River boundary, there was nothing for the confederates to discuss with the commissioners at Lower Sandusky. The American commissioners left for Fort Erie the next day.[52] There would be no peace without further war.

The renewal of the conflict in the Ohio and Illinois countries was a terrifying prospect for British officials in Canada. The outbreak of war between the British Empire and Revolutionary France in February 1793 had heightened security concerns in Britain's North American provinces. Not only did ethnically French Canadiens of questionable loyalty form a majority of the population of Lower Canada, but imperial officials feared that the United States would come to the aid of its sister republic. While the United States was far from a formidable foe on the global stage, it enjoyed regional superiority over the mighty British Empire along the border of Upper Canada, where 4,000 U.S. troops faced only 1,325 British regulars.[53] Simcoe had no doubt but that diehard American republicans had set their sights on his province. He predicted that "should the scepter of the United States fall from the feeble grasp of Washington, I doubt not but that Republic would enter into a treaty with France, and divide the Canadas between them." Simcoe also feared that an American victory over the confederacy would embroil the British Empire in war, as the confederates would use Upper Canada as a base from which to "continue a perpetual Warfare." If Simcoe was to doom the confederacy to defeat by withholding military aid, however, the colonists of Upper Canada would fall victim to the vengeful wrath of the "untutored savage."[54] The ongoing war also devastated Montreal's fur trade. The lieutenant-governor argued that "the serious Inconveniences in the Commerce View of this Unfortunate War ... tend to one point, our interest in an immediate Pacification."[55] Simcoe's and McKee's decision to support the militant faction in the confederacy had helped sustain Indian unity, but it had also made the failure of their negotiations with the United States almost certain. As such, the pair had inadvertently created a security crisis for Upper Canada from which there was no easy escape.

The only solution that Simcoe and Lord Dorchester could hit upon was to continue aiding the confederates while also being careful not to antagonize the United States by appearing to openly sponsor attacks on American colonists and soldiers. This did not prove easy. Rumors reached Dorchester in February 1794 that "General Wayne intends to march to Detroit."[56] Recognizing that the defense of Canada depended on the unity of the confederacy, the governor-general delivered a bellicose speech to the Seven Nations of Canada, a federation of Iroquois villages in the St. Lawrence River Valley. Dorchester explained that he would "not be surprised" if the United States went to war with the British Empire in the course of the year, and if such was the case, "a Line must then be drawn by Warriors."[57] Alexander McKee attested to the transformative power of Dorchester's speech among the king's Indian allies, which, along with the governor-general's decision to rebuild Fort Miami near the Maumee Rapids, promised to promote "a very extensive union of the Indian nations."[58] The speech did not play out so well in Philadelphia or Whitehall, where the American government denounced Dorchester's warmongering and the British government disavowed the governor-general's rhetoric, which, Home Secretary Henry Dundas chided Dorchester, "may not rather provoke Hostilities, than prevent them."[59]

The actions of Major William Campbell, the commander of Fort Miami, soon revealed the contradiction between the efforts of British colonial officials to aid the confederacy and their resolve to avoid going to war with the United States. After two years of careful preparations, U.S. general Anthony Wayne finally led his troops into battle on the humid morning of August 20, 1794. At the cost of $1 million, Wayne's Legion represented perhaps the last gamble that the United States could afford to take in its efforts to colonize the Northwest Territory.[60] If Wayne should fail, as had Harmar and St. Clair before him, it was by no means clear that the Washington administration could afford to mount a fourth campaign against the Indian confederates. Wayne did not falter. His superior numbers and well-trained troops routed the confederates and allied traders from Detroit, whose ranks included the trader John Askin, Jr. All was not yet lost, however, for the retreating confederates headed up the Maumee River to seek refuge from their pursuers in the earthen walls of Fort Miami.

As streams of retreating men hove into view, Major William Campbell was faced with the most important decision of his career: open the fort's doors to his allies and risk starting a war with the United States, or leave the retreating men to suffer their fate at the hands of the pursuing American forces. Campbell chose the latter. The outbreak of war with Revolutionary France in 1793 had fundamentally changed the mathematics of British geopolitics. Simply put, the defense of Canada and opposition to U.S. imperialism were not as important to the British Empire as waging war against the radical Jacobinism of the French Republic. Campbell knew that his masters in Whitehall had no desire to initiate a war with the United States, which would be a costly distraction from the main event in Europe. The gates of Fort Miami remained shut tight against the fleeing confederates. Campbell's betrayal, rather than Wayne's modest victory at the Battle of Fallen Timbers, fractured the confederacy, paving the way for the American general to dictate the terms of the Treaty of Greenville in 1795. To retain at least a part of their homelands, the confederates had to accept the American interpretation of the treaty of 1783: the international border had weakened both Native autonomy and possession of the land.

John Jay arrived in England on June 8, 1794, as part of the Washington administration's last-ditch effort to prevent a British-American conflict.[61] The outbreak of war in the Revolutionary Atlantic World meant that longstanding tensions in British-American relations assumed new and more threatening forms. While it had been possible for the American and British governments to largely ignore the ambiguous relationship between their territories and peoples during the cold war of the 1780s and early 1790s, these contentious boundaries threatened to spark armed conflict by the summer of 1794. Britain's continued occupation of the western posts and the Royal Navy's seizure of American merchant vessels both struck at the heart of the United States' claim to nationhood and imperial dominion. Moreover, they threatened to draw the fragile American Union into the French Revolutionary Wars.

When the French Republic declared war on the British Empire in February 1793, the Washington administration hoped to preserve peace by pursuing a policy of strict neutrality. The U.S. government was determined to avoid becoming embroiled in a European war that could easily spell disaster for the survival of the American Union. Not only was the fledgling republic too militarily weak to take on either the French Republic or the British Empire on anything like equal terms, but the polarization of American politics in the wake of the radicalization of the French Revolution threatened disunion, with Americans dividing into pro-French and pro-British camps. Neutrality was also an expression of national independence for the United States. It was a means of distinguishing the American Republic from the belligerent powers by proving that the United States would not become a British or French proxy.

It soon became painfully clear to Washington that proclaiming neutrality was easier said than done. French efforts to mobilize American citizens as combatants in the war against the British Empire and Britain's increasingly aggressive efforts to control maritime commerce both threatened to draw the United States into the conflict, no matter how vigorously the U.S. government tried to resist. Edmond Genet, the first minister to the United States from the French Republic, began commissioning privateers and set up a maritime prize court to condemn captured British merchant vessels almost as soon as he set foot in Charleston, South Carolina, in April 1793. Crewed and financed nearly exclusively by American nationals, these privateers violated the Neutrality Proclamation that Washington had issued on April 22, which prohibited U.S. citizens from taking part in hostilities for or against the belligerent powers. Genet's audacious behavior soon convinced even the Francophile secretary of state Thomas Jefferson that the Washington administration would have to demand his recall.[62] Although less colorful, the British Royal Navy's efforts to blockade the French West Indies proved more damaging to the United States. Washington received word in March 1794 from the U.S. consul at St. Eustatius in the Dutch West Indies that the Royal Navy had seized 250 American merchant ships in a matter of a few months. The consul's report coincided with rumors from Lower Canada of Dorchester's belligerent speech to the Seven Nations.[63] It seemed that war with the British Empire was imminent in the spring of 1794.

Rather than prepare for war, Washington decided to nominate U.S. Supreme Court chief justice John Jay as a special envoy to Great Britain.[64] Washington tasked Jay with securing compensation for the "vexations and spoliations" committed against American commerce, settling "all points of difference between the United States and Great Britain, concerning the treaty of peace," and framing a commercial treaty based on "reciprocity of navigation," which was to include gaining direct access to the British West Indies for American merchants. Jay was supposed to accomplish all of this without compromising the United States' treaty obligations to France.[65] It seemed like a tall order.

The failure of British-American negotiations to agree to anything since the preliminary peace articles in 1782 did not bode well for Jay's mission. Nevertheless, there was good reason to hope that a diplomatic solution to the ongoing conflicts between Great Britain and the United States could be found. Above all, neither side wanted to go to war. The Pitt ministry wanted no distractions from Britain's struggle against radical Jacobinism, which threatened not only to engulf Europe but also to incite revolution at home. The war was going badly for Britain and its European allies. French forces had won a series of victories in the Low Countries during June 1794, driving the coalition back across the Rhine.[66] British foreign secretary Lord Grenville was prepared to make a series of important concessions to the United States, including offering relief for Royal Navy seizures and agreeing to evacuate the western posts, before Jay even set foot in England.[67] Peace with America would help Britain's war effort against France.

The negotiations between John Jay and Lord Grenville that began in July 1794 offered another path to a border settlement. Merchants celebrated Jay's arrival in London. They had long hoped that British-American diplomacy could resolve the ambiguity surrounding the boundary of 1783. Montreal merchant James McGill reported the latest news from London to his Detroit correspondent John Askin in January 1794. McGill warned Askin that it was "the general opinion that the Posts will be given up" but that the British government would only agree to the evacuation if it could ensure that "the Indian Trade will be free within the American line to us."[68] McGill's partner, Isaac Todd, wrote Askin from London the following April with much the same news. While Todd expressed his disappointment that "there was not a Peace concluded between the Americans & Indians," he was "certain either by treaty or otherwise the Americans will in a few years get the Posts." The merchant believed that handing over the posts to the United States would be "no great injury to the Country" so long as the British Empire and the American Republic could amicably resolve their differences, "leaving the Trade free to all." Indeed, Todd predicted that an open commercial border with the United States meant that Upper Canada "would benefit by the Indoustry and ingenuity of the Americans," who would rely on the province's merchants to convey their produce to the Atlantic marketplace via the St. Lawrence River.[69] The way that the border functioned would be more important than its location.

As Jay and Grenville began their negotiations in London, Canada merchants recognized that the British government would have to agree to evacuate the western posts in order to establish a new border settlement with the United States. While they had consistently lobbied the British government against handing over the forts, they quickly realized that the negotiation of an open trade zone in the Great Lakes could compensate for the loss of the posts. Two years earlier, Montreal merchants had suggested that George Hammond propose to the United States that both nations adopt a "neutrality or reciprocity of Trade with the Indians inhabiting *within the limits of each.*"[70] Three days before the merchants' memorial came to hand, Alexander Hamilton told Hammond that "he doubted not" that his government would "consent to grant to the subjects of the crown a free intercourse of commerce with the Indians dwelling within the American territory" provided that American citizens would enjoy reciprocal access to the Indian trade in the Canadian provinces.[71] It seemed that the groundwork had long been in place for finalizing a new border settlement. Even as traders from Detroit fought alongside the confederacy at Fallen Timbers to defend Native homelands in the Ohio and Illinois countries, merchants in Montreal and London had largely given up on the idea that the Jay-Grenville negotiations would relocate the border. Rather, they hoped that the diplomats would ensure that the boundary functioned to their advantage by protecting border crossings.

During the course of August and September 1794, Jay and Grenville framed an agreement that granted British subjects and American citizens reciprocal commercial access to the Indian trade of the United States and British Canada. Jay sent Grenville an initial "outline of a treaty" on August 6, which "recognized ratified and forever confirmed" the boundaries of the United States as set down in the Treaty of Paris. The American envoy demanded that the British government remove its troops from the western posts by June 1, 1795. Colonists and traders living in the environs of the posts could choose to become U.S. citizens or they could take up to two years to settle their affairs before leaving the United States. Jay also proposed that the British and American governments appoint a joint commission to resolve ongoing geographic disputes over the running of the northern border where it met the Mississippi River.[72] Jay's outline seemed to offer few concessions to the Montreal fur trade.

Grenville countered Jay's proposal with one that would grant commercial and residential privileges to British subjects engaged in the Montreal fur trade. He agreed to evacuate the British garrisons but not until the summer of 1796, a year later than Jay had suggested. The foreign secretary was also careful to ensure that the cession would not interrupt the "the usual course of communication and Commerce between the Two Canadas and the Indian Nations who are to the Southward and Eastward of the Lakes." He proposed that merchants and traders at the posts should be allowed to continue in the enjoyment of their property "so long as they think proper to remain." Moreover, Grenville proposed that "it shall at all times be free" for British subjects and Native peoples "to pass and repass with their Goods and Merchandizes" for commercial purposes "without any hindrance or molestation from the Officers or Citizens of the United States." He also looked to establish the neutrality of the lakes, rivers, portages, and roads that ran adjacent to the border to ensure that "no impediment or obstacle shall be given to the passage of goods or merchandize of any kind, nor shall any duty be attempted to be levied upon them."[73] While Grenville offered to evacuate the western posts, he only did so on the condition that U.S. officials would not interfere with free movement across the border.

The American envoy was largely receptive to Grenville's proposal. As the Montreal merchants had anticipated, Jay demanded that American citizens enjoy reciprocal access to the Indian trade of British Canada, and that Native peoples residing in the British Empire should also be free to cross into the territory of the United States for the purpose of trade. The American envoy did question the feasibility of allowing British traders to import Indian trade goods into the United States without paying customs duties. Not only would it be difficult to prevent the fraudulent import of merchandise by traders who meant to sell it to colonists in the trans-Appalachian West, but even if the arrangement could be strictly enforced, the U.S. treasury would lose revenue without receiving any reciprocal benefit. Grenville suggested a compromise that would exempt from duty all furs, goods, and effects owned by Indians who crossed the border.[74] Jay was prepared to agree to create an open commercial border that would allow British subjects and American citizens reciprocal access to the Indian trade of the West, but he was not prepared to go so far as to create a free-trade zone devoid of all customs barriers.

The most important question that remained unresolved in the border negotiations was what to do with the merchants and traders who chose to remain at the western posts after the British evacuation. Jay asked Grenville, "In what capacity are they to remain? As British Subjects or American Citizens?"[75] Grenville proposed that the merchants and traders should "not be compelled to become Subjects of the United States, or to take any oath of Allegiance to the Government thereof," but if they should choose to become

American citizens, they must make this election within a year of the British evacuation.[76] Jay essentially agreed to Grenville's proposed new article but with the proviso that anyone who did not announce their decision to remain a British subject living on American soil would be "considered as having elected to become citizens of the United States."[77] Grenville rejected additional "desirable" proposals by Jay that would have demilitarized the border and the Great Lakes, and committed both governments to renouncing the use of Native allies in time of war.[78] By the end of September, the British and American governments had essentially agreed on the final border settlement contained in the second and third articles of the Jay Treaty.

In part, Jay's and Grenville's agreement conformed to long-established norms of the kinds of commercial and residential privileges that European merchants enjoyed in cosmopolitan trading communities across Europe and in the Ottoman and Mughal Empires in the late eighteenth century. The Jay Treaty's third article ensured that "it shall at all Times be free" for all British subjects, American citizens, and Indians, regardless of their place of residence, to "pass and repass" the boundary between the United States and British North America to "freely carry on trade and commerce" in perpetuity.[79] Beginning in the fifteenth century, European monarchies began brokering temporary agreements with the Ottoman emperor to allow their merchants to trade in commercial centers, such as Aleppo, in present-day Syria.[80] This practice was repeated by European traders in the Mughal Empire and in a web of commercial agreements made among European nations in the sixteenth and seventeenth centuries.[81] Traditionally, European monarchies had been far more protective of their colonial trade, with Spain and France in particular adopting their own regulatory systems, akin to Great Britain's Navigation Acts, to exclude foreign merchants from trading with their American colonies. In the Caribbean, at least, Great Britain, France, and Spain all liberalized their colonial commercial policy to allow limited foreign trade with their European rivals in the 1780s and 1790s.[82] In this sense, then, the commercial provisions of the Jay Treaty as they applied to the Montreal fur trade were nothing out of the ordinary. But in the context of the unfinished business of disentangling the American and British peoples after the American Revolution, these commercial privileges ensured that the border would not differentiate American citizens from British subjects. Two of the core rights of nationality—residence and free movement—would not distinguish nationals from foreigners.[83]

The Jay Treaty differed from European traditions of commercial diplomacy by allowing the residents of the western posts to choose their nationality, exempting them from the regular rules and processes of naturalization. The point of the commercial agreements—whether European treaties, Ottoman "capitulations," or Mughal *farmans*—that provided a legal basis for foreign merchants to live and trade within the borders of the state was that these individuals were foreigners. The eighteenth-century Swiss theorist of international law Emer de Vattel distinguished the "inhabitants" of a country from its "citizens." Inhabitants possessed some privileges, particularly "perpetual inhabitants" who were "a kind of citizen of an inferior order," and some duties, including observing the law and helping in the defense of their host state. But, according to Vattel, the law of nations did not require inhabitants to submit to "all the commands of the sovereign" because, unlike citizens, they were not members of civil society.[84] Vattel's "inhabitants" are what twenty-first-century political theorist Elizabeth F. Cohen calls "semicitizens": individuals who possessed some but not all of the rights of citizenship.[85] Although divided by two hundred years, Vattel and Cohen both recognized that states govern populations comprising individuals who enjoy different degrees of membership in society. By allowing individuals to elect to choose British subjecthood or American citizenship, the Jay Treaty obscured the distinction that Vattel tried to make between inhabitants and citizens. The treaty allowed inhabitants to become citizens without being naturalized. Unlike diplomatic agreements that granted foreigners commercial and residential privileges in other parts of the world, the Jay Treaty not only granted some rights of nationality to foreigners but granted individuals the capacity to choose their nationality.

The signing of the Jay Treaty on November 19, 1794, unquestionably cemented peace between the United States and the British Empire. But at what cost? In terms of the instructions that Washington had given Jay, the American envoy did broker a deal with the British government to establish a commission to administer compensation for American merchants who had suffered from Royal Navy seizures. But Grenville would not agree to a joint definition of neutral trading rights during wartime. Jay managed to secure the British withdrawal of the garrisons from the western posts, which was one of the most controversial issues that lingered on from the peace treaty of 1783. The London negotiations also established a joint commission to resolve the geographical uncertainty surrounding the St. Croix River and the northwest boundary of the United States. Jay and Grenville further settled the problem of prewar debts owed by American citizens to British merchants by establishing a compensation commission, though there would be no such commission to adjudicate the claims of American slaveholders against the British government for the enslaved peoples who escaped to freedom during the War of Independence. The treaty promised "a reciprocal and entirely perfect Liberty of Navigation and Commerce" between the British Empire and the American Republic, which did include direct commercial access for American citizens to the British colonies in the Caribbean and East Indies. Despite this, the treaty's temporary commercial articles placed restrictions on American trade to the West Indies. American merchants could not employ vessels over seventy tons in the carrying trade nor could they re-export the most lucrative items of the British West Indies, including sugar, molasses, and coffee, to other parts of the world. Nevertheless, scholars usually agree that the Jay Treaty inaugurated a period of prosperity for the American economy, that Jay did the best that he could in brokering this deal with Grenville, and that any deficiencies were well worth the price of preserving peace for the fledgling republic.[86]

Using Jay's instructions to tally up what he did and did not achieve does not reveal the hidden costs of the Jay Treaty. The privileges that Jay granted to both British subjects and Native peoples as part of the treaty's border settlement had important, though unintended, consequences for American nationhood and empire. The concessions that the treaty granted foreigners may have been common practice in European commerce. But in the North American context, in which Americans and Britons remained tightly intertwined, the privileges that British subjects and Native peoples enjoyed in the United States ensured that the American national state could not use the border to distinguish between its own nationals and foreigners.

The inability of U.S. officials to determine who was and who was not a legitimate member of the body politic posed significant dangers to the survival of the republic. It undermined the United States' claim to sovereignty and an equal status among the European nations of the Atlantic World. If the American government did not have reliable means of knowing who was and who was not a citizen, it cast doubt on the founding claim of the republic—laid out by Thomas Jefferson in the Declaration of Independence— that the American people represented a distinct nation. In more concrete terms, the ambiguous boundaries of citizenship threatened to introduce dangerous foreign influences into the domestic affairs of the republic. There was growing concern in both the Federalist and Republican Parties about the political implications of liberal immigrations laws in the 1790s. Republican fears of "aristocrats" and Federalist concerns about "Jacobins" brought the parties together in framing a more restrictive naturalization bill in 1795.[87] The difficulty of distinguishing American nationals from foreigners posed particular problems for American imperial ambitions in the northern borderlands. Volatile allegiances and inter-imperial competition with rival European empires meant that the U.S. hold over Euro-American colonists and Native peoples was particularly tenuous in the trans-Appalachian West. To its critics, the border established by the Jay Treaty gave license to foreign agents to incite rebellion against the United States among both Euro-American colonists eager to access the economic opportunities of the Atlantic marketplace and Native peoples who sought to maintain their political autonomy in opposition to American efforts to control and contain them within imperial boundaries. The Jay Treaty may have saved the United States from fighting a war that it could not win in the 1790s, though the British government was certainly not spoiling for a fight, but it did so by creating significant problems that imperiled the long-term survival of the American Union.

The Jay Treaty is one of the most controversial treaties in the history of the American Republic. Political reaction to the agreement played a crucial role in the crystallization of the first political parties and profoundly changed ideas about popular politics in the United States.[88] Republican critics of the treaty unquestionably viewed the accord through the partisan lens of their Anglophobia, particularly in their vigorous opposition to the treaty before word of its terms were even made public. But their criticisms were not simply a visceral reaction to any agreement with the British Empire that recognized the inequality of power between the former mother country and the American Republic. Rather, Republicans rightly protested the rights of commercial access, residence, and citizenship that the treaty granted British subjects in the Northwest Territory.

The debate that took place in the U.S. House of Representatives over the bill to fund the enactment of the Jay Treaty in 1796 reveals the pragmatic approach of supporters of Jefferson and Madison toward commerce and empire which cut against the grain of European experiments with a more liberal colonial trade policy in the Caribbean. While many Republican politicians supported liberal commercial policies toward foreign merchants in America's Atlantic port cities, they opposed similar concessions in the rising commercial centers of America's imperial domain in the West. In the former case, international trade promoted American Empire by forging ties of mutual interest between western colonists and eastern merchants; in the latter, foreign trade threatened American Empire by establishing commercial connections and political channels between the British Empire and Native peoples and colonists. James Madison, U.S. representative from Virginia, argued that the Jay Treaty rendered useless American possession of the western posts. The value of the posts, in Madison's estimation, lay in controlling the Indian trade by monopolizing the portages associated with them. The treaty, however, guaranteed that the "carrying places are to be enjoyed in common." Madison recognized that equal access did not mean equal facility. British merchants and traders possessed superior capital to their American competitors. Moreover, the merchant houses of British Canada could import goods from Great Britain duty-free through Montreal. These advantages, Madison predicted, would deny American citizens the bounty of the western trade and allow the British government to maintain its political influence among the western Indian nations. Albert Gallatin, a congressman from western Pennsylvania, was "at a loss" to understand why the treaty's second article allowed British traders to reside on American soil without becoming citizens of the United States and "without being subject to any control from our Government."[89] Far from solving American security concerns in the West, Republicans argued, the western provisions of the Jay Treaty had created new and more insidious challenges for American imperialism by ensuring that foreign agents were free to conspire with Native peoples against the United States.

The Federalist supporters of the Jay Treaty saw things differently. Horrified by the violent excesses of the French Revolution, they saw the British Empire as a bulwark against Jacobin extremism in Europe. In more pragmatic terms, Federalists saw Great Britain as a natural trading partner, and the privileges offered by the treaty as a usual practice among European nations. As such, Federalists believed that the Jay Treaty validated American nationhood. Massachusetts representative Benjamin Goodhue argued that the United States had nothing to fear from foreign traders. He reasoned that if the British government was willing to grant American citizens access to the fur trade of Upper Canada, then the United States should not worry about allowing British subjects into its western territories. Of course, New England Federalists like Goodhue believed that their constituents had much to gain from the Jay Treaty's promise of expanding maritime trade between the United States and the British Empire. Indeed, Federalists had a track record of sacrificing imperial ambitions in the West to further maritime trade in the East: John Jay's negotiations with Spain in the mid-1780s had sparked outrage among colonists in Kentucky when it appeared that the United States would abandon its navigation rights on the Mississippi River for trading privileges in Spanish America. Federalists from western districts, however, also supported the treaty, convinced that it would promote economic development.

New York representative William Cooper, the patriarch of Cooperstown, believed that his community would benefit from the growth in trade in the Hudson River Valley, which had traditionally been the main thoroughfare of western trade in colonial British America before the fall of New France in the 1760s.[90] In the end, this was a debate that the Federalists won both in Congress and in public discourse. The Senate and President Washington ratified the treaty and the House of Representatives voted the necessary appropriations for the agreement to go into effect. Thirteen years after the end of the War of Independence, the American Republic and the British Empire had succeeded in working through many of the ambiguities contained in the Treaty of Paris. But in separating their respective territories, the British and American governments had brokered an agreement that would make it increasingly difficult to distinguish the rights of American citizens from British subjects on the border.

The British evacuation of the western posts hung in the balance in the spring of 1796. The British and American governments had ratified the Jay Treaty, and Federalists had defeated Republican opposition to the treaty's appropriations bill in the U.S. House of Representatives. But Lord Dorchester contemplated delaying the evacuation of the British garrisons because he saw a conflict between the Treaty of Greenville—the peace terms dictated to the defeated confederates by Anthony Wayne in July 1795—and the western provisions of the Jay Treaty. Dorchester informed Alexander McKee about the expected change of plans in April 1796. He explained that U.S. regulation of the fur trade, which the United States asserted under the eighth article of the Treaty of Greenville, violated the free commercial access of British subjects to the Indian trade. The governor-general considered it "indispensably necessary" that the British minister in Philadelphia receive a satisfactory explanation from the Washington administration to remove "all doubts and misconception" over the operation of the western provisions of the Jay Treaty before he would order the withdrawal of the British garrisons.[91]

The conflict that Dorchester saw between the two treaties reveals the duality of the border settlement of the 1790s. It was an agreement of two parts: it defined the location of the boundary *and* how the border would function once in place. In terms of location, both treaties essentially reaffirmed the territorial border of 1783. The Jay Treaty finally agreed to the transfer of the posts, as well as setting up a joint British-American commission to resolve the disputed running of the boundary in the Northwest. The Treaty of Greenville ceded Native homelands in most of present-day eastern and southern Ohio to the United States, casting aside the alternative Ohio River boundary and any hope of a neutral Indian state for almost a generation. As such, there was no longer any serious dispute over the location of the border.

The way that the border would function under the Jay Treaty, however, meant that there would be no such clear divide between the peoples of the American Republic and the British Empire. The boundary would not distinguish British subjects from American citizens, nor would it contain Native peoples as domestic dependents of either state. Dorchester finally issued orders to evacuate the British garrisons once he received confirmation from Philadelphia that the British consul, Phineas Bond, and U.S. Secretary of State Timothy Pickering had agreed to a supplementary article explicitly protecting the "rights of free intercourse, and commerce" that British subjects and Native peoples enjoyed under the Jay Treaty's third article.[92] It was only by guaranteeing that the boundary would not discriminate between British subjects and American citizens that the British government would agree to its location.

The Battle of Fallen Timbers and the Treaty of Greenville were significant developments in the history of American Empire. Certainly American Indians never forgot what happened on the banks of the Maumee River. Over a decade after the defeat, the rotting remains of Fort Miami reminded the Potawatomi chief Nanaume "of our fathers, who fell on those fatal plains" and "of the ingratitude of the British; how they shut the Gates against us when we were flying to them for protection."[93] Nevertheless, the 1790s left a more complex legacy for the future of American imperialism than scholars have recognized. If the Indian cession of lands in present-day southern and eastern Ohio and the transfer of the western posts cleared the way for the United States to bring more land under territorial governance, then the Jay Treaty limited the ability of U.S. agents to exert control over the peoples who traveled and inhabited these lands. The northern border might divide the territories of the United States and the British Empire, but the boundary regime framed by the Jay Treaty made it more difficult than ever for government agents to distinguish between their own nationals and those belonging to other nations.

As British officials prepared to evacuate the posts, they tried to convince their Native allies that the location of the border mattered much less than how it would function. On reflection, Dorchester believed that the king's Indian allies had not the "least ground of umbrage with us" for the "attention which has been paid to their Interests in forming the late Treaty with the United States." Indeed, he believed that there was "much cause of gratitude for the King's friendly interference in relieving them from the servitude they had submitted to in their own Treaty with Mr. Wayne."[94] Few Indians agreed with the rosy picture that Dorchester painted for his masters in Whitehall. There were not many things that Joseph Brant and Blue Jacket could agree on, but they both knew that the British government had sacrificed the confederacy for its broader geopolitical interests.[95] The way that the boundary would function did matter, even as its location was a disaster for many Native peoples in the Ohio River Valley. The inability of the American national state to use the border to discriminate between its own citizens and foreign nationals was a significant obstacle to American imperialism, and the continued freedom of cross-border movement and trade made it much easier for a new pan-Indian movement lead by Tenskwatawa and Tecumseh to forge a new alliance with the British government in the years before the War of 1812.

3

"TO GUARD THE NATIONAL INTEREST AGAINST THE MACHINATIONS OF ITS ENEMIES"

General James Wilkinson declared martial law in Detroit on July 12, 1797, a year and a day after the United States occupied the town. "To guard the National Interests against the Machinations of its enemies, secret or ouvert, Foreign or Domestic," Wilkinson resolved to treat "all persons resorting to or residing within the limits" of Detroit as "followers of the army." Wilkinson's proclamation received the support of the magistrates and sheriff of Wayne County, who entertained "disagreable apprehensions from the dangers that at present MENACE its tranquility from an approaching Ennemy, as well as from internal and increasing factions."[1] No matter Wilkinson's later maverick behavior as an agent of the Spanish government, he was no loose cannon in 1797: civil officers at Detroit agreed that the authority of the U.S. government was under threat in the largest population center in the Northwest Territory.[2]

When U.S. troops arrived in Detroit in July 1796, they were foreigners entering a strange land. Founded by Antoine de La Mothe Cadillac in 1701, generations of Detroiters had lived and died under the French and British Empires. Until 1796, Detroit's residents had never been American citizens; the town had never before been part of the United States. For Detroiters, the arrival of the Americans was no homecoming: it was an occupation little different from the arrival of the British regime thirty-three years earlier. And, it might prove just as transitory. While the colonization of Native homelands by migrants from the eastern states was an important part of U.S. imperialism, it is important not to overlook the significance of places like Detroit for understanding American Empire. These long-established communities, the legacies of both French and British colonialism in the West, posed different challenges to American colonization. The United States would need to find ways to attach the loyalty of polyglot and multiethnic populations to the well-being of the American Republic to guard against separatist conspiracies sponsored by rival European empires. This was particularly urgent in Detroit, given the proximity of the British Empire across the narrow straits that gave the town its name.

The Jay Treaty made the American occupation of Detroit more perilous than it otherwise would have been. The rights of movement protected by the treaty created a porous border that was a constant source of anxiety and frustration for U.S. officials trying to construct a colonial regime in Detroit. The treaty's second permanent article granted British subjects the privilege of residing and engaging in commerce in the Northwest Territory, while the third permanent article ensured that British subjects, U.S. citizens, and American Indians were free to travel back and forth across the border for the purpose of trade.[3] These privileges in themselves were not extraordinary in the context of the traditional customs that governed global trade outside of the Atlantic World. Indeed, British merchants enjoyed similar rights in cosmopolitan commercial centers from the Indian Ocean to Portuguese Brazil.[4] But context matters. Diasporic polities of merchants outside of the Americas were usually culturally alien communities, separated from the indigenous population by ethnicity, language, and religion.[5] Not so in Detroit. The town represented a potent combination of the strange and the familiar, which complicated the ongoing challenge of disentangling the American and British peoples. Detroit's residents included an influential Anglophone minority of Britons and a Francophone majority who were strangers to the cultural and legal underpinnings of the American regime. The presence of an influential foreign population of merchants and traders who shared some rights of American nationality was uniquely problematic in the American West.[6]

The Jay Treaty also created the conditions for individuals to become citizens of convenience. The second permanent article allowed the residents of Detroit and of the other western posts the right to choose their nationality. This privilege not only allowed them to sidestep the naturalization process established for new immigrants to the United States, which was becoming increasingly stringent in the late 1790s, but, in practice, it exempted the residents of the western posts from any effective government regulation of nationality in the West. After 1796, merchants and traders claimed or rejected American citizenship and British subjecthood as part of a strategy to evade government regulation of the Montreal fur trade. In doing so, they demonstrated the porous nature of the territorial border between the British

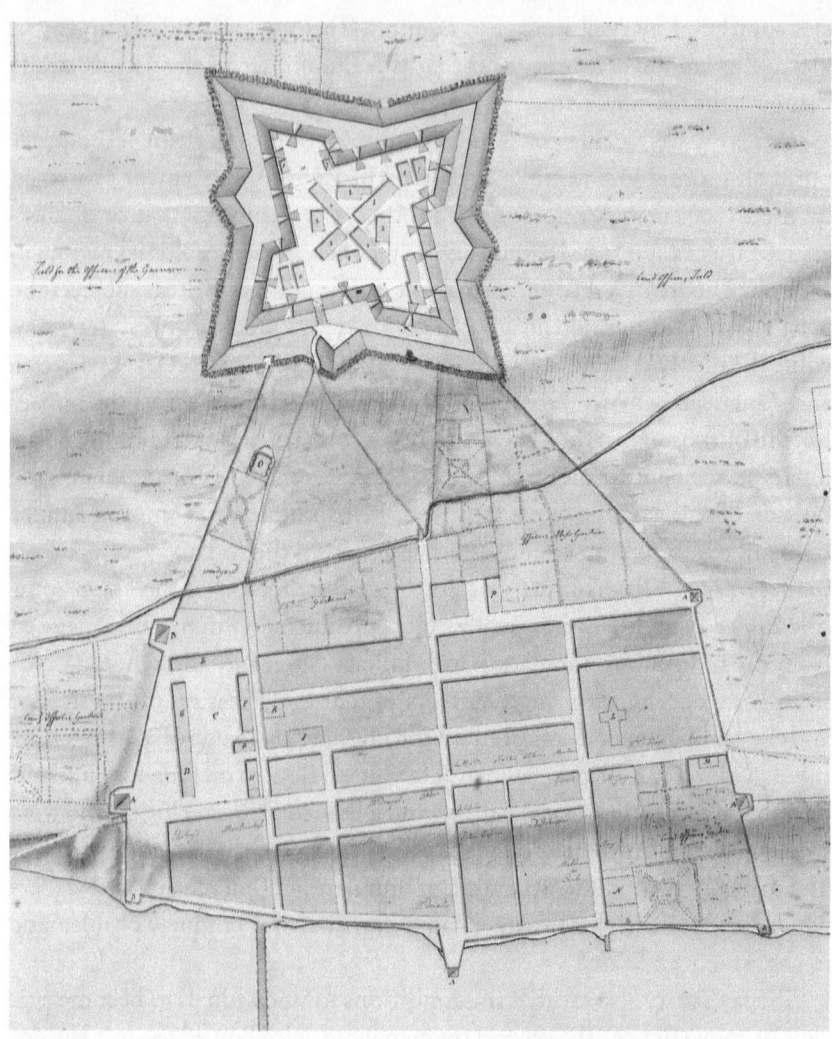

Detail from *Plan of the Town of Detroit and Fort Lernoult, situated on the Strait between the Lakes Erie and Huron . . . Taken from Actual Survey, August 1st, 1792*. A defensive perimeter wall connected Fort Lernoult and the town of Detroit. This plan, sketched by a British officer, recorded the storehouses of prominent merchants, including John Askin, alongside military buildings and the local parish church. Merchants estimated that they owned three-fourths of Detroit's fixed property when U.S. general James Wilkinson placed the town under martial law in 1797.
(Archives of Ontario, F 47-5-1-0-11)

Empire and the American Republic through the movement of goods, capital, and labor, and ensured that it was difficult, if not impossible, for U.S. officials to determine who was and who was not an American citizen or a British subject.

The fluid territorial boundary and the indeterminate membership of the body politic both created a series of problems for U.S. officials seeking to establish government authority on the periphery of the United States. Wilkinson declared martial law "to baffle the Arts of Seduction which have led to numberless desertions from the Public Service and to restrain licentiousness, and the infamous habits of drunkenness encouraged among the Troops, by the disorderly conduct of the venders of ardent Spirits." He blamed local merchants for encouraging soldiers from the U.S. garrison to escape across the border into Upper Canada where these same merchants, serving as justices of the peace, administered the deserters with oaths of allegiance to the British Crown.[7] The magistrates of Wayne County accused a malevolent British faction of corrupting the minds of the Canadien majority in the town by alienating "their affections from the Government of the States." Consequently, they urged Winthrop Sargent, the territorial secretary and acting governor, to invest Wilkinson with the power to "check the progress of the present prevailing faction, and to prevent the further corruption of the Inhabitants."[8] U.S. officials believed that the presence of an alien faction within the body politic threatened the security of the United States by weakening its military power and fomenting opposition to the new American regime.

The western provisions of the Jay Treaty reframed the problem of American nationhood. They resolved two longstanding issues that had contributed to the ambiguous character of the border since 1783: the treaty concluded a commercial agreement with Great Britain that established regulations for the movement of people, commodities, and credit between the American Republic and the British Empire, and, by securing the withdrawal of the British garrisons from the western posts, it cleared the way for an American state presence along the border. But, it also granted British subjects commercial and residential privileges and destabilized nationality by exempting residents of the western posts from the usual process of naturalization. Taken together, these provisions of the Jay Treaty ensured that U.S. officials could not use the border to make "legible" an American people.[9] The critical challenge facing American nationhood after 1796 was to find a way to properly differentiate American citizens from British subjects.

Colonel John Francis Hamtramck and the troops of the 1st Regiment of the U.S. Army marched into a foreign town on July 11, 1796. The arrival of the army in Detroit marked the second regime change in living memory; many of the town's residents could recall when British soldiers took possession of Detroit in 1760, during the conquest of New France. Detroiters responded to the American occupation in different ways. For some, the regime change offered new opportunities. Patrick McNiff had worked as a surveyor for Upper Canada in the 1790s. On the outs with Lieutenant-Governor John Graves Simcoe and the British commandant of Detroit, he lost his job in 1794. For McNiff, regime change provided a fresh start, and he quickly offered his services to the Americans.[10] Others were less hasty to collaborate with the United States. The merchant John Askin chose to accompany Lieutenant-Colonel Richard England to the mouth of the Detroit River to bid the departing British commandant farewell, rather than to stay in town to welcome Hamtramck and his troops.[11] While the United States certainly had friends in Detroit, July 11, 1796, was no homecoming for the American regime.

The divisive nature of the American occupation of Detroit was not soon resolved. As the first anniversary of the British evacuation of the western posts approached in May 1797, the merchant George Sharp circulated a petition among the townspeople of Detroit. The document offered an opportunity for all British subjects who wished to remain residents of the United States to record their election to do so. When Sharp registered the declaration with Peter Audrain, the prothonotary of Wayne County, at the end of the following month, 113 male heads of household in Detroit had signed or made their mark. One-third of the adult male population of the town of Detroit—one-fifth of all of Wayne County, which included the present-day state of Michigan, in addition to portions of Wisconsin, Indiana, and Illinois—alienated themselves from the body politic of the United States.[12] While they declared themselves foreign nationals, they were determined to continue to live and do business in the United States.

The scale of Sharp's petition shocked U.S. officials. Moreover, the petition also made it clear that ethnicity did not determine loyalty. While Anglo names were disproportionately represented among the signatories, 44 percent of those who attested their intention to remain British subjects had French names.[13] Likewise, not all natural-born subjects of the British Crown eschewed American citizenship. The merchant James Abbott, for example, was born in Ireland but chose to become a U.S. citizen and served as a justice of the peace for Wayne County.[14]

U.S. officials collapsed the complexity of loyalty into a simple story of conspiracy. They accused a small cabal of British merchants of hoodwinking weak-minded Canadians into subscribing to the petition without knowing what they were doing. The justices of the criminal Court of Quarter Sessions twice quizzed the merchant John Askin about his alleged role in instigating this anti-American conspiracy.[15] While Askin and his fellow merchants vigorously denied these accusations, Peter Audrain concluded that "great pains have been taken by some of Leaders of the british side to get Signatures from poor, ignorant People who have either signed or made their marks through fear or threats, others without Knowing what they were signing."[16] The Wayne County magistrates agreed with Audrain, complaining to Sargent that "Twelve months ago, we Knew of no more than Ten of its Inhabitants that were avowed British Subjects." In the meantime, the magistrates claimed, this handful of merchants had "with Some other Emissaries, found means by indirect insinuations and circulating-papers to corrupt the minds of the Inhabitants and alienated their affections from the Government of the States."[17] For American officials in Detroit, it was simply unthinkable that so many people would reject republican citizenship without some kind of skullduggery at work.

For the signatories of Sharp's petition, however, their decision made perfect sense. It allowed them to enjoy the residential and commercial privileges that the Jay Treaty had extended to British subjects in the United States, protecting the transnational connections underpinning the Montreal fur trade. Many of those who signed or attested Sharp's declaration had familial and commercial ties to Montreal. Eighteen of Detroit's most prominent merchants signed the declaration, as did Captain John Fearson, whose sloop, the *Saguinah,* depended on the Montreal fur trade for its cargo. The Indian trader Gabriel Hunot, who wintered in the Ohio country, made his mark. Mathew Dolson, a Detroit tavern-keeper and farmer, also signed the declaration. Dolson regularly supplied merchants with wheat and Indian corn to provision the fur trade northwest of Lake Superior. The livelihoods of Dolson and his fellow farmers in Detroit's agricultural hinterland might not depend on the Montreal fur trade, but the sale of their produce helped them obtain some of life's comforts.[18] The petition also allowed the signatories to gamble on the future of Detroit. Given the geopolitical uncertainty in the Revolutionary Atlantic World, it was by no means certain that the United States would hang on to Detroit forever. If, or when, the British returned, the Crown would surely reward its loyal subjects in Detroit. Even if there was no return to British rule, the signatories hoped that the government of Upper Canada would reward them with more extensive land grants in the new townships being laid out in the Western District on the Canadian shore of the Detroit River. Being a British subject in the United States held out a number of advantages to Detroiters in 1797.

While the presence of foreign merchants in cosmopolitan commercial centers like Cadiz, Lisbon, or even Philadelphia was numerically insignificant, the decision of one-third of the adult male population of Detroit to reject the civic responsibilities of U.S. citizenship posed significant problems for the everyday running of government in the town.[19] British subjects refused to serve on the Wayne County Grand Jury after an incident in March 1797 when one of the judges abused the British Crown from the bench, "which very naturally hurt the feeling of many of the Jurors." The magistrates and sheriff of Wayne County complained to Winthrop Sargent in July that "it was with difficulty that the Sherrif could procure a Jury of real Citizens to attend the last Sessions, or Ballifs to do their duty."[20] Patrick McNiff, a justice of the peace for Wayne County, considered civil government in Detroit to be "unequal to counteract the Machinations of the present prevailing factions." Such was the sense of alarm that McNiff urged Sargent to abandon civil government in Wayne County in favor of limited military rule.[21] The body politic was simply not healthy enough to support republican government.

The militia, too, suffered from a shortage of manpower. Chalbert Joncaire, the lieutenant colonel of the Wayne County militia, declared the military force unreliable in the winter of 1796. Only 29 of 111 men on the town's roster of two companies mustered arms. Moreover, the delinquent militiamen had refused to pay their fines for failing to appear because "they considered themselves as British Subjects" or informed Chalbert's sergeants that "they had business of their own to attend to." Chalbert blamed "a few Carreactors of the Town in the Mercantile line" for preventing the Canadien residents of Detroit from fulfilling their civic duty. Whatever the cause, the lieutenant colonel declared that he would not muster the militia until "some forceable measure is adopted to compel the Citizens of the Town to do their duty." The situation had not improved by July 1797, when the local magistrates informed Sargent of their "reason to fear, that little or no dependence can be put in the Militia of the County if called upon."[22] The citizen militia, the bulwark of liberty, could not be relied upon to defend the republic.

The U.S. garrison proved no better. Security concerns led Wilkinson to declare martial law in Detroit because of an alarming spate of desertions from the garrison at Fort Lernoult. Wilkinson was increasingly suspicious that British subjects were aiding the "dismemberment of the military force & the dispersion of a desperate band of Villains among these settlements, ripe for revolution, & ready to ride on any tempest which may be excited."[23] Desertion was not a uniquely American problem: British soldiers exploited the porous border to seek refuge in the American Republic.[24] But Wilkinson believed that civil officers of the Crown were complicit in the recent acts of desertion. Moreover, the magistrates of the Western District of Upper Canada were mostly residents of Detroit who had subscribed to Sharp's declaration. Wilkinson accused the magistrates of administering oaths of allegiance to the British Crown to "citizens of the United States, deserters from its colours" as soon as they crossed the river into Upper Canada, rather than returning the absconders to face military justice. This was particularly troubling to Wilkinson because he believed in the summer of 1797 that the government of Upper Canada and the Northwest Territory shared a common interest in opposing western conspiracies.[25]

While historians usually interpret the late 1790s as a period of improved imperial fortunes for the United States following the Battle of Fallen Timbers and the Treaty of Greenville, U.S. officials at the time felt less confident about the future. They viewed these military and diplomatic victories as indecisive, and they continued to fret about separatist conspiracies sponsored by rival foreign powers. In May 1796, President Washington had received word that "there are certain persons employed & paid to visit the Western Country for the purpose of encouraging the people of those parts to secede from the union and form a separate connection with a foreign power."[26] U.S. general Anthony Wayne feared that these agents of the French Republic meant to "feel the political pulse of the French & other inhabitants in the Western Country & particularly in the vicinity of our posts."[27] Later that year, a conspiracy involving U.S. senator William Blount of Tennessee and the U.S. Indian agent John Chisholm proposed a scheme to Robert Liston, the British minister to the United States, to capture Spanish Florida and Louisiana. While British Foreign Secretary Lord Grenville informed Liston that the government would not support the plan, the John Adams administration made public news of the "Blount" conspiracy in 1797.[28] The western provisions of the new treaties with Great Britain and Spain had not alleviated the threat that foreign powers would intervene on behalf of western separatists.

The political situation in the Northwest Territory remained unsettled in the summer of 1797, as Sharp's petition gathered the signatures and marks of Detroiters. Spanish officials in Louisiana refused to honor the terms of Pinckney's Treaty, protecting the commercial access of American citizens to the Mississippi River and the port of New Orleans. Wilkinson saw this refusal as a "precursor of serious consequences."[29] Rumors circulated in Philadelphia and the West that Britain and Spain meant to defile American sovereignty by marching their armies across the Ohio and Illinois countries to attack one another's North American possessions in Upper Canada and Louisiana.[30] More disturbing news came from Lexington, Kentucky, of the arrival of "Mr. D'Orleans, the legitimate heir of the late Duke, with his two Brothers." Wilkinson was convinced that this "relic of Blood Royal" meant to "debauch and detach the people of the Western Country from their Obligations and relations to the United States, and to embark them in the mad Projects of the French."[31] Fearful of the loyalty of the Canadien population, the general requested permission to prevent D'Orléans from traveling to Detroit. He wrote Winthrop Sargent, "you know, full well, what Influence the Rank of D'Orleans would give him over the ignorant credulous Canadians;—it might well turn their weak heads, and occasion no small difficulty."[32] Putting aside the delicious irony of Wilkinson, who was in the pay of the Spanish Crown, questioning the loyalty of Canadiens, other American officials shared the general's concern about the political allegiance of westerners who had only recently come under the jurisdiction of the United States. The Detroit magistrate Patrick McNiff warned Sargent that "the first leaders of the faction are all connected in Canadian families and have no real attachment to the Government of Britain any more than to that of the States." Rather, "their expectations have been and still are very Sanguine in favour of the States of France in getting possession of this Country; in this case they conceive it their Interest at a convenient time to abandon the British Government as well as that of the united States." McNiff saw Sharp's petition as part of a duplicitous scheme by a malevolent faction who sought to "establish their credit the more with the french when they might arrive . . . by alienating the attachment of the Canadian from the Government of the States."³³ Martial law, then, was necessary to protect U.S. authority in Detroit from domestic and foreign enemies bent on its destruction.

Detroit merchants saw things differently: Wilkinson's declaration of martial law violated "many invaluable priviledges" under the Jay Treaty, "the sacred source of a public and solemn treaty." They presented Wilkinson with a formal petition protesting martial law as an unprecedented measure in the town that "enjoys at least a prescriptive Charter of rights incompatible with the Idea of a Military Garrison." Moreover, the petitioners argued that the suspension of civil authority at Detroit violated the eleventh article of the Jay Treaty, which promised that "the Merchants and Traders on both sides shall enjoy the most complete protection and security for their Commerce." The merchants concluded that their present situation, as owners of "three fourths of all the property of a fixed or moveable nature within the Town of Detroit," was "repugnant to the feelings and Dignity of human nature as to the mutual harmony and friendship so strongly to be cultivated between Great Britain and America."³⁴ Wilkinson disagreed. While he promised to forward the merchants' petition to President John Adams, he informed them that martial law "has for its object the security of your persons and your property," which meant that his declaration "invades no single privilege of Citizenship, or right of Treaty valuable or invaluable."³⁵ Wilkinson's declaration of martial law did help stem the flow of deserters fleeing across the Detroit River to seek refuge in Upper Canada, but the response it provoked from the town's British subjects helps to reveal the extent to which the boundary failed to disentangle the American Republic from the British Empire.

U.S. territorial officials blamed British merchants for causing a split between civil and military officers at Detroit during the winter of 1797–98. Captain Peter Curry of the U.S. Navy and a file of troops from the U.S. garrison forced entry into the kitchen of Peter Audrain to apprehend the sailor Cornelius Mahoney. Curry had left Mahoney in charge of his effects in Detroit while the captain supervised the shipyard on the Rouge River. On his return, Curry discovered that Mahoney had "stolen & drank his liquor &c.," for which conduct the naval captain administered a severe beating. The frightened sailor ran away, seeking refuge in the home of Audrain, before Curry turned up to arrest him at bayonet point.[36]

Mahoney's arrest touched off a battle between the civil and military establishments at Detroit. Prior to forcing his way into Audrain's kitchen, Curry had appeared before the criminal Court of Quarter Session to answer for "beating his servant barbarously," and he had given bond to keep the peace for a year. Judge Louis Beaufait demanded that Colonel David Strong, the commander of the U.S. garrison, hand over Curry for breaching the terms of his bond. While Curry did turn himself in, the incident further soured deteriorating relations between military and civil officials. Audrain reported that Strong "received the Court with a cold politeness and rather with an apparent displeasure. . . . His resentment was particularly directed to Justice May, and fair warm expressions on both sides ensued."[37] Strong denied that he had obstructed the civil authorities in the execution of their duties, and he claimed that Curry's actions were from "irritation, and not from disrespect or Contempt."[38] Audrain was not so sure. He wondered in a letter to Sargent "if the military can enter the house of an officer of the Court, what will they not do with us?"[39]

Despite his suspicions about the tyrannical ambitions of the U.S. military establishment at Detroit, Audrain thought that the ultimate blame for the strife in the town lay with the British community. He believed that local merchants had been scheming to undermine the authority of territorial officials in the eyes of U.S. military officers. He explained to Sargent that "for some time past the british faction have been at work," but failing to find grounds to criticize the courts and civil officers, they had turned "the whole of their Strength Towards effecting a disunion amongst the Citizens themselves." The British faction succeeded in this aim through "an Easy conquest of certain Officers of the army who through foly or want of prudence, have involved themselves in debts, and have felt the Severe and impartial Justice of Court." To Audrain, the Curry incident revealed that these "officers have joined heart and hands with a party whose objective is to depress the dignity and destroy the respect due to our Magistrates."[40] Curry, Strong, and other military officers were not inherently hostile to the exercise of civil authority. Rather, British merchants had manipulated them into attacking the dignity of territorial officials.

Division and mutual suspicion seemed to infect every aspect of the lives of Detroiters. Winter was traditionally the social high season for communities tied to the Montreal fur trade. Audrain complained that merchants and officers from the garrison formed "a Separate and distinct Society for this Winter's amusements to which no Citizens of any respectability has been or is to be admitted." The insidious influence of faction also found its way into the confessional lives of Detroiters. Audrain reported to Sargent that "the british faction have carried their intrigue as far as the roman Catholic Church" by "effecting a misunderstanding between the respectable & rev'd Monsr. Levadoux, pastor of this parish, and the wardens of the Church." In preaching a sermon celebrating George Washington's birthday and extolling the virtues of the U.S. Constitution as "the best in the World," Father Michael Levadoux questioned whether British subjects could serve as parish wardens. In particular, Levadoux queried whether Philip Belangé could serve a third term in this capacity. The *curé* referred the question to the magistrates of Wayne County, who decided that Belangé "could not serve in any office of Trust." The decision sparked a violent demonstration among Belangé's supporters, who only dispersed after "the riot act was read in English & french." Audrain reported that "Phillip Bellengié makes no secret that he was advised & supported by John Askin Senr. George Meldrum & others."[41] The presence of British subjects in Detroit divided confessional and social life in ways that undermined the health of the body politic. Conflict made it all the more difficult for territorial officials to integrate the community into the American Empire.

In the fall of 1797, John McDonald left Detroit to make his way down the Maumee River with a "pirogue loaded with Goods to a pretty large amount" to trade at the Odawa towns near the Auglaize River. He did not make it past Fort Defiance, which stood at the confluence of the Maumee and Auglaize Rivers. U.S. soldiers stopped McDonald on the orders of James Wilkinson and forbade him from trading with Indians. McDonald returned to Detroit where news of Wilkinson's order met with the vocal opposition of local merchants, who claimed that the American general had violated the Jay Treaty by trespassing on their right of free and equal access to the Indian trade of the United States. The merchants claimed that the garrison had acted illegally by forbidding McDonald to trade with the Indians, while Wilkinson, it was rumored, had "granted an exclusive priviledge for trading with the Indians at and in the neighbourhood of Defiance to Mr. Hunt of Cincinnati, and a similar one to Mr. George McDougall for all the ottawa

Towns." "This report," Peter Audrain wrote Winthrop Sargent, "has produced a great deal of uneasiness at this place amongst the british merchants, that they make a common cause of it, and publicly assert that if the Commander in chief does not grant redress in the premises, they are determined to carry their Complaint to a Superior authority."[42]

Merchants and traders looked on the commercial and residential privileges that they enjoyed under the Jay Treaty as a charter of rights, the terms of which the government of the United States was duty-bound to honor.[43] McDonald's employers, the Detroit firm of Leith, Shepherd & Duff, dispatched James Leith to carry their protest to Wilkinson at Fort Wayne. The petitioners explained that they had "put themselves to a very great expence in making arrangements for trading with the Indians especially at the Ottawa Towns" because they were confident that "no partiality would be shown betwixt Citizens of the United States and british Subjects, as agreeable to the Solemn Treaty of Amity and commerce." The merchants asked Wilkinson to allow Leith to carry on trade at the Odawa towns until allegations of wrongdoing leveled against McDonald could be brought to trial.[44] Wilkinson agreed. He explained to the merchants that McDonald had "been represented to me, as a man mischievously disposed to toward the Government of the United States, and who had countenanc'd the purchase of stolen Horses from the Indians." The general, however, did not deny that the "preference to Mr. McDougal was founded on the presumption of his services to the Government . . . and the manifest confidence reposed in him by my predecessor in Command, and the acting Governor of the Territory." Nevertheless, Wilkinson assured the merchants that he would not trespass "on the rightful pretensions of any foreigners whatsoever, much less to offer Wanton injury to an individual."[45] While McDonald's fate remained undecided, Wilkinson's reply seemed to resolve the complaint of Leith, Shepherd & Duff.

News of Wilkinson's response actually created further alarm among merchants because the general claimed the right "to regulate within the Military reservations."[46] The Jay Treaty's third article stated that "it shall at all Times be free to His Majesty's Subjects" to "pass and repass" the border between the United States and the provinces of British Canada to "freely carry on trade and commerce."[47] Merchants argued that this clause meant that they ought to enjoy unfettered access to the Indian trade of the United States. The importance that both merchants and the British government placed on the right of British subjects to enjoy free access to the Indian trade had almost delayed the transfer of the western posts in 1796. Governor-General Lord Dorchester was worried that the Treaty of Greenville would provide a loophole for U.S. agents to exclude British merchants and traders: that treaty's eighth article granted the United States the right to regulate intercourse with the western Indian nations, which Congress enacted in the Indian Intercourse Act in 1796. The British evacuation of the western posts only went ahead as scheduled because U.S. secretary of state Timothy Pickering and British consul Phineas Bond quickly agreed to a supplementary article that reaffirmed the "rights of free intercourse, and commerce, secured by the aforesaid third article."[48] By claiming authority to regulate the Indian trade on the military reserves, the merchants argued, Wilkinson was violating an international agreement.

Regulating the Indian trade of the Northwest Territory was an important part of the U.S. imperial project after 1796. The expansion of the U.S. Indian factory system in the late eighteenth and early nineteenth centuries was part of a paternalist scheme to secure the attachment of Native peoples to the American Republic by offering them trade goods at rock-bottom prices. Unlike "unscrupulous" private traders, U.S. factors did not need to turn a profit when trading for furs. Consequently, American policymakers looked forward to a time when the government would hold a monopoly over the fur trade by driving private companies out of business. But the U.S. Indian factory system was not simply about making Native peoples dependent on the U.S. government for manufactured goods; it was also part of a larger scheme to acquire more land by undermining Native culture. The Treaty of Greenville may have fractured the unity of the Indian confederacy, but many individual nations and villages remained opposed to selling their homelands to the United States after 1795.

U.S. policymakers designed Indian factories to wrest more land from Native peoples. Established under the Washington administration but expanded during Thomas Jefferson's presidency, the network of U.S. Indian factors peddled cheap goods as a form of cultural imperialism aimed at convincing American Indians to abandon hunting in favor of commercial agriculture and domestic manufacture. According to Jefferson, Indians were only reluctant to sell land because they wanted to protect vast hunting grounds. When they realized that they could enjoy a better standard of living with less land by engaging in farming and manufacturing, Jefferson reasoned, Native peoples would drop their opposition to land sales.[49] If nothing else,

U.S. factors could pressure Indians into ceding land to settle the debts they racked up by buying trade goods from the U.S. government.[50] The factory system also promised to isolate Native peoples from the commercial and diplomatic networks of the Atlantic World, which had strengthened Indian resistance to U.S. imperialism in the 1780s and 1790s.[51] A government monopoly would come at the expense of foreign traders, like McDonald, who Jefferson accused of "constantly endeavouring to excite, in the Indian mind, suspicions, fears, and irritations towards us."[52] Regulation of the fur trade, then, promised to advance the colonization of the West by driving foreign traders out of business and forcing Indians to become farmers and mechanics. Military conquest was not the only means by which U.S. imperial policy would bring more land into the public domain.

Wilkinson worried that the dangerous restrictions that the Jay Treaty placed on his ability to regulate the fur trade threatened U.S. security in the West. The Treaty of Greenville had been painfully divisive for American Indians. The land cessions in Ohio had hardened the longstanding animosities among the militant and conservative factions that had always existed in the confederacy. As late as 1802, Joseph Brant chided militant Ojibwas, Odawas, and Potawatomies that they had "yourselves only to blame" for their misfortunes because they listened to "the English & the Shawamies" and foolishly ignored his advice to negotiate with the United States in 1793.[53] Nations and villages divided against themselves. Blue Jacket and Red Pole were among the first confederate leaders to meet with Anthony Wayne after Fallen Timbers, while Captain Johnny continued to lead a pro-British faction of Shawnees at Swan Creek near Fort Miami. Indeed, Blue Jacket set up a new home near Fort Wayne, paid for by the United States, and he and Red Pole accompanied Colonel Hamtramck's expedition to occupy Fort Miami and Detroit in 1796, in part to guard against any interference from Captain Johnny and other pro-British Indians.[54] Despite the divided nature of Indian politics, and having secured newfound allies among several former confederate leaders, U.S. officials remained worried about American Indian resistance to their colonization schemes. A generational split between older confederate leaders and younger warriors meant that violence against American colonists continued unabated in the Mississippi River Valley.[55] The political divisions among American Indians ensured that British Indian agents could still find allies, to whom they distributed presents from the newly established military forts that quickly sprung up on the Canadian side of the border after 1796.⁵⁶ Wilkinson warned Winthrop Sargent that "there is nothing more certain than that the natives imbibe the prejudices & politicks of their Traders." Wilkinson excluded McDonald from the Indian trade because he had it on "good authority" that the trader was "a principal Actor in all the Scenes of Blood & rapine on our frontiers, who cherishes the disaffection of the Indians towards us, and encourages the theft of Horses."⁵⁷ To Wilkinson, the Jay Treaty's protection of subversive criminals like McDonald was a recipe for disaster.

Wilkinson had particular cause to fear the worst in 1797. The general had spent the preceding summer and fall gathering "evidences of foreign Interference to excite Indian Hostility." He was not talking about the British government but about the audacious schemes of the French Republic. Wilkinson was convinced that "whatever may be the exterior of the Indians, it is certain that some secret plan has been in agitation among them for several months past," hatched by foreign traders in the pay of the French and Spanish governments, who were "insinuating themselves among the Indians to prevail on them to act both against the british and Americans."⁵⁸

The Mohawk leader Joseph Brant inadvertently helped give currency to these rumors. Brant traveled to Philadelphia in the summer of 1797 to consult with the British minister Robert Liston about the government of Upper Canada's refusal to allow him to sell Mohawk land on the Grand River to American speculators. Rumors reached Liston that Brant was prepared to offer the services of the Mohawks to the French minister, Pierre Adet, to aid in overthrowing the British Empire in Canada. Moreover, yet more stories reached the U.S. secretary of war, James McHenry, that Brant had been affronted by his reception by the Washington administration and that he was willing to aid French designs against the United States in the West. Brant did not start these rumors, but he embraced them as an opportunity to get what he wanted from the British government, adding his own account of "evil messages" about the French and Spanish that he had received from the Odawas and Shawnees at Michilimackinac.⁵⁹ Multiple reports from different sources all suggested that trouble was brewing in the Northwest Territory.

The conflict between Detroit merchants and Wilkinson over the commercial rights that British subjects enjoyed under the Jay Treaty became a diplomatic incident. The merchants complained to Peter Russell, who was administering the government of Upper Canada in Lieutenant-Governor Simcoe's absence, that Wilkinson's exclusion of McDonald and alleged regulatory power over the military reservation was "incompatible with the Treaty of Amity, commerce & navigation." They called on Russell to employ "the energy and justice of Government" to secure "a re-establishment of our Rights." Wilkinson's regulatory claims threatened the security of their trade. The military reserve, the merchants explained, "comprehend generally all the Trading Posts where the Indians live or resort to for trade, and which nature has pointed out as the most eligible for establishments of a commercial description." Consequently, unless "the principle of Military Jurisdiction be fully & unequivocally abandoned and the right of Trade according to the Treaty as amply supported," the petitioners argued, "no man of common sense will hazard his person or his property in situations liable to the injuries & indignities arising from the whim or caprice of a Military Commandant." Allowing Wilkinson the right to regulate the Indian trade, then, would mean that the Jay Treaty "so far as it respects His Majesty's Subjects trading to the Territory N. West of the Ohio, becomes little more than a pleasing dream."[60] Russell forwarded the petition to Robert Liston for him to seek redress from Timothy Pickering.

The Adams administration upheld the rights of Detroit merchants to engage in the fur trade without interference from Wilkinson. There were a number of reasons why the U.S. government did not share Wilkinson's view that British subjects posed a security risk in the Northwest Territory. Pickering had been a leading advocate of the Jay Treaty when he served in Washington's cabinet, and he had coauthored the supplementary article of 1796; Pickering knew the intent behind the Jay Treaty's western provisions better than anyone. Pickering and McHenry also viewed the local conflict at Detroit within the broader context of the United States' position in the Revolutionary Atlantic World. When Liston presented the Detroit merchants' complaint in early 1798, it seemed that France and Spain harbored hostile intentions toward the United States. In February 1798, news arrived in Philadelphia that a French privateer had violated American neutrality by seizing a British merchantman in Charleston Harbor; the following month, the XYZ dispatches arrived from Paris, describing how French officials in Paris had insulted the national honor of the United States by demanding payment from American diplomats before opening peace negotiations.[61] Combined with the rumors from the previous summer that French and Spanish agents were trying to enlist the support of colonists and Indians in the Northwest Territory to attack both the United States and Upper Canada, the Adams administration saw the British Empire as a likely ally rather than an enemy. Consequently, Pickering and McHenry reassured Liston that they had issued orders to Wilkinson "to preclude the further interference of that Officer in Commercial Matters."[62]

Montreal's fur trade grew under the protection of the Jay Treaty during the late 1790s. The conflict between the United States and the confederates in the 1780s and 1790s had proved damaging to the fur trade. Native peoples were busy protecting their homelands rather than hunting. Native and U.S. forces used the same river networks that formed the highways of the fur trade to prosecute the war, closing off wintering grounds in the Wabash and Maumee River Valleys to traders, who were unwilling to risk their lives trying to trade in a warzone. But it was not just the restoration of peace in the Ohio country that aided the recovery of Montreal's fur trade. Merchants and traders also benefited from the new territorial court system established by Winthrop Sargent in 1796. Merchants frequently used the new Wayne County Court of Common Pleas to recover debt and enforce contracts. While Audrain fretted about the general state of civil government in Detroit in the spring of 1797, the Court of Common Pleas provided a rare bright spot in his frequently foreboding reports to Sargent: "We have had Several Jury Trials at our last court of Common Pleas," which Audrain took "great pleasure in having it in my power to assure you that they have proved generally satisfactory to all parties; and that is not saying litle for a place like this." The court in Detroit proved more accessible than the Western District courts across the river in Upper Canada. The prothonotary added that he had "heard a British mercht. say publicly that in the course of one Term he had received from our laws more benefit than he ever had in Seventeen years under the british laws."[63] The numbers bear out Audrain's story. British subjects filed one-fourth of the cases heard by the Court of Common Pleas between 1796 and 1804, and fifteen Detroit merchant houses accounted for one-fifth of these cases.[64] The peace and stability that the American national state brought to the Northwest Territory after 1796 strengthened the transnational network underpinning the Montreal fur trade.

Detroit merchants expanded their commercial operations after 1796, hoping to make good the losses they had suffered over the previous decade. John Askin entered into a new agreement with the Fort Miami trader John Anderson in September 1796. He reassured his Montreal patron, Isaac Todd, that his new venture "will not run the smallest risk."[65] Askin's fellow

Detroiter Angus Mackintosh employed Antoine Lafond to "carry on the trade at Sandusky with vigor" in July 1800, allowing him to send John Connor to new hunting grounds.[66] The renewed investment in Indian trade goods and supplies was felt in Montreal where Askin's patrons James and Andrew McGill (the successors to Todd, McGill & Company) doubled their order of trade goods from their London suppliers John and Laurence Brickwood, and Phyn, Ellices & Inglis between 1797 and 1799.[67] The growing confidence of merchants involved in the Montreal fur trade may have encouraged the formation of the rival New North West Company in 1795. Several partnerships, including Forsyth, Richardson & Company and Todd, McGill & Company formed an opposition to Simon McTavish's North West Company. The rivalry spurred growth in the market for supplies and shipping on the Great Lakes, as the two Montreal groups vied for Indian corn, flour, and access to ships to transport these essential supplies to Grand Portage.[68] The late 1790s seemed like halcyon days for the Montreal fur trade after the misery of the previous decade of decline.

Merchants were in no doubt that they had the Jay Treaty to thank for their newfound prosperity. Queenston merchant Robert Hamilton prepared a memorandum for Peter Russell in November 1798 that explained how the treaty had promoted trade between Upper Canada and the Northwest Territory. Operating a monopoly of the government portage on the Canadian side of the Niagara River in partnership with Kingston merchant Richard Cartwright, Hamilton was as good a judge of trends in the Montreal fur trade to the Southwest as anyone. He estimated that Upper Canada's trade "in the territory of the United States about Detroit, and towards the Illinois & Mississippi" was currently worth about £100,000 a year and growing. Fur returns from Detroit had increased year-on-year for the past three years. And all this was exclusive of the trade in the upper Mississippi River Valley through Michilimackinac. "So far from having lost anything by the American Treaty," the merchant wrote, "the Trade of this Country has visibly increased by that Mutual and unrestrained Intercourse which has taken place between the Americans and us in consequence of this Treaty."[69]

Hamilton also anticipated that the Jay Treaty would ensure that the merchants of Upper Canada would benefit from the American colonization of the Northwest Territory. He informed Russell, "the demand for Goods of all kinds from this Province must further increased with the progress of American Settlements which are forming along the Southside of the River

St. Lawrence and the Lakes." The merchant explained, "the natural, we may indeed say the only outlet for all the produce of these settlements is by the river St. Lawrence, whose Waters are sufficient to carry the largest Rafts of lumber to the Sea Ports of this Province." Hamilton looked forward to the diversification his trade in concert with the economic development of the western country. He predicted that colonists would float rafts of lumber up the St. Lawrence "and this lumber which is itself a valuable Article of Commerce may at the same Time be made a vehicle for transporting their Wheat, Flour and Pot Ash to Market."[70] With an open border between Upper Canada and the United States, it no longer mattered to merchants which country garrisoned the western posts after 1796.

Geography, capital, and the multiethnic networks of family and friendship that underpinned the Montreal fur trade also ensured that Canada merchants and traders faced no serious competition from American merchants. Hamilton boasted that "it is Notorious that no established Mercantile house in the States hath yet engaged in this Trade. The few Articles which are brought are generally brought by Adventurers who seldom appear a second time." The merchant celebrated the geographical advantages that the St. Lawrence River held over both the Hudson and Ohio Rivers for the Montreal fur trade's commercial ascendancy over the West. Hamilton estimated that the carriage of a "Barrel of three hundred weight" from Montreal to Kingston cost between "three to three and a half Dollars," while the cost of transporting the same cargo from Albany to Oswego by the Mohawk River was "from nine to Ten dollars."[71] The Montreal merchant Alexander Henry confirmed Hamilton's claim. He found freight charges from "Schenectady very High," with a boat to Niagara costing "£80 York Currency—which will be half a Dollar near pr. Gallon on Liquor."[72] In addition to enjoying cheaper transportation costs than their potential rivals in New York or Philadelphia, merchants supplied from Montreal imported British manufactured goods into the United States duty-free.[73] In theory, the Jay Treaty was meant to ensure that American citizens and British subjects enjoyed equal access to the fur trade. But in practice, equal access did not mean equal facility for U.S. merchants trying to break into the Indian trade of the Ohio and Illinois countries.

Where American merchants were involved in the Montreal fur trade after 1796, their enterprise benefited Montreal merchants. By opening direct trade between the United States and British North America, the treaty allowed merchants in Montreal and Quebec to establish commercial connections with their American counterparts in New York, Philadelphia, and Baltimore. Before the Jay Treaty, American merchants had little choice but to purchase furs from the Ohio and Illinois countries via London. The New York merchant John Jacob Astor, for example, first traveled to Montreal in the winter of 1787 to purchase furs, but the British navigation system required that his consignment had to cross the Atlantic twice—from Montreal to London and then London to New York—before he could sell them on the American market.[74] After 1795, American merchants were more often associates, rather than competitors, of Montreal merchants. It was easier for merchants such as Astor to avoid the trouble and expense of direct competition with the long-established Montreal fur trade. The association between Montreal and American Atlantic port cities also helped Canada merchants to break into the China trade by evading the Crown monopoly enjoyed by the East India Company. Montreal merchants worked around this monopoly by forming partnerships with American merchants. In July 1794, William Hallowell, an agent and future partner in the North West Company, was in New York to discuss cooperating with the houses of John Jacob Astor, Hamilton and Reid, and Seton and Maitland. By 1798, the Montreal partners had purchased the ship *Northern Liberties* for exclusive use in the China trade. The following year, William McGillivray opened the New York office of the North West Company on Day Street, between Broadway and the North River, not far from Astor's establishment at 149 Broadway.[75] The Montreal merchants' maneuvering over the China trade reminds us that their claims to nationality were strategic. To protect their free access to the Indian trade of the trans-Appalachian West, the merchants loudly proclaimed their rights as British subjects under the Jay Treaty, but to open trade between British North America and China, they quietly shipped their bales from New York to Guangzhou under American colors.

In 1800, the electors of Wayne County voted in the Northwest Territory's second election to send a representative to the territorial legislature in Chillicothe. By 1798, U.S. territorial officials determined that the adult, white male population of the Northwest Territory had reached the threshold of five thousand, established by the Northwest Ordinance, which allowed the territory to advance to the second stage of territorial governance. While American colonists had lived under the colonial rule of an appointed governor and territorial officials, who had governed through ordinance since 1788, voters could now participate in governance by electing representatives from among their own ranks to the territorial legislature. As such, the late 1790s marked an important marker in American colonization of the West, as the Northwest Territory advanced toward statehood and equal membership in the American Union. Territorial elections, then, were meant to signal the maturation of political society in the Northwest Territory from a primitive, colonial state. Participation in elections was the key moment in defining the boundaries of the body politic in a white, patriarchal republic. While partisan division was an integral part of electioneering, the pageantry and spectacle of early American elections also promoted solidarity among voters by demonstrating the racial and gendered hierarchy of politics in the early American Republic.

Far from demonstrating the health of political society, the election of 1800 in Detroit revealed how the Jay Treaty exacerbated the problem of distinguishing who was and who was not a member of the body politic. Six candidates stood for election, with George McDougal, Chalbert Joncaire, and Jonathan Schieffelin defeating Benjamin Huntington, Joseph Cissne, and James May to claim the county's three seats in the territorial House of Representatives.[76] Huntington contested the election results on the grounds that Schieffelin was ineligible to run for office because he had signed Sharp's declaration in 1797. The defeated candidate protested that his rival was "not a citizen of the United States, but a subject of his Britanic Majesty." It was inconceivable to Huntington that Schieffelin would claim "the right of remaining here a citizen of the United States and of filling a seat in our Legislature under (what you call) the taut implications of our Treaty with the British Government." Allowing an avowed British subject to sit and vote in the legislature represented a dangerous intrusion "on the domestic affairs of this Government" and "an illegal attempt to influence its deliberations."[77]

The Court of Quarter Sessions heard Huntington's petition on October 19 in "rather noisy" proceedings that lasted "from ten o'clock in the forenoon until five o'clock in the afternoon."[78] While legal proceedings over the contested election continued until December 1802, Schieffelin traveled to Chillicothe to take his seat in the House of Representatives for the opening of the second General Assembly on November 23, 1801.[79] Schieffelin's election to the territorial House of Representatives helps to reveal the ways in which American nationhood remained ambiguous at the turn of the nineteenth century. He had signed Sharp's declaration as a British subject in 1797, served in the employ of the U.S. government in 1798, and was a voting member of the territorial legislature in 1801 without ever having become a naturalized citizen of the United States. Despite this, the House of Representatives of the Northwest Territory was satisfied that he was an American citizen because the Jay Treaty had allowed Schieffelin to claim citizenship without having to follow the naturalization rules and procedures established by Congress in the 1790s. Unlike a foreigner in the eastern states who had to register the decision with an American court, all that Schieffelin had to do to become an American citizen was to swear an oath.

The Jay Treaty created the conditions for individuals to claim and refute American citizenship and British subjecthood as they pleased. Given that Schieffelin had signed a public petition stating his intention to remain a British subject, it seems strange that he was able to convince the territorial legislature in Chillicothe that he was a fellow citizen. But the petition organized by George Sharp was a purely voluntary act, neither required nor mandated by the U.S. government. Indeed, this was the rub: the treaty's second article exempted the residents of the western posts from the naturalization process established by Congress that would otherwise have allowed U.S. territorial officials to distinguish between foreigners who enjoyed some of the basic rights of nationality (residence and free movement) and U.S. nationals. Some subscribers to Sharp's petition soon developed strategies to exploit the ambiguity of the Jay Treaty to advance their own interests. During the discontented winter of 1797–98, Peter Audrain fretted that British subjects meant to run him out of office by becoming U.S. citizens. He warned Winthrop Sargent that the British subjects in Detroit promised to have "every person now in Commission turned out of office" because they planned to "fill the vacancy by remaining on our side and taking the oath of allegiance to the United States."[80] The ability of individuals to claim American citizenship by the simple utterance of an oath meant that it was difficult for officials to determine who was and who was not a member of the body politic.

While U.S. territorial and military officials often spoke of their intention of excluding foreigners from office or benefiting from government contracts, in practice they were unable to exclude British subjects. James Wilkinson was determined "to prevent the money of the United States going into the British Citizens," but he was unable to find American merchants to supply his troops in July 1797. Wilkinson's determination "to forbid any

Intercourse with Traders or Dealers, who do not make their remittancy to the Atlantic States" proved impossible.[81] The U.S. government was a regular customer of John Askin, who sold firewood, hay, and various building materials to the U.S. Commissary and the U.S. engineers at Detroit.[82] Several signers of Sharp's declaration held commissions in the U.S. military. Jonathan Schieffelin, who replaced Colonel Return Jonathan Meigs as the garrison engineer for Fort Lernoult; Hugh Heward, who served as a commissary; and Jonathan Nelson, the commander of the sloop U.S.S. *Detroit*, had all subscribed to Sharp's document.[83] While Wilkinson had promised to remove from office any British subjects employed by the U.S. government, this proved more difficult than he anticipated. William Henry Harrison, the governor of the Indiana Territory, which Congress carved from the Northwest Territory in 1800 in anticipation of Ohio statehood, employed a number of British subjects in civil government. The trader John Johnston served as the U.S. customs agent at Sault Ste. Marie; Charles Reaumé, also a trader, served as a justice of the peace at Green Bay; the merchant Robert Dickson received an appointment to serve as a justice of the peace at Prairie du Chien on the upper Mississippi River.[84] The difficulty of differentiating between citizens and subjects was a consequence both of the Jay Treaty's western provisions and the practical demands of governance in a sparsely colonized region.

The problem of distinguishing between foreigners and American nationals meant that the realms of domestic and international politics were one and the same. Patrick McNiff wrote Albert Gallatin, the new treasury secretary in Thomas Jefferson's cabinet, of the rise of an "aristocratic" Federalist faction in Detroit in the fall of 1801. Addressing Gallatin because of his support for Jefferson in the disputed presidential election of 1800 against a "Nefarious and daring faction of Aristocrats Introduced by foreign (I mean British) Influences," McNiff explained to the Pennsylvanian that Jefferson's supporters encountered an equally dangerous movement in local politics. The Detroit Republican described an alliance between "Bandittis" from Pittsburgh and "a number of British Subjects still remaining among us [who] have formed one faction giving themselves the appellation of Aristocrats." McNiff accused the faction, led by Matthew Ernest, of using "every artful means in their power to bring over undiscerning Ignorant people to their principles," and decried their occupation of civil offices at Detroit.[85] McNiff's letter to Gallatin was unquestionably motivated by his ambition to secure the lucrative position of U.S. customs collector for the port of Detroit. But his argument also demonstrates the ways in which citizens of convenience poisoned the body politic. When it was impossible to determine who was truly an American citizen, the loyalty of the entire community became suspect. In such a toxic atmosphere, partisan politics and personal rivalries could soon descend into bitter acrimony as opponents resorted to accusations of treason and foreign intrigue.

Just a few months before Ohio achieved statehood in 1803, Peter Audrain continued to worry about British subjects in Detroit. By December 1802, many of the town's leading merchants had established new homes across the river in Upper Canada. Angus Mackintosh moved his family to their new residence near Sandwich in September 1799, while John Askin followed later in April 1802.[86] Nevertheless, Audrain reported the aggravating presence of British subjects in Detroit who went about denigrating the character of President Thomas Jefferson to promote disaffection among the town's Canadien residents. Reflecting on the state of civil society in the settlement after six years of American rule, Audrain thought it best that Detroit would not be part of the new state of Ohio. He wrote John Cleves Symmes that the U.S. government had made a wise decision by allowing the town and its environs to remain a "Colony of the United States," as he considered the local population, including the "illiterate" Canadiens, "not fit for a Self Government."[87]

American Empire remained a work in progress in 1802. Incorporating places like Detroit into the United States was not simply a case of raising the stars and stripes. The town had never been part of the American Republic, and its majority Francophone residents had never been U.S. citizens. In the best of circumstances, securing the attachment of this alien population to the American Republic would be no easy task. But the Jay Treaty ensured that the U.S. occupation of Detroit occurred in difficult conditions. The residential and commercial rights that British subjects enjoyed in Detroit might have been little different from the kinds of privileges that foreign merchants exercised in numerous cosmopolitan trading centers around the globe, but they clearly proved a serious irritation for U.S. territorial and military officials trying to establish the authority of the United States in the newly occupied town. Moreover, the ability of individuals to claim U.S. citizenship under the Jay Treaty outside of the regular system of naturalization gave rise to more serious problems for American Empire. Some Detroiters took advantage of the ambiguity surrounding the Jay Treaty to pursue a strategy of claiming and rejecting nationality according to their interests. These citizens of convenience created a volatile situation in which it was impossible for U.S. officials to distinguish between American citizens and British subjects. By 1802, then, it no longer mattered how many or how influential the avowed British residents of Detroit were. With U.S. officials unable to tell who was a national and who was a foreigner, the damage to the body politic had already been done.

4

"THE EQUIVOCAL ATTRIBUTES OF AMERICAN CITIZEN AND BRITISH SUBJECT"

· · ·

Troubling news arrived in Montreal from Michilimackinac in February 1803. Forsyth, Richardson & Company and Parker, Gerrard, Ogilvy & Company sent an urgent memorial to Lieutenant-Governor Peter Hunter of Upper Canada to complain of the actions of David Duncan, the new collector of customs for the port of Michilimackinac. They "learnt with infinite concern" that Duncan "had set out from thence for Saint Marys, with an intention of seizing a quantity of Merchandise" worth five thousand pounds belonging to the New North West Company (better known as the XY Company). The collector claimed that the company had violated the new Customs Act passed by Congress in 1799 because "the Vessel which carried the Goods had not previously touched at Michilimackinac."[1]

The Montrealers protested that Duncan's seizure was "contrary to the Spirit of the Treaty with America." Moreover, they explained that accepting the collector's argument that they must enter their goods at Michilimackinac before proceeding through the Saint Marys River into Lake Superior "would be ruinous to the fair Trade of your Memorialists."[2] The U.S. collector's determination to levy duties on goods crossing Grand Portage had opened a new front in Montreal's civil war between the North West Company and the New North West Company. Under the direction of the ruthless Simon McTavish, the original company attempted to put their rivals out of business by controlling the British shore of the Saint Marys River and constructing a new portage at Kaministiquia (renamed Fort William in 1807).[3] The entrepreneurial McTavish hoped to mobilize U.S. customs agents to defeat his commercial enemies.

To speed along the restoration of their goods, the XY Company also sent "an unofficial application" to the British minister in Washington, D.C., Edward Thornton. The merchants explained that "a delay of Restoration of their Property; (as the Articles cannot be replaced from hence in time) would be as injurious to their interests almost as eventual forfeiture." Delay was nearly as damaging as permanent loss because the Montrealers needed to convert their trade goods into furs to be able to pay their accounts in London.[4] Thornton managed to recover the company's property without much difficulty. The minister wrote the merchants in April 1803 that U.S. Treasury Secretary Albert Gallatin had ordered Duncan to return their property and made "an explicit declaration that no Duties were or are meant to be levied at St Marys." But Montreal merchants would hope in vain that they could in the future "avoid the risk of a Robbery under pretext of Law, similar to what the recent conduct of the American Collector seems to aim at."[5]

The competition between the rival Montreal companies proved short-lived: McTavish's nephew William McGillivray helped effect a reunion of the North West Company after his uncle's death in 1804.[6] But Duncan's seizure was merely the opening salvo in an escalating entrepreneurial battle waged between the Montreal fur trade and U.S. agents on the northern border of the American Republic. Congress passed the Customs Act in 1799, designating six new inland ports of entry in the trans-Appalachian West, including Detroit and Michilimackinac.[7] While the Jay Treaty's third article protected British subjects from paying discriminatory customs duties, the U.S. customs establishment, in keeping with the common practice of early modern states, rewarded agents who found innovative ways to enforce revenue laws by paying them a percentage of collected duties and the proceeds of condemned chattel. As such, the creation of an inland customs establishment pitted two sets of entrepreneurs against one another: merchants and traders, who looked for ways to evade paying customs duties, and U.S. collectors, who benefited from the effective collection of revenue from cross-border trade.

The local innovations of U.S. agents on the border were increasingly welcomed in Washington, particularly following the election of Thomas Jefferson as president in 1800. Jefferson appointed two of the Jay Treaty's leading critics to important cabinet positions in 1801: Albert Gallatin became secretary of the treasury, whose responsibilities included overseeing customs collection, while James Madison headed the State Department. The Jefferson administration was not prepared to openly violate the treaty with Great Britain—doing so would undermine the United States' claim to be a treaty-worthy nation—but the president and his cabinet were eager to limit and eventually renegotiate the Jay Treaty's western provisions. The Jefferson administration could confirm or deny the local innovations of its agents according to geopolitical circumstances without undermining the U.S. government's claim to possess the authority to enforce treaties with foreign nations.

The Louisiana Purchase of 1803 raised the stakes in the contest between U.S. agents and Canada merchants to truly continental proportions. The addition of the vast Louisiana Territory to the imperial domain of the United States meant that American officials and merchants and traders were fighting over the geopolitical future of a vast swath of North America, ranging from the Mississippi River to the Rocky Mountains. While oft-celebrated as Jefferson's greatest accomplishment, the Louisiana Purchase posed significant challenges, as well as opportunities, for American Empire. As with Detroit in 1796, the American occupation of St. Louis eight years later exposed the ambiguity of nationality in the West. It was not simply that the Louisiana Purchase extended an already contested boundary into unsurveyed territory that was peopled by Indian nations and foreign colonists who were strangers to the United States. Rather, merchants and traders argued that the acquisition expanded the operation of the Jay Treaty into the region purchased from France, granting them important rights of access and residence in the trans-Mississippi West. Traders managed to evade the attempts of local U.S. agents to exclude foreign nationals from the Indian trade of the Missouri River by claiming American citizenship under the Jay Treaty's second article. Unable to distinguish U.S. nationals from foreign aliens, General James Wilkinson, the Canada merchants' old nemesis, now governor of Upper Louisiana, decried a situation in which individuals could "acquire the equivocal attributes of American Citizen and British Subject."[8]

Merchants and traders became citizens of convenience as they developed their own strategies to counter the innovations of U.S. customs and territorial officials. These schemes formed part of the western dimension of an imperial struggle between the American Republic and the British Empire. Empire lay at the heart of a broad argument between the two countries about rights of free navigation and nationality in the Atlantic World, which became increasingly urgent with the renewal of the European war in 1803. As historian Alan Taylor has argued, the British and American governments traded positions on these questions.[9] When discussing navigation on the inland waters of the West, the British government was a strong advocate of free trade in favor of its subjects. In the Atlantic Ocean, by contrast, Great Britain employed ever narrower definitions of what constituted the trading rights of neutral merchants at the same time that it sought to enforce the exclusive and indefeasible definitions of British nationality that underpinned the Royal Navy's policy of pressing sailors into service.[10] For the United States government, the opposite was true: they were vocal proponents of free trade and more permeable boundaries of American citizenship on the high seas but not on the Great Lakes.

The two governments embraced the contradictions inherent in their respective positions because policymakers were concerned with imperial pragmatism, rather than ideological consistency. The United States accepted free movement in the Atlantic World because maritime trade was an engine of American imperialism that helped to connect eastern merchants with western colonists. It opposed free movement on the northern border because foreign merchants and traders threatened American Empire by "fomenting" rebellion among colonists and Indians alike. Deadlocked in a death struggle with the Napoleonic Empire, the British government restricted free movement of maritime trade to protect its global empire. By contrast, the Crown supported free movement on the border as the king's ministers recognized that the defense of Britain's North American colonies depended on military alliances with American Indians. The conflicting imperial interests of the American Republic and the British Empire ensured, however, that only a grand deal between the two governments was likely to resolve the Canada merchants' complaints.

Such a deal looked like it might happen in 1806. The expiration of the temporary commercial clauses of the Jay Treaty meant that the Jefferson administration dispatched William Pinkney to aid James Monroe, the American minister in London, to negotiate their replacement. The negotiations that continued into 1807 promised to reaffirm and extend the Jay Treaty to protect the access of British subjects to the trans-Mississippi as well as the trans-Appalachian West. But resolution of border disputes ultimately proved elusive because British and American diplomats could not agree on a comprehensive deal that resolved the contradictions in their own policies toward navigation and nationality.

By 1808, merchants and traders were losing confidence in the Jay Treaty's ability to protect their right of free movement across the border. After 1807, the entrepreneurial contest along the northern border became an important front in the economic war that the United States waged against the British Empire through the Embargo and Nonintercourse Acts. Technically, the Jefferson administration honored the commercial privileges that British subjects and Native peoples enjoyed under the Jay Treaty by exempting the Montreal fur trade from the Embargo Act and its supplementary acts passed by Congress in 1807 and 1808, which prohibited commerce between the United States and British North America (and the rest of the outside world). The violent seizure of boats from the Michilimackinac Company in the Niagara River in spring 1808, however, made it clear to Montreal merchants that the U.S. government was determined to destroy their trade.

In February 1804, the Montreal firm of Forsyth, Richardson & Company consulted Phineas Bond, the British consul in Philadelphia, about "differences of Opinion upon the Mode of calculating Duties payable ad Valorem."[11] While the creation of the U.S. customs regime in the Great Lakes after 1799 meant that it was no longer possible to legally import goods into the United States duty-free, business continued much as before the passage of the Customs Act. Montreal merchants continued to export manufactured goods into the United States, destined for Indian Country, and imported furs and peltries. The third article of the Jay Treaty guaranteed that British subjects would pay "no higher or other Duties" than American citizens when importing the same goods through the eastern Atlantic ports, and the treaty explicitly exempted furs from paying "any Impost or Duty whatever."[12] Consequently, Montreal merchants quite reasonably believed that "as British Subjects claiming the Benefit of the Treaty... we are to pay precisely the same, and no more, than an American."[13] Instead, the U.S. customs collectors at Detroit and Michilimackinac engaged in local innovations that employed a sleight of hand in calculating ad valorem duties, which meant that British subjects paid higher customs duties than American citizens.

The entrepreneurial activities of U.S. customs collectors on the northern border in the first decade of the nineteenth century were an important part of American empire-building in the West. The Jay Treaty was meant to create an even playing field for British and American merchants to compete in the fur trade. But the established commercial and kinship networks of the Montreal fur trade, which stretched from the wintering grounds of the American West to the great merchant houses of the City of London, meant that American merchants enjoyed equal access to the fur trade without sharing equal facility with their competitors in Montreal. U.S. territorial official Patrick McNiff lamented the continuity of trade in Detroit in a letter to U.S. treasury secretary Albert Gallatin in October 1801. He estimated that at least 90 percent of the merchandise on hand in Detroit came from Montreal despite the new Customs Act.[14] Montreal retained its position as the Atlantic entrepôt and commercial capital of the fur trade of the American West.

There were some changes. Merchants obtained more of their tobacco and liquor supplies from the United States because these commodities paid particularly high duties when imported from Upper Canada. In October 1800, for example, Angus Mackintosh made sure to divide his liquor order with McTavish, Frobisher & Company between those parts he planned to sell in Upper Canada, to be shipped from Montreal, and those parts for use in the United States, to be dispatched from New York.[15] The Customs Act helped to level the playing field between New York and Montreal, but even when merchants in the trans-Appalachian West ordered liquor or other commodities from New York, they did so through their patrons in Montreal. A transnational web of patronage, debt, and credit ensured that Montreal retained its ascendency over the Indian trade.

Merchants in Detroit and the neighboring township of Sandwich, Upper Canada, made the best of the Customs Act by pursuing new commercial ventures. The shift toward using American, rather than West Indian, liquor meant that Native peoples increasingly demanded whiskey rather than high wines after 1800. The growth of grain production in the Detroit and Thames River Valleys meant that local merchants established their own whiskey distilleries. Angus Mackintosh employed George Jacobs of the Thames River Valley to form a distillery on a "modest scale" in January 1801. Mackintosh ordered two copper stills and "a man of good character, who understands the business of distilling perfectly well" from Pittsburgh the following month. His distillery proved highly successful. He supplied the North West Company with 1,500 gallons of "double-distilled whisky" in June 1802.[16] Other merchants followed suit. By 1806, Mackintosh, John Askin, and the houses of Leith, Shepherd & Duff and Pattinson and McGregor all operated stills with a combined capacity of over 1,600 gallons.[17] Distilling became an integral part of the ancillary economy supporting the Montreal fur trade as its center of gravity shifted further westward during the early nineteenth century.

On its own, the creation of customs establishments on both sides of the border had minimal impact on the movement of people, capital, and commodities between the British Empire and the American Republic. Nevertheless, merchants and traders probed for legal loopholes as part of their perennial battle to reduce the cost of doing business. In 1801, merchants tried to avoid paying customs duties on goods they sent to St. Louis in Spanish Louisiana. They argued that the rivers and carrying places that connected Detroit to the Mississippi River constituted one long portage; the third article of the Jay Treaty specifically exempted goods carried over portages from payment of customs duties. Treasury Secretary Albert Gallatin rejected this argument as "too dangerous to be tolerated." He explained to Comptroller John Steele that the Maumee and Wabash Rivers led "into the heart of the United States." Consequently, "to lay that passage open, would render all the provisions of our revenue Laws nugatory," for Gallatin was convinced that the goods were "exclusively intended for consumption of the Indians living within the Territory of the United States, and even of the American settlements on the waters of the Ohio."[18] The merchants accepted Gallatin's decision without protest.

Merchants also tried to use the Jay Treaty to evade paying duties in Upper Canada, which responded to the Customs Act by creating its own system of collection districts after 1800.[19] McTavish, Frobisher & Company claimed that their annual tobacco consignment to Grand Portage, which lay on the American side of the border on the northwest shore of Lake Superior, should be exempt from payment. They petitioned Lieutenant-Governor Peter Hunter in 1802 to complain that the collector of customs at Queenston had illegally demanded payment of over £220 on the 12,000 pounds of tobacco they had imported from the Albany firm of Caldwell, Fraser & Company. The merchants argued that customs duties should not be levied on goods that temporarily crossed into Upper Canada for the sake of portaging. To collect duties on goods destined for Grand Portage, the memorialists proclaimed, was "prejudicial to the rights of Individuals, to the Interest of Commerce, and to that amicable intercourse and good neighbourhood which was meant to be promoted by the aforesaid Treaty of Amity and Commerce."[20] Their arguments found traction, and merchants would no longer pay customs duties on tobacco consigned to Grand Portage.[21]

The terms of the Customs Act were not of themselves a threat to Montreal's fur trade, but the U.S. customs establishment was organized to encourage innovation among its agents. The local efforts of U.S. customs agents to enforce revenue laws on the border would quickly bring them into conflict with merchants and traders. The Customs Act mobilized the private interest of agents toward national ends by ensuring that collectors received 3 percent of the import and tonnage duties paid in their district, as well as receiving payment of a tariff of fees ($1.50 for each entering vessel of under one hundred tons, for example) and a share of the fines, penalties, and forfeitures collected from customs violations.[22] Matthew Ernest, a patriot war veteran, defeated the aspirations of both Peter Audrain and Patrick McNiff to secure the lucrative appointment as collector for the port of Detroit in January 1800. Ernest wasted little time in collecting duties once he received instructions from the Treasury Department. He sent a circular letter to local merchants, calling for the retroactive payment of duties on all the spirits, wines, and teas that they had imported since the passage of the Customs Act.[23] On occasion the system proved all too accomplished in exciting the avarice of collectors. Ernest absconded owing the U.S. government more than $7,500 of customs receipts in 1805, accompanied by David Duncan, his counterpart at Michilimackinac, who made off with almost ten times as much.[24] Peter Audrain shared the "Common Report" with Gallatin that "Duncan is in london rolling in his chariot, and that Matthew Ernest is now quartermaster in the british service, in one of the west-Indies Islands."[25] The Treasury Department's annual auditing system may have provided the duplicitous Ernest and Duncan with the opportunity to defraud the U.S. government, but their abuse of public funds did not detract from the incentive that the Customs Act provided for agents to engage in border surveillance.

Ernest and Duncan both pursued local innovations that challenged the right of British subjects to import goods into the United States on equal terms with American citizens. Through sleight of hand in calculating ad valorem customs duties, they succeeded in charging British subjects importing goods through the Great Lakes 5.5 percentage points higher charges than American citizens importing the same goods through the Atlantic seaports. Or, to put it simply, £100 of goods imported from London paid £22 of duties when imported into the United States through Detroit and only £16.10.10 when imported through New York or Philadelphia. Ernest and Duncan achieved this by including the cost of transportation in their calculation of the value of goods at Detroit and Michilimackinac. Consequently, they reasoned that £100 of London goods was worth £133.3.8 in Montreal and £146.13.4 in Detroit, compared to only £110 in New York.[26] The collectors financially benefited from finding ways to discriminate against British subjects by pushing the boundaries of the Jay Treaty.

After consulting with Phineas Bond, Forsyth, Richardson & Company sent a complaint to Anthony Merry, the British minister plenipotentiary to the United States. Merry protested the actions of Duncan and Ernest to Albert Gallatin in April 1804. Gallatin was dismissive of Forsyth's and Richardson's complaint, explaining that the Jay Treaty's third permanent article was only meant to exempt British subjects from the payment of "the Foreign Extra Duty" that amounted to an additional charge of 10 percent; the treaty did not obligate the U.S. government to fix the same value on goods imported through the Great Lakes and the Atlantic seaports. The treasury secretary supported Ernest's and Duncan's practice of including the cost of transportation when calculating the value of goods imported through the Great Lakes.[27] Gallatin and Madison gladly endorsed the local innovation of U.S. customs collectors when they could be defended against British protests under the letter of the Jay Treaty.

After 1803, the conflict along the border merged with a more general dispute in British-American relations about the character of free trade and nationality. American complaints against the Royal Navy's impressment of sailors and its seizure of neutral merchant vessels reemerged with the renewal of the war in Europe and worsened with the return of William Pitt to the British premiership in 1804. Moreover, Pitt's appointment of the unpopular Anthony Merry as minister plenipotentiary to the United States only made it more difficult for the complaints from Montreal to receive a sympathetic hearing in Washington, D.C.[28] Merry, whose insistence on observing social rank succeeded only in alienating himself from Washington society, attempted to convince Gallatin in conversation that "the Amount of Duties paid was in Fact greater at one Place than at another, let the Mode of estimating them be what it may, it must be considered that the Spirit of the Treaty was not fulfilled." Merry concluded that the stubborn refusal of Gallatin and Madison to entertain his arguments reflected "the Wish of this Government to check as far as possible the Importation of Goods through Canada into the North Western Part of the United States." A point which gave the minister "equal Reason to take the Liberty to suggest that it may eventually be very much for the Interest of His Majesty's Government to afford every Protection to that Trade." With Merry and the Jefferson administration at an impasse over their conflicting interpretations of the

Jay Treaty, the British minister concluded that only "a formal Discussion between the Two Governments" would resolve the dispute.[29]

On April 25, 1805, two boats of the North West Company, loaded with trade goods, pushed away from Lachine. Below the rapids of the St. Lawrence River, which prevented direct traffic from Montreal to the Great Lakes, Lachine served as a major transportation center for the river vessels of the Montreal fur trade. The boats, under the command of Joseph Labelle, were destined for the company's storehouse at Kaministiquia, on the northwest shore of Lake Superior. Labelle guided them by the "accustomary and usual rout of Navigation," following the border down the St. Lawrence, across Lake Ontario, through the Niagara River Valley, then across Lake Erie, through the Detroit River Valley, and across Lake Huron to the Mackinac Straits and the Saint Marys River entrance to Lake Superior.[30]

They never made it into Lake Superior. Labelle and his boats encountered "waves and great swells" when they entered the Mackinac Straits, at the northern tip of Michigan's lower peninsula, on June 11. "From stress of weather, & with a view for the safety of said Boats & cargoes, and to preserve the same, as well as his life as well as the lives of the Boatmen & passengers," Labelle put in at Grosse Isle on Michilimackinac Island around four o'clock in the afternoon to wait out the storm. Labelle moored the boats a few feet offshore, landed a tent, and set about building a fire to make some tea to warm the boatmen. Three hours later, David Duncan and a squad of troops from the island's garrison arrived on the scene, seizing the two North West Company boats and their cargoes on suspicion of smuggling.[31]

William and Duncan McGillivray, the North West Company's agents at Saint Joseph's Island, immediately protested Duncan's seizure as a contravention of the free navigation of the Great Lakes as protected by the Jay Treaty. The McGillivrays argued that Duncan had no grounds for his seizure because the boats were merely seeking shelter from a storm and had not landed any of their goods on American soil. "Had any Part of their Cargoes been landed, & a Sale attempted," the agents pointed out, "the Thing would have been totally different: but stopping merely within a few Feet of the Shore, and only for a Couple of Hours, cannot surely give you a Right to make a Seizure of Property." If they were to accept such a right, the McGillivrays pointed out, "with the same Propriety might our Vessels be seized in the River Sinclair or in the Streights of Saint Marys; a Situation in which it was never contemplated by the Treaty to place British Subjects." Duncan refused to discuss the seizure with the North West Company agents, referring them instead to the territorial Supreme Court in Detroit for the resolution of their case.[32] The local innovations of U.S. customs officials were not just burdening the Montreal fur trade by demanding the payment of higher customs duties than merchants believed they ought to pay; Duncan had now demonstrated the capacity of the American national state to destroy the Montreal fur trade by capturing its trading vessels and confiscating its valuable cargoes traversing the commercial highways of the Great Lakes.

In August 1805, a brigade of traders from Montreal made their way through the Great Lakes bound for the Missouri River. They entered their goods and paid duties with David Duncan at Michilimackinac. From the Mackinac Straits, the traders crossed Lake Michigan to the portage at the future site of Chicago before making their way through the Des Plaines and Illinois Rivers to its confluence with the Mississippi River to the north of St. Louis. "To their utter astonishment," the traders found their passage across the Mississippi River to St. Louis barred by a proclamation issued by their old advisory, James Wilkinson. The governor of the Upper Louisiana territory ordered that "no person the Citizen or Subject of a foreign Power, will be permitted to enter the Missouri River for the purpose of the Indian trade." Moreover, the traders complained, Wilkinson had imposed "the most extraordinary test that was offered to any, but more especially to British Subjects; nothing less than abjuring their Allegiance and Faith to their lawful Prince & Sovereign, or to be excluded from that Trade."[33] Rather than successfully banning British traders from accessing the Missouri River fur trade, Wilkinson's proclamation spurred Montreal traders to engage in their own entrepreneurial innovations. Exploiting ambiguity in the Jay Treaty, traders became citizens of convenience, claiming American citizenship in St. Louis and British subjecthood in Montreal.

U.S. territorial officials and local residents approached one another with caution and a measure of mutual suspicion when Captain Amos Stoddard conducted the ceremonies marking the transfer of St. Louis from France to the United States on March 10, 1804.[34] This was the third time in forty years (and the second time in two days!) that St. Louisans had witnessed their hometown changing hands between competing empires.[35] In 1763, Pierre de Lacléde Liguest and his common-law stepson Auguste Chouteau had traveled north from New Orleans to select a site for the town on the western Spanish shore of the Mississippi River. St. Louis was a town built on trade. Laclède selected its location near the confluence of the Mississippi and Missouri Rivers, and only 135 miles north of the mouth of the Ohio River, because these three great rivers formed a major crossroads of Native America.[36] News of France's cession of the trans-Appalachian West to Great Britain by the 1763 Treaty of Paris convinced many French families to leave the Illinois country for St. Louis, which remained a culturally French city despite the arrival of a handful of Spanish officials in 1767. By 1804, the town boasted two hundred houses and a cosmopolitan population, which included merchants from Italy, Germany, and the Netherlands, as well as Frenchmen drawn from around the Atlantic World. St. Louis, like Detroit and other places in the creole corridor, was a foreign city, unacquainted with U.S. governance and populated by aliens. But unlike the transfer of Detroit by the Jay Treaty, the Treaty of Cession made all free, adult male St. Louisans citizens of the United States. This troubled both parties. St. Louisans worried that the United States would levy higher taxes and demand the performance of more onerous civic duties from its citizens than had the Spanish regime without providing the same level of security. U.S. officials and policymakers, including President Thomas Jefferson, worried about whether Catholic Frenchmen would prove equal to the demands of republican citizenship or remain loyal to the United States.[37]

By 1804, St. Louis had long-established commercial ties with the Montreal fur trade. New Orleans served as the Atlantic entrepôt of St. Louis during its first two decades, connecting the town's merchants to the French port cities of La Rochelle and Bordeaux. After the American Revolution, however, local merchants faced fierce competition from the Montreal fur trade in the Upper Mississippi and Missouri River Valleys. Before long, traders from Michilimackinac and Prairie du Chien had cut the profit margin of St. Louis merchants by as much as sixfold.[38] Arthur St. Clair, the governor of the Northwest Territory, described the Mississippi trade in 1791 as being "almost entirely in the hands of the british—even much the greatest part of the merchandise for the trade of the Misouri River is brought from Michilimackinac by that of the Illinois, partly by spanish Subjects themselves, and partly by british Traders."[39] St. Louis merchants soon adapted to the new economic environment by forging commercial ties with Montreal and London in the 1790s. Indeed, many merchants discovered that their furs fetched more money on the Montreal market than in New Orleans.

St. Louis's leading merchants, Auguste and Pierre Chouteau began doing business with Todd, McGill & Company, employing Andrew Todd as their agent at Michilimackinac, after Auguste's brother-in-law Charles Gratiot visited London in 1793.[40] A decade later, the Chouteaus learned about the Louisiana Purchase from their Michilimackinac agent George Gillespie, who reported "the news of the day is that the French have ceded Louisiana to the Americans for 6 million piastres, part in money, part in bad debt. I cannot believe it although it is generally admitted here."[41]

The regime change in St. Louis presented both risk and reward to the Chouteaus. On the one hand, the United States could reward the brothers with patronage and, perhaps more importantly, trading privileges among the Native peoples of the Missouri River, ensuring that they would no longer have to share the proceeds of the fur trade with their Montreal patrons. On the other hand, the new regime could favor the Chouteau's political and commercial rivals in St. Louis, or abruptly sever the trade connection with Montreal, either of which would severely damage their business interests. The Chouteaus hedged their bets. Auguste maintained his relationship with Gillespie and other British merchants after 1804, while Pierre looked for ways to ingratiate himself with the new American regime.[42] After traveling to Washington, D.C., with a deputation of Osage leaders in 1804, Pierre Chouteau managed to secure his appointment as U.S. Indian agent for the Upper Louisiana territory, while Governor William Henry Harrison chose Auguste to serve as a justice of the peace and judge of the Court of Quarter Sessions.[43] Securing the services of the Chouteau brothers was an important victory for the United States in its efforts to integrate St. Louis into the American Empire. They were powerbrokers among the French and Native populations of Upper Louisiana. As with many of their colleagues in the Montreal fur trade, the Chouteau brothers married into Indian kinship networks to access commercial opportunities in the fur trade. Under the Spanish regime, they had enjoyed a trading monopoly with the Osages, and the Chouteaus continued to exercise considerable influence in tribal politics, notably with the Osage leader White Hair, whom the brothers had helped to secure the position of the principal civil chief of the northern band in the 1790s.[44] Still, with the Chouteaus' commercial interests keeping them in the orbit of the Montreal fur trade, U.S. officials could not be sure how enduring the brothers' professed loyalty to the American Republic would prove.

Montreal merchants hoped that the U.S. occupation of St. Louis and the

Upper Louisiana Territory would create greater stability for their trade west of the Mississippi River. Under the Spanish regime, the illicit trade across the river had depended on the complicity of local officials or the readiness of Spanish subjects to smuggle goods across the river from Kaskaskia. Montreal merchants believed that the Louisiana Purchase had expanded the operation of the Jay Treaty to include the trans-Mississippi West, protecting their access to the trade of the Missouri River Valley. Eager to exploit the regime change in the Upper Mississippi and Missouri River Valleys, they imported three-fourths more merchandise through Michilimackinac for the Indian trade of the Missouri River after 1804.[45] Newly arrived governor James Wilkinson, however, was determined that U.S. imperial expansion would thwart, rather than advance, the commercial ambitions of the Montreal fur trade.

American policymakers believed that control over the fur trade was essential to establishing U.S. hegemony over the peoples of the Missouri River Valley. U.S. territorial officials encountered a volatile situation in Upper Louisiana in the early 1800s. The regional supremacy of the Osage people had been on the decline since the 1790s when their traditional allies, the Missouris, suffered severe losses from Indian raiding parties from the Illinois country and a smallpox epidemic. Spying an opportunity to gain the upper hand over the Osage, Spanish colonial officials recruited Shawnees and Delawares to migrate across the Mississippi River. Border crossings continued into the 1800s, with Potawatomis, Kickapoos, and Sacs and Foxes clashing repeatedly with the Osage. Originally viewing Upper Louisiana as a Native enclave, U.S. authorities pushed Indian nations in the Ohio and Illinois countries to move west of the Mississippi River. Shawnees, Delawares, Miamis, Potawatomis, Kickapoos, Odawas, Wyandots, Chickasaws, and Cherokees all migrated to Upper Louisiana during the early years of American rule. Establishing new villages in the Ozarks, these newcomers penetrated deep into Osage territory. By 1807, some Shawnee villagers called for a pan-Indian campaign to drive out the Osage.[46]

Wilkinson recognized that his ban on foreign traders was "somewhat extrajudicial," but he believed that his actions were justified because he blamed these individuals for promoting Indian hostility to the United States. "It is well known," Wilkinson explained to Secretary of War Henry Dearborn, "that the Indian trade, from Hudsons Bay and the St. Lawrence, to the remotest streams of the lakes, the Mississippi and the Missouri is nearly monopolized by British Traders, their factors Agents and Engagées." The governor considered the commercial loss suffered by the United States "a trifling ill, when compared to the transcendent influence, which is thus acquired and perpetuated by a foreign power, over the aborgines within our national limits."[47] Wilkinson's conviction that regulating the fur trade was a central part of the U.S. imperial project had stuck with him since his time in Detroit. It was a view he shared with President Jefferson, who saw the expansion of the U.S. Indian factory system as an important part of "civilizing" Native peoples and neutralizing their resistance to U.S. colonization by isolating them from rival empires in North America and, ultimately, assimilating them into American agrarian society.[48]

Wilkinson's attempt to differentiate between American citizens and foreign nationals drove the evolution of citizens of convenience, as Montreal traders searched for ways to evade the governor's attempts to exclude British subjects from the Missouri River. Wilkinson's proclamation helped to reveal the ambiguous bounds of American citizenship by provoking traders to exploit the overlapping rights of American and British nationality that they enjoyed under the Jay Treaty. This "accursed instrument," the governor explained, allowed individuals to shift between citizenship and subjecthood. Wilkinson complained to Dearborn that traders had "availed themselves of an extraordinary clause in the treaty... to acquire the equivocal attributes of American Citizen and British Subject, which they acknowledge or deny as may best suite their interests." In short, these individuals were British subjects in Montreal and American citizens in St. Louis. "A Mr Aird a Scotchman has just arrived with a considerable quantity of goods from Michilimackinac, and A Mr. Dickson his Countryman, is daily expected with a large Cargo from the same Place," Wilkinson reported in September 1805. On arriving in St. Louis, James Aird, an employee of Robert Dickson & Company, had "claimed the right of Citizen-ship, under the last clause of the British Treaty," and Wilkinson expected that "Mr. Dickson will no doubt follow his example."[49] The proclamation failed to exclude two of the most influential British traders from accessing the Missouri River.

The western provisions of the Jay Treaty did not create dual nationality or permit individuals to move between subjecthood and citizenship. Rather, the treaty exempted residents of the western posts from the regular system of naturalization that normally would record an individual's election to become a full citizen of the United States. The most recent Naturalization Act of 1802 required aliens to announce their intention to become American citizens three years before their naturalization in court, for which they were qualified after five years of residence in the United States.[50] Nothing compelled claimants under the Jay Treaty to follow this procedure. Wilkinson complained that he had no effective means of querying Aird's and Dickson's claims to citizenship. He recognized that "I can barely require proof of residence, which I have no doubt they will find, coming as they do prepared for this occasion." Consequently, he called for "some extraordinary provisions . . . to detect or repel the impositions daily practiced by persons calling themselves American Citizens, but who are in fact Zealous British Partizans." Wilkinson questioned the ease with which Aird and Dickson claimed American citizenship. He asked Dearborn whether it was "proper to admit such Characters to take the oath of Allegiance and abjuration? Or is this Oath sufficient, to intitle them to all the Privileges of American Citizenship?"[51] The fluid boundaries of American citizenship allowed Aird and Dickson to maintain their transnational trade between British Canada and the United States.

While the likes of Aird and Dickson found ways to evade Wilkinson's proclamation, their patrons in Montreal worked to have the Jefferson administration rescind the order. They addressed a memorial to Thomas Dunn, the administrator of Lower Canada in the absence of Lieutenant-Governor Sir Robert Milnes, protesting Wilkinson's actions as a particularly spiteful violation of the Jay Treaty. They claimed that the governor had timed his proclamation to coincide with the arrival of their traders at the mouth of the Missouri River. This threatened to inflict grievous losses on them by ensuring that they already had purchased and imported goods into the United States that would not realize returns from the Missouri hunting grounds. Moreover, the suddenness of the proclamation had made it necessary for the traders to hire a new set of canoe men in St. Louis to continue the voyage up the river. The Montrealers informed Dunn that the additional expense of employing American citizens in St. Louis "will amount to a prohibition of the Trade." If British officials could not hold the Jefferson administration to the Jay Treaty's assurance that "no distinction" would be made between British subjects and American citizens in the prosecution of the Indian trade, British merchants would lose an annual return of furs worth "upwards of Forty thousand pounds" from the Missouri River Valley.[52]

With Dunn's strong endorsement, merchants George Gillespie and

Pierre Rocheblave carried their complaints to Anthony Merry in the winter of 1805. The memorial formed part of a litany of treaty violations that Merry presented to James Madison in January 1806. First, he protested Wilkinson's proclamation as an unprecedented intervention in the Missouri River trade, unknown under Spanish rule and a violation of the "positive Right" of British subjects to trade within the territory of the United States. Second, Merry renewed his complaints against the local innovations of U.S. agents, which constituted "a Contravention of both the Letter and Spirit of the Third Article of the Treaty of 1794." To the dispute over the calculation of customs duties, the minister added the unreciprocated "alien Tonnage Duty" levied on British vessels entering American inland ports and the regulations that required traders to pay six dollars for a license to trade among Native peoples.[53] In a second letter written the following day, Merry protested Duncan's seizure at Michilimackinac and called for Madison to order the restoration of the North West Company's property. Merchants continued to wait for their case to be heard in Detroit, while the condemned goods accumulated interest with their patrons in London. Merry appealed to Madison "in the just Hope and Expectation that not only by this Means it will meet with a more prompt and favorable Decision, but that such Directions will be given to the Collector as shall prevent a repetition of similar vexations to the British Trade."[54] In sum, the British minister asked the U.S. government to repudiate the local innovations of its agents and embrace a more expansive interpretation of the rights the king's subjects enjoyed under the Jay Treaty.

The Jefferson administration, however, saw Merry's protest as an opportunity to curb the rights of British subjects. Jefferson was in no doubt that "the British have clearly no right to trade with the Indians in Louisiana." The president explained to William Henry Harrison, the governor of the Indiana Territory, that the United States must "govern" the Sacs, Foxes, Kickapoos, Sioux, "& other Indians residing on the borders between the British and us" by monopolizing the fur trade through government Indian factories. "By taking their pelts & furs at higher prices, & selling them goods at lower prices than the trade will bear without loss," U.S. Indian factors would "let them see their own interest in an exclusive adhesion to us."[55] Madison had long been an outspoken critic of the Jay Treaty; in concert with Gallatin he had helped lead opposition to the treaty in the House of Representatives in the 1790s. The secretary of state was also disinclined toward reaching an accommodation with Merry because of Britain's increasingly belligerent maritime policy and growing security concerns in the trans-Appalachian West. While the British Royal Navy continued its impressment of American seaman, the Board of Trade in Whitehall advocated a more aggressive policy against neutral merchant shipping, which some policymakers accused of maintaining the colonial trade of Britain's enemies under false flags. H.M.S. *Cambrian* excited popular protests in the summer of 1804 when its captain violated U.S. territorial waters by searching vessels outside of New York Harbor. The *Essex* decision handed down by the Lords Commissioners of Appeals in the spring of 1805 made it more difficult for merchant vessels to claim neutral status when trading with the French and Spanish Empires. The decision, combined with the British victory over the Franco-Spanish fleet at Trafalgar in October 1805, sparked an increase in maritime seizures by the Royal Navy, including as many as four hundred American vessels between 1805 and 1806.[56] British violations of neutral trading rights in the Atlantic Ocean made it difficult for Madison to stomach the Montreal merchants' complaints against American infringements of their commercial rights along the border.

In the trans-Appalachian West, American officials blamed British traders for orchestrating the growing resistance of Native peoples to the United States' piecemeal efforts to dismantle the Greenville peace settlement of 1795. Beginning with the Treaty of Fort Wayne in 1803, William Henry Harrison worked aggressively to acquire Native homelands in the Illinois country. While Harrison and other U.S. Indian agents had succeeded in making common cause with most Native leaders, Tenskwatawa, the Shawnee prophet, spoke a nativist message of resistance to American imperialism. His movement gained increased authority after he correctly predicted a solar eclipse on June 16, 1806.[57] Harrison, however, blamed British traders for the growing popularity of Tenskwatawa's message. West of the Mississippi River, Wilkinson reported that the Sacs, Foxes, and Iowas were "certainly disposed for war, and beyond all doubt are excited by their Traders—from Canada a[nd] I believe also from this place." He counseled that "the most conclusive mode, for humbling those Refractory nations, and all others, and for correcting the traders would be to interdict all trade the next Season," while he advised that "certain villainous French and half breed Interpreters, should be forced to leave the Indian nations, and held in confinement until they could find security not to return."[58] To accede to Merry's demands, then, would be to strengthen Native resistance to American imperial ambitions in the West.

Madison's reply to Merry offered a narrow construction of the rights that British subjects enjoyed under the Jay Treaty, while also being careful not to appear to undermine the United States' commitment to honoring its treaties with foreign powers. He upheld Wilkinson's proclamation excluding foreign nationals from the Missouri River on the grounds that the Jay Treaty's western provisions applied only to the "boundary of 1783," not to territories subsequently acquired by the United States. Madison did offer some consolation to the North West Company: he promised to order the release of their seized merchandise on the condition that the merchants pay a security bond in case the court condemned the property when the case finally came to trial. The secretary of state deferred answering Merry's complaints about the local innovations of Ernest and Duncan until "some further time," to allow the government to consider the minister's arguments.[59] Madison responded to Merry four months later, forwarding the opinion of U.S. attorney general John Breckinridge that the mode that Ernest and Duncan had employed in calculating customs and tonnage duties was legal; Breckinridge did, however, uphold Merry's complaint against U.S. agents' demanding payment for Indian trade licenses, though he insisted that British subjects were not exempt from the laws regulating the Indian trade.[60] While the Jefferson administration did not reject outright Merry's complaints, the major issues concerning the equity of customs duties and access to the Louisiana Territory remained unresolved.

Merry expressed his frustration at the impasse to Foreign Secretary Henry Phipps, the earl of Mulgrave. The minister was convinced of the justice of the merchants' complaints and the "Importance of that Trade, in which... Two Hundred Thousand Pounds of British Capital, and the Labour of Thirteen Hundred British Subjects were annually employed." Merry bemoaned his failure to "obtain a favorable Decision" from Madison, which he attributed to "the unfriendly Temper of the present moment" and to the American government "being desirous to put a stop altogether, if possible, to the Trade from Canada within the United States."[61] Merry forwarded his entire correspondence with Madison to Whitehall in the hope that a new treaty with the United States would codify a more expansive interpretation of the Jay Treaty; it was clear to him that diplomacy in Washington had run its course.

The conflict along the border continued. In June 1806, George Hoffman, the new collector at Michilimackinac, detained several canoes in the service of James and Andrew McGill for over a week before he allowed them to enter the United States on payment of a thousand-dollar bond.[62] Three months later, Hoffman provoked the ire of the North West Company by refusing to release the property seized by his predecessor, David Duncan, the previous year unless its agent, William McGillivray, posted a bond for the value of the goods and customs duties. McGillivray refused to pay duties on goods that were destined for Fort William in Upper Canada. Moreover, he found the company's boats "broken in Pieces, and parts of the goods missing and part of them injured."[63] McGillivray immediately wrote Merry to seek redress from the U.S. government, which was not forthcoming. Albert Gallatin, who had still not received a report of the seizure, ruled that the North West Company must either pay duties on the goods or a bond that the merchandise would not enter the United States.[64] The territorial supreme court in Detroit finally heard the North West Company's case in the fall of 1806. The court ruled in the merchants' favor, ordering Hoffman to restore their merchandise to them. Hoffman, however, was not ready to give up the fight. He requested permission from Gallatin to appeal the case. After consulting with the new U.S. attorney general Caesar Rodney, the treasury secretary denied Hoffman's request.[65] Nevertheless, Hoffman's zeal underlined the uncertainty surrounding the Montreal fur trade so long as the British and American governments remained at loggerheads over the meaning of the Jay Treaty.

Merchants were particularly sensitive to risk of seizure in the first decade of the nineteenth century because of economic uncertainty in the broader Atlantic World. In the optimistic 1790s, many merchants had invested heavily in the Indian trade in the hope of clearing the debts they had accumulated during the postwar recession. They were to be disappointed. An oversupply of trade goods in the trans-Appalachian West and business failures in Europe threw the Montreal fur trade into crisis. Merchant Alexander Henry wrote John Askin of the sense of panic in Montreal during the winter of 1799–1800. Henry passed on troubling accounts from London that "most of the furr buyers are bankrupts owing to several Houses in Hamburg failing, which has bankrupt all the foreign Houses in London, and several in New York."[66] The European war only made things worse. Napoleon's attempt to close the European continent to British trade after 1805 denied merchants access to important fur-buying markets in the German and Baltic States. Henry wrote Askin in March 1807 of reports from London that "all the deer, Bears, Raccoons, Martins, which went home last fall cannot be sold at any price, therefore they have put them in the King's stores & Bonded them, to save paying the dutys until Bonepart makes peace or dies."[67] While the European conflict seemed intractable, merchants had good reason to hope that forthcoming negotiations in London to frame a new British-American commercial agreement would provide an opportunity to resolve the ambiguity of the border. The Jay Treaty might not currently work as they wished, but there was reason to believe that new negotiations could make it do so.

There was optimism on both sides of the Atlantic as William Pinkney arrived in London to begin negotiating a new treaty of amity, commerce, and navigation in late June 1806. Relations between Great Britain and the United States seemed to be on the mend. The Fox-Grenville ministry of "All the Talents," which replaced William Pitt after his death in January, had already demonstrated a more conciliatory policy toward the United States. Whitehall recalled the hated Merry from Washington, replacing him with the more amiable David Erskine. Moreover, the British government signaled its goodwill by placing trade between the United States and the British West Indies on a more regular footing and quietly backing away from enforcing the more aggressive seizure of neutral merchant shipping that was authorized by the *Essex* decision.[68] On the surface, at least, there was every reason to believe that the forthcoming negotiations would settle the differences between Great Britain and the United States on both the North American continent and in the broader Atlantic World.

Canada merchants meant to grasp this opportunity to rid themselves of the vexatious innovations of U.S. agents and restore the border settlement of 1794. They sent a deputation to confer with William Eden, Baron Auckland, and Henry Vassall-Fox, Baron Holland, who would negotiate on behalf of the British ministry, shortly after discussions began with Pinkney and James Monroe, the U.S. minister to the Court of St. James. The "Merchants of London trading to Canada" advised the British negotiators about the "interruption" of their trade in Louisiana and the calculation of customs duties at Michilimackinac and Detroit, "which give a great advantage to the United States in the Indian trade." Impressed by the deputation's arguments, Auckland and Holland asked them to "prepare certain Documents for the information of their Lordships."⁶⁹ The merchants presented them with an extensive memorial, recounting the history of the border from the Treaty of Paris in 1783 to the Jay Treaty and supplementary article of 1796, which were intended to "establish the most perfect freedom of commerce and intercourse and to avoid all vexatious impediments." Under this protection, the memorialists explained, "the Canadian Fur Merchants from their experience, superior capital and knowledge of the business also from some local advantages of which they are not yet deprived have continued to command a larger portion of the trade which is now carried on from the settlements formed on the British side of the Boundary line."⁷⁰

The merchants drew directly on their experience at the hands of U.S. customs and territorial officials over the previous few years in framing their complaints. First, the United States had prohibited access to the trade west of the Mississippi River to "all persons who will not abjure their native allegiance and become Citizens of the United States." The supplementary article of 1796 had guaranteed that no subsequent treaties agreed by either party with another power would in any way mitigate the Jay Treaty. The merchants argued that this meant that the Louisiana Purchase ought not to restrict their commercial access to all the territories of the United States. Second, the memorialists censured "the revenue officers of the United States," calling on Auckland and Holland to "secure the neutrality of the Lakes and Waters to prevent any future seizure of vessels of any description upon pretext of their too near approach to any particular Post of Shore." Third, they complained about the unequal tonnage duty imposed on British and American vessels, "a very trifling acquisition to the revenue of the United States" and "a vexatious and frivolous obstruction to the inland Trade." Fourth, the merchants protested the charges collected on "every canoe which bring down Furs from the interior on the American side." Lastly, the memorialists explained how the goods that they imported into the United States paid duties "amounting to more than 20 pr. Cent," while American merchants managed to "supply Canada with Teas, East India Goods of all sorts, West Indian Productions, and also various articles of European and American Manufacture" without paying provincial customs duties. The inevitable outcome of this litany of obstructions to free navigation, "which are so industriously thrown in the way" of the merchants by American officials, was that "the Fur Trade from Canada notwithstanding the advantages and experience there possess'd, cannot long be conducted to advantage."⁷¹

The memorialists proposed four measures for Auckland and Holland to pursue in their negotiations with Monroe and Pinkney. First, a new agreement ought to renew "the freedom of commerce and intercourse by Land or inland Navigation" promised by the "third Article of the Treaty of 1794," including all territory acquired "subsequent to that Treaty." Second, all vessels navigating the "lakes and river forming the boundaries of the United States" should not be subject to any tonnage duty or pay customs duties unless they made entry at a port or break bulk with the explicit intention of landing their cargoes without legal entry. Third, all goods imported into Canada from the United States ought to pay the same duties as the same goods imported from Great Britain into the Atlantic ports. Fourth, the United States ought not to charge higher duties on goods imported through the inland ports than were charged in their Atlantic ports.[72] In essence, the merchants hoped to close the loopholes in the Jay Treaty that U.S. agents had discovered over the previous years.

Auckland soon realized that Madison had instructed Monroe and Pinkney to kill, rather than breathe new life, into the Jay Treaty. When Auckland raised the Canada merchants' memorial with the American commissioners on September 22, Monroe "suggested that it might be expedient to draw a line which should separate the respective Fur Trades of the two Countries." Such a border would "prevent all disagreements & all grounds of suspicion that the British Traders might sometimes endeavour to indispose the Indians towards the Citizens of the United States."[73] Monroe drew his argument from instructions that Madison had sent the commissioners to help them convince the British government to amend the third article of the Jay Treaty "in such a manner as will mutually authorize the parties to confine the Indian trade within their respective limits to their own traders." As the article currently stood, the secretary of state considered "its operation to be very seriously detrimental to the United States" because it allowed British traders to excite the opposition of Native peoples to U.S. imperial ambitions without offering "any real reciprocity of advantage to American traders."[74] Auckland found the idea of a closed border "quite fallacious" as it hurt the interests of British subjects without benefiting American citizens. The two sides agreed to adjourn their discussion, and Auckland handed over the merchants' memorial to Monroe and Pinkney to study "several other allegations of Injury," which the British government requested them to "explain or redress by an Article in the proposed Treaty."[75]

Auckland and Holland refused to drop the merchants' complaints. They sent "an extraofficial statement of the Injuries which the Canada Merchants complain of having sustained from the government & servants of the United States" to Monroe and Pinkney during the long hiatus of conferences that followed Foreign Secretary Charles James Fox's death in mid-September.[76] Auckland and Holland noted to Foreign Secretary Charles Grey, Viscount Howick, that "this is an extremely complicated subject," with Monroe's proposed amendment to the third article of the Jay Treaty being "quite inadmissible." Nevertheless, the British commissioners reiterated their commitment to "provide some additional security to our Traders against the vexations and grievances of which they complain."[77] As the negotiation of new commercial clauses drew to a close in early December, Monroe and Pinkney tried to convince Auckland and Holland to put off discussion of an "Article respecting the Fur Trade at the back of Louisiana" to "subsequent negotiations." The British commissioners held firm, warning their American counterparts that pushing off an agreement on the fur trade would have "an unbecoming appearance on their part" and occasion a reciprocal postponement "either of the East Indian Article, or of the Article relative to the Trade of the British Colonies."[78] Auckland and Holland finally agreed to delay discussion of the merchants' complaints only four days before signing the new treaty. They did so with the understanding that Monroe and Pinkney would apply to Washington for instructions "without delay" to allow them to frame an article in the new commercial convention that would accompany the treaty.[79] When the commissioners signed the Treaty of Amity, Commerce, and Navigation on New Year's Eve 1806, they left the fate of the border unresolved.

The merchants of Montreal spent an anxious winter awaiting news of the outcome of the negotiations in London. With such high stakes involved, James McGill bemoaned the lack of news from Europe since the previous September in a letter he penned to his London patron John Brickwood in January 1807. After all the useless complaints sent to the British minister in Washington, McGill recognized that "a right understanding with our Neighbours can only be settled by our Commissioners and their Plenipotentiaries now in *London,* and we shall be anxious on this side till we know the result." He hoped that Auckland and Holland would "obtain a certainty of free Trade in the Indian Territory depending on the U States, whither on the East or West side of the Mississippi as low down as possible, but by all means to include the Missouris to its sources." If the American commissioners would not agree to these terms, McGill believed that the merchant houses of Montreal would have to quit the Indian trade.[80] The future of the Montreal fur trade hung in the balance.

McGill's anxiety about the uncertainty surrounding the border did not stop him and his fellow merchants from gambling on the outcome of the London negotiations. On the same day that the British and American commissioners signed the new treaty, four of Montreal's leading merchant houses concluded an agreement to form the Michilimackinac Company for the sole purpose of carrying on the Indian trade in the United States. James and Andrew McGill & Company, Parker, Gerrard, Ogilvy & Company, Forsyth, Richardson & Company, and William and Duncan McGillivray & Company pooled capital of $800,000 to form a ten-year co-partnership, which McGill expected to yield him "yearly returns of Furs to the extent of £20,000 Stg."[81] The Montreal fur trade had upped the ante in their entrepreneurial contest with U.S. agents along the border.

In London, the Michilimackinac Company's gamble looked like it would pay off. Lord Howick (soon to be Earl Grey) dispatched a copy of the new treaty to David Erskine in Washington, "together with a Copy of a Note delivered previous to the signature by the Lords Holland and Auckland relative to the Complaints of the Canada Merchants." He assured the British minister that "every means will be taken to obtain Redress for the Removal of the Inconveniences complained of."[82] Moreover, Monroe and Pinkney were willing to offer concessions on the fur trade. The diplomats pointed out to Madison that the British commissioners had refused to make new arrangements for trade between the United States and British North America "in consequence of our declining to admit their Canada and Hudson Bay traders into Louisiana." They counseled compromise. Any concessions that Monroe and Pinkney were to offer the British government in Louisiana would be short-lived: the commercial convention would have a limited lifespan, and by the time the treaty expired, the pair were "confident that our population will have so far spread over the whole surface of that country . . . [so] as to supersede the necessity of renewing it."[83] As negotiations began again in 1807, Auckland and Holland intended to press the merchants' complaints, and Monroe and Pinkney were ready to cut a deal.

Negotiations dragged on but the project of additional and explanatory articles that Monroe and Pinkney sent to Madison in April 1807 answered the merchants' complaints. The lengthy seventh article agreed to extend the "privileges of intercourse and trade by land or inland navigation" that had been embraced in the third article of the Jay Treaty and the explanatory article of 1796 "to all the territories belonging to either of the high contracting Powers on the continent of America," with the exception of the settlements and their environs of the Hudson's Bay Company. The article created a massive British-American trade zone from the maritime provinces of British North America to the source of the Missouri River in present-day Montana. It also prescribed the method for calculating customs duties to ensure that customs officers would assign the same value to goods imported through the inland ports of the United States as would be the case for goods entered in the Atlantic ports from overseas. Finally, the article guaranteed that British traders would no longer have to pay for fur trade licenses.[84] The protections offered by this article were precisely what Canada merchants had been clamoring for, for so long. It seemed that their troubles were finally over.

The agreements brokered in London stood no chance of survival in Washington, D.C. David Erskine was the first to receive a copy of the treaty, which he carried to James Madison's office in the State Department on March 3, 1807. Madison had instructed Monroe and Pinkney to secure two main objectives. First, he wanted an agreement ending impressment. Second, the secretary of state charged the pair with protecting the United States' re-export trade. Monroe and Pinkney found the former impossible. They explained to Madison that it was politically unfeasible for Prime Minister Lord Grenville to publicly agree to end impressment, but the cabinet had signed a note that promised to observe strict caution in impressing only British seamen. The American ministers did manage to secure some protections for the re-export trade. The British government agreed to relax the *Essex* decision, which effectively had outlawed the re-export of goods from France or Spain to their respective colonies in the Americas. Instead, the treaty determined that the payment of minimal duties for goods landed in the United States was sufficient to break the continuity of a voyage, allowing American merchant ships to trade with the French and Spanish Empires. This was not good enough for Jefferson and Madison. The president refused to send the treaty to the Senate for ratification, and the secretary of state returned the agreement to Monroe and Pinkney, conveying Jefferson's views and outlining six points for renegotiation.[85] It was still not impossible, however, that some kind of agreement could be salvaged from the London negotiations.

Jefferson's rejection of the treaty meant that the British and American commissioners put aside the North American fur trade deal. Moreover, when Madison received the details of the agreement, he rejected the concessions that Monroe and Pinkney had offered to British traders in Louisiana. These individuals threatened the security of the United States while few American citizens would benefit from access to the Hudson's Bay Company's territory. Nevertheless, Madison did instruct Monroe and Pinkney that they could agree to the equitable calculation of duties described in the seventh supplementary article, as well as to the stipulation that Indian trade licenses would be granted free of charge.[86] A deal could still be done that would offer merchants some protection from the innovations of U.S. agents. David Erskine certainly thought so. He wrote Thomas Dunn, the administrator of Lower Canada, not to despair over Jefferson's rejection of the treaty. Indeed, he was "happy to inform" Dunn that he had received assurances that "the point of dispute with the Canada Merchants relative to the mode of estimating the duties levied upon European goods from Canada ... will be settled favourable to the views of the Canada Merchants."[87] It seemed it was only a matter of time before British-American diplomacy would resolve at least some of the merchants' complaints.

The U.S.S. *Chesapeake* let slip its anchor on June 22, 1807, bound for the Mediterranean. H.M.S. *Leopard* hailed the American warship shortly after it left Norfolk, Virginia. Under orders from Vice-Admiral Sir George Berkeley, Captain Salusbury Humphreys demanded that Commodore James Barron, who commanded the *Chesapeake,* hand over Royal Navy deserters among his crew. Barron was unmoved by Humphreys's arguments. The British captain first fired a warning shot across the bow of the American frigate and then fired into the warship itself. Three American sailors lay dead, with a further eighteen wounded. The *Chesapeake* struck its colors, and a boarding party from H.M.S. *Leopard* seized four seamen accused of deserting from the Royal Navy.[88]

The *Leopard-Chesapeake* affair sparked a diplomatic crisis between Great Britain and the United States that overshadowed the ongoing commercial negotiations. The unprovoked attack on an American warship off the coast of Virginia caused an outpouring of popular hostility against Great Britain in the Atlantic states. The Virginia militia patrolled the coast of the Chesapeake Bay to ensure that Royal Navy warships could not draw supplies from their state. In New York City, a mob set about dismantling a British ship, removing its rudder and rigging and destroying its gun carriages. With the Jefferson administration unprepared for war, British and American diplomats were preoccupied with avoiding armed conflict, rather than framing new commercial clauses, during the summer of 1807.[89]

The popular clamor for war in the Atlantic states had largely subsided by the fall, but there was still little prospect of a renewal of commercial negotiations. The *Leopard-Chesapeake* affair was a deadly illustration of the ways in which Royal Navy impressment undermined American sovereignty. The Jefferson administration was more determined than ever to force the British government to end this pernicious practice. London, however, was in no mood to treat with the United States. George Canning, the foreign secretary in the Tory ministry that replaced the Fox-Grenville coalition in 1807, informed Monroe and Pinkney that he was not prepared to negotiate a revised treaty.[90] The opportunity for a new British-American treaty solving the merchants' complaints had passed for now.

In the late spring of 1808, twenty boats "laden with merchandise, solely intended for the indian trade" of the Michilimackinac Company left Lachine for Michilimackinac. U.S. troops fired on the boats as they made their way through the Niagara River on May 21. While no one was killed, the soldiers helped John Lees, the U.S. customs collector for the port of Niagara, to seize two boats and set the Canadien boatmen "adrift to cross the river to the British side in the best manner they could."[91] Learning that more boats were heading toward Niagara, Lees sent additional soldiers from the Niagara garrison to intercept them on Lake Ontario. U.S. authorities seized eight boats and merchandise worth over £5,000.[92] The Michilimackinac Company estimated that the incident cost them £26,000, approximately a quarter of their annual operating budget.

The merchants followed what had become a well-established pattern of complaint. First, Robert Hamilton, the Michilimackinac Company's agent at Queenston, protested Lees's seizure to Captain Nathaniel Leonard, who commanded the American garrison at Niagara. He explained to the officer that the company had received assurances in Washington, D.C., that their trade was exempt from the most recent supplementary Embargo Act. The Jay Treaty ought to have protected them from Lees's seizure. The merchant

Canoe Manned by Voyageurs Passing a Waterfall, Frances Anne Hopkins, 1869. Although depicting *voyageurs* of the Hudson's Bay Company, this painting gives a sense of the size of the canoes that U.S. customs collector John Lees captured in the Niagara River in 1808. The eight vessels of the Michilimackinac Company that he apprehended formed part of a brigade of twenty canoes. (Frances Anne Hopkins Fonds, Library and Archives of Canada)

demanded that the American officer return the seized merchandise and allow the boatmen to continue on their way. Leonard refused.[93] With his efforts frustrated at Niagara, Hamilton and his fellow agent Thomas Dickson appealed to Francis Gore, the lieutenant-governor of Upper Canada, to "make a proper representation to the Government of the United States" to secure the release of the boats and goods. In addition, the company's Montreal partners petitioned Governor-General Sir James Craig, also sending a copy directly to David Erskine in Washington, D.C.[94] The merchants needed British officials to speedily resolve their complaint if they were to stand any chance of getting the trade goods to the hunting grounds before winter closed off communication.

The confrontation on the Niagara River did not merely jeopardize the fortunes of the Michilimackinac Company, but its consequences, in Erskine's words, also threatened to "seriously affect the Harmony and good understanding between His Majesty's Provinces of Canada & the Adjacent Territories of the United States." Erskine protested Lees's violent seizure as a "gross & unprovoked outrage towards the Persons of His Majesty's Subjects" and a "flagrant Insult" against "His Majesty's Government in Canada."

Erskine demanded that Lees immediately return the company's property, and he asked James Madison to order U.S. agents on the border "to respect the Rights of His Majesty's Subjects & forbear from such acts of violence towards their Persons." Moreover, the minister reaffirmed the British government's commitment to upholding the principle of free navigation on the inland waters that comprised the border between the British Empire and the American Republic.[95]

Albert Gallatin ordered Lees to return the company's property on payment of surety, but Madison contested the Michilimackinac Company's right of free navigation. The secretary of state argued that the company's boats ought to have reported to Lees before proceeding through the Niagara River, as was required by U.S. law.[96] The British minister vehemently denied that the king's subjects were subject to U.S. laws when they had "cleared out from one of their own Ports and being bound to another situated upon Waters, to the free Navigation of which, they had a most unquestionable Right." While he welcomed Gallatin's order, Erskine also warned Madison of the "Serious consequences" that could easily follow from "the appearance of a Military Force drawn up in Battle Array for the hostile purpose of making an Attack upon His Majesty's Subjects while engaged in a lawful Undertaking and conducting themselves in a peaceable manner."[97] With only the narrow Niagara River separating the British garrison of Fort George from the American fortress at Niagara, border frictions could ignite a full-scale conflict.

By 1808, the merchants of Montreal were convinced that the U.S. government was conspiring to put them out of business. In yet another memorial presented to Governor-General Craig, they explained that they had "for some time seen progressing, with extreme concern, a systematic plan to drive the British Indian traders from the American territory, by every species of vexation." Aside from the unlawful seizures perpetrated against them by the collectors at Michilimackinac and Niagara, the merchants complained that they had "long suffered under the requirement of passes, extortion in duties, and vexations in various ways."[98] Lees's seizure of the eight boats was the boldest step in an escalating entrepreneurial war fought between U.S. agents and Montreal merchants and traders.

Hoping to coax the British government into action, the merchants framed Lees's seizure as Canada's *Chesapeake* affair. It was an affront to the "national dignity," as well as "an attack upon the rights and property of British subjects." U.S. troops firing on unarmed boatmen within sight of Fort George was not unlike Captain Humphreys's loosening a broadside into the U.S.S. *Chesapeake* off the coast of Virginia. But it was the *Chesapeake* affair pulled inside out. For Montreal merchants, this meant that the United States was the aggressor in the Niagara River. The memorialists found it "not a little extraordinary that those who are so clamorous for general free navigation in cases neither authorized by the law or practice of nations should themselves so arrogantly violate the rights of free lake navigation when specifically secured by a compact to which they are a party." They also enjoyed the irony of "those who were so irritable in the case of the Chesapeake, where a provocation not to be borne was previously given by them, should so unfeelingly fire, without any notice upon armed men who never offered them even a shadow of pretense for doing so."[99] The lesson was clear: the Canadien boatmen were the unfortunate casualties of American hypocrisy, for if the U.S. government meant what it said about protecting sailors' rights and free trade, the incident would never have occurred.

But the Montreal merchants had got it wrong. U.S. policy toward navigation and nationality was not truly Janus-faced. It was a pragmatic response to the exigencies of empire rather than an inconsistent ideological commitment to republican principles of free trade. Jefferson embraced free movement in the Atlantic World as a vehicle for American Empire. Colonization of the West depended on Americans gaining access to foreign markets. The free movement of foreign traders in the West, however, threatened the U.S. imperial project by bolstering rebellion and resistance among colonists and Indians alike. The U.S. government rewarded its agents for finding ways to collect revenue in the international rivers and lakes that comprised the shared border with British North America, while protesting the Royal Navy's claimed authority over the ships, cargos, and bodies of American merchant seamen as part of a coherent imperial policy. It would be no easy business to convince the Jefferson administration to rein in their entrepreneurial agents on the northern border.

5

"WE OUGHT TO HAVE THE TRADE WITHIN OUR AWEN COUNTRY"

The New York merchant John Jacob Astor made his way north to Montreal in September 1808. This was a familiar journey for Astor, who had regularly attended the town's annual fur auctions for over twenty years. This trip was different, for the New Yorker meant to purchase more than furs. He intended to buy the Michilimackinac Company. Keen to court the favor of the Jefferson administration, Astor wrote Albert Gallatin about his negotiations in terms of economic nationalism. In Astor's telling, he was not merely offering to buy the company's furs; he was brokering a deal that would see the "Boundarys of 1783" mark a territorial division between the commercial activities of British subjects trading under the banner of the North West Company and American citizens employed by Astor's American Fur Company.[1] As much as any of the formal negotiations that took place between British and American diplomats, the commercial bargaining in Montreal proposed a settlement in which the border would distinguish British subjects from American citizens.

Astor found himself in a position to make a credible offer to buy the Michilimackinac Company because of the American national state. And he knew it. Entrepreneurial U.S. agents had found innovative ways to control border crossings at important junctions, such as the Niagara River Valley and the Mackinac Straits. With the passage of the first of the Jeffersonian Embargo Acts in November 1807, Montreal merchants feared that the U.S. government would use the border as a tool of economic nationalism to exclude British subjects from the Indian trade. The geopolitical uncertainty of the Revolutionary Atlantic World meant that they could no longer predict whether the goods that they ordered from London one year would reach American hunting grounds the next.

In a dramatic reversal, the merchants of British North America—a committee formed of London and Montreal houses—publicly declared their opposition to the western provisions of the Jay Treaty. Nathaniel Atcheson, the merchants' political agent in London, authored the treatise *American*

Portrait of John Jacob Astor, Gilbert Stuart, c. 1794. An immigrant to New York City from Germany, Astor was an associate of the Montreal fur trade for over twenty years before he launched his scheme to create a transcontinental commercial empire with the American Fur Company in 1808. (© Peter A. Juley & Son Collection, Photograph Archives, Smithsonian American Art Museum)

Encroachments on British Rights in April 1808, which criticized the "ambiguity of the treaty of 1794" for placing "Canadians in a very hopeless situation respecting their commercial intercourse with the United States." Entrepreneurial American agents had proven far more adept in exploiting loopholes in the Jay Treaty than had their fur trade opponents. And the British government's neglect of Canada was responsible for the U.S. agents' successes because the ineffectual diplomacy of the king's ministers had left the explanation of the Jay Treaty to the "revenue officers of the United States," who enjoyed the full support of the U.S. government.[2] British subjects could no longer rely on the privileges that they formerly claimed under the Jay Treaty to protect their border crossings.

The American Fur Company did not receive its name by chance. Astor recognized that he would need the U.S. government's sponsorship to make good on his dreams of a transcontinental trading monopoly.[3] He was careful from the beginning to couch his private ambitions in terms of American nationalism and imperial expansion. By supplying the wants of Native peoples, the American Fur Company would conciliate the attachment of the nations and villages of the vast territory of the Louisiana Purchase to the United States and exclude the insidious influence of foreign traders. Astor's enterprise played into the U.S. government's growing security concerns, which increasingly focused on Tenskwatawa's opposition to American Empire.[4] U.S. Indian agents wrongly blamed British traders for the rising Native opposition to American imperialism, rather than the aggressive land grabs of William Henry Harrison in Indiana and William Hull in Michigan. The interests of national security spoke to the wisdom of Astor's assertion that "we ought to have the trade within our awen country."[5] For their part, Astor expected the U.S. government to strengthen his bargaining position in Montreal by pursuing policies of economic nationalism on the border to discriminate against his foreign rivals.

The stakes were high for both Astor and Montreal. The two sides were not simply haggling over the diminishing returns of the Ohio country but about the largely untapped fur reserves of the Pacific Northwest. The outcome of these negotiations, then, would help realize American and British imperial ambitions not only on the far side of the North American continent but also in the Pacific World: both parties hoped to lay claim to the Columbia River as a base for colonization in the Pacific Northwest and expanding transoceanic trade with China. This was an important reason why Montreal turned down Astor in the fall of 1808. The Michilimackinac Company was prepared to ignore its mounting losses east of the Rocky Mountains in the hope of securing the future riches of the fur trade on the Pacific Coast. The partners recognized that changing geopolitical conditions could just as easily favor their commercial ambitions as they could Astor's. The likelihood of war with the United States in the immediate aftermath of the *Leopard-Chesapeake* incident in 1807 had made British officials in North America and Whitehall mindful of the king's Indian allies, who would play a critical role in the defense of Canada.[6] Atcheson exploited these imperial security concerns in *American Encroachments on British Rights*. He emphasized the role that the fur trade played in cementing the military alliance between Great Britain and the Native peoples of the Great Lakes which would prove critical to repulsing an American invasion. Atcheson argued that the private interest of Canada merchants was also a public good, protecting the security of British North America and advancing the Crown's future imperial ambitions in the Pacific Northwest.[7]

While Astor returned to New York City empty-handed in 1808, he did not give up his imperial scheme. Republican commercial policy provides the key to understanding the sporadic negotiations that continued for the next three years. The passage, repeal, and suspension of the Embargo and Nonintercourse Acts reflected shifts in British-American diplomacy as the Jefferson and Madison administrations hoped to pressure the British government into recognizing liberal definitions of navigation and nationality on the Atlantic Ocean. Jefferson and Madison overestimated the effectiveness of economic coercion as a geopolitical tool, and they underestimated the willingness of individual citizens to suffer privations in pursuit of the collective good. But their commercial policies shaped the course of the negotiations between Astor and the Montreal merchants.[8] By January 1811, the unpredictable ebb and flow of the Embargo and Nonintercourse Acts convinced the Montreal merchants to accept Astor's revised offer of an international partnership as the only means of protecting their trade from falling prey to entrepreneurial American agents.

The meaning of the South West Company, the name chosen for the joint venture, for American nationhood and empire was ambiguous. The deal was not the stroke of economic nationalism that Astor had promised Gallatin. While the company would import the majority of its merchandise through New York City, it would continue to rely on the labor and expertise of British subjects. Moreover, the agreement was limited to east of the Rocky Mountains. While Astor's men had moved first to establish a fort at the mouth of the Columbia River, the imperial contest in the Pacific Northwest remained undecided when Congress declared war on Great Britain in June 1812.

Astor shared his imperial ambitions with New York governor DeWitt Clinton as he moved to charter the American Fur Company in Albany in 1808. The merchant explained how he intended to form a company capable of engrossing the entire fur trade of the United States—from New York State to the Columbia River on the Pacific Coast—within the next four or five years.[9] Success would depend not simply on meeting the logistical challenge of conducting business on a continental scale, no mean feat in early nineteenth-century America, but also on defeating his rivals in Montreal, who had dominated the fur trade since before the Revolution. Astor needed the support of the U.S. government if he was to stand any chance of realizing his grand scheme of commercial empire.

This was why Astor was writing Governor Clinton, the nephew of the vice president of the United States, George Clinton: he needed to mobilize the power of the American national state in his commercial contest with the Michilimackinac and North West Companies. Astor described the present absurdity of the British-dominated American fur market, which required merchants in Boston, Philadelphia, and Baltimore to "draw ¾ of our furrs for ham [home] consumption from Canada." He estimated that American merchants annually imported $400,000 worth of furs "collected on the Mississippi and Missourie" from Montreal and London. But it was the important role that the American Fur Company would play among Native peoples that convinced Astor that his enterprise would be "pleasing to our government & that they would give me very considerable aid to Insure its success." He explained to Governor Clinton that he envisioned the American government withdrawing the U.S. Indian factories in favor of awarding his company "the exclusive right of Trading in the Lusiananas & Missourie." Such an arrangement would not just save the government money, but "the cultivation of Intercourse & good will with all the natives would it self be a gr[e]at object to the country."[10] Private enterprise and public interest would unite in the American Fur Company.

Astor wrote Thomas Jefferson the following month, hoping to solicit the president's support for his imperial scheme. He explained how his company meant to "embrace the greater part of the fur trade on this Continent the most which passes now through Canada." In doing so, Astor would be doing work of national importance, for he promised that "the views & wishes of government in thire relation with the Indians" would guide his every action. Astor explained to the president that he could not be assured of wresting the fur trade from British merchants and traders without the help of both the national and state governments. Through DeWitt Clinton, Astor was already pursuing a corporate charter from the state of New York. He wrote

Jefferson to secure "the countenance and good wishes of the Executive of the united States." Astor did not specify what this meant in practical terms. Rather, he asked for the "entire approbation of government" without which, he warned Jefferson, "the business could not Succeed neither would I wish to engage in it." The New Yorker was also careful to direct the president to consult with George Clinton, should Jefferson "wish for anny Information concerning my character of knowledge of the trade," safe in the knowledge that the vice president was briefed on the virtues of Astor and his scheme.[11]

Astor's plan intrigued Jefferson. The transcontinental ambitions of the American Fur Company dovetailed with the Virginian's own vision of an expanding empire of liberty. Moreover, Vice President Clinton vouched for Astor's character. Secretary of War Henry Dearborn reported that the vice president believed Astor to be "a man of large property & fair character, and well acquainted with the fur & peltry business."[12] Satisfied that Astor was both honorable and experienced in the Indian trade, Jefferson offered his qualified endorsement of the American Fur Company in April 1808. While he was eager to exclude British merchants and traders from the fur trade, the president was not prepared for this to come at the price of awarding a government monopoly to Astor. Monopoly smacked of corruption and was anathema to republican government.[13] Nevertheless, Jefferson promised to use "every reasonable patronage & facility in the power of the Executive" to throw "great advantages" to American merchants and traders operating west of the Mississippi River. It was the policy of the Jefferson administration "to get the whole of this business passed into the hands of our own citizens & to oust foreign traders who do much abuse their privilege by endeavoring to excite the Indians to war on us."[14] The American Fur Company might not enjoy a government monopoly to protect it from homegrown competition, but it could rely on the support of the U.S. government in defeating its foreign foes.

Just how far the American government was willing to go to support U.S. merchants remained unclear. Astor traveled to Washington, D.C., in July 1808 to attend a private meeting with the president and his cabinet. He later claimed that Jefferson had pledged military support to defend Astor's traders from British attack if the need ever arose. Certainly the meeting encouraged the president to recommend the American Fur Company to the "particular attention" of Governor Meriwether Lewis in St. Louis. Jefferson wrote Lewis about the formation of a "powerful company . . . for taking up the Indian commerce on a large scale... under the direction of a most excellent man, a mr Astor mercht. of N. York." Jefferson was confident that the success of Astor's enterprise would mean that "the English Mackinac company will probably withdraw from the competition," something he believed was essential to securing peace between the United States and Native peoples on both sides of the Mississippi River.[15] By the time Astor traveled north to Montreal in the fall of 1808, he had the security of a corporate charter from the New York State Assembly and the potential military backing of the U.S. government to bolster his bargaining position.

The Montreal partners were not yet desperate enough to accept Astor's offer. The status of the Montreal fur trade was unclear under the shifting terms of the Jeffersonian Embargo. Congress passed four different Embargo and Supplementary Acts between December 22, 1807, and April 25, 1808, the last of which specifically exempted Indian trade merchandise and furs that were "the property of British subjects" from the Embargo.[16] Moreover, Montreal merchants had reason to hope that a new British-American accord would resolve the longstanding problems of navigation and nationality. In Washington, D.C., David Erskine, the British minister plenipotentiary, was optimistic that the incoming administration of James Madison would welcome the opportunity to settle its differences with the British government. In London, the American minister William Pinkney suggested that his government would accept British Foreign Secretary George Canning's proposal to repeal the latest order-in-council if the United States would agree to freely admit British trade to American ports, while excluding France, and allow the Royal Navy to enforce the ban on French trade.[17] If Congress repealed the Embargo Acts in response to an agreement with Great Britain, there would be no reason to cut a deal with Astor.

Traders also continued to exploit the uncertainty of citizenship in their entrepreneurial struggle with U.S. agents on the border. At Michilimackinac, customs collector George Hoffman refused to grant clearance to boats commanded by British traders bound for Montreal. He was, however, prepared to let American citizens carry British property across the border. But Hoffman found it difficult to distinguish one from the other. James Aird again claimed American citizenship under the Jay Treaty, as he had done three years earlier in St. Louis to evade James Wilkinson's attempt to exclude British subjects from the Missouri River trade. Moreover, Aird had sworn an oath of allegiance to the United States the previous year to obtain an Indian trade license in St. Louis.[18] Nevertheless, his true allegiance remained suspect. While Hoffman felt compelled to grant clearance to Aird, he was convinced that the trader "certainly is a British subject" and "one of the members of the Michilimackinac Company." Aird might "claim under the Jay's treaty all the rights & privileges of an American citizen," but the collector was in no doubt that Aird's "interest is connected & interwoven in that of many powerful British fur traders, and he considers himself as one of the King's loyal subjects."[19] The problem with the ambiguity of nationality was that agents like Hoffman could not assume that individual claims to American citizenship reflected attachment to the government of the United States. Aird might be a wolf in sheep's clothing, or he might not. What was certain was that Aird and other traders managed to keep the Michilimackinac Company going through fair means and foul.[20] Hoffman reported that traders carried 1,700 packs of furs worth over $110,000 across the border between July and September 1808.[21] He accused local traders of smuggling goods through the Mackinac Straits. There was no other way for Hoffman to explain the "astonishing" decline in the district's customs revenue, which had more than halved from $22,441 in 1807 to $10,508 in 1808.[22] The collector had it on good authority that the Michilimackinac Company was still importing a large volume of goods from London—over £22,000 (approximately $100,000) in 1808.[23] What else could have happened to the goods? The Montreal fur trade continued, albeit under a cloud of uncertainty.

Developments in Washington, D.C., the following spring suggested that the Montreal partners had been right to refuse Astor. On March 1, 1809, Congress passed the Nonintercourse Act, which prohibited the ships and merchandise of the British and French Empires from entering the ports of the United States from May 20. At the same time, the act lifted the Embargo for all other nations, raising the prospect that Montreal might find a way to access the Indian trade through foreign intermediaries.[24] Gallatin not only assured Erskine that the act would not impact the export of American peltries into British North America but also suggested that British merchants should send their boats to Oswego to ensure that their merchandise entered the United States before the law went into effect.[25] Certainly the fur markets in London reacted favorably to the news, with a precipitous rise in peltry prices.[26] Whitehall responded to the repeal of the Embargo by issuing a new order-in-council that targeted Napoleon's empire, opened up the German and Baltic States to American commerce, and offered some other concessions that Prime Minister Spencer Perceval hoped would improve relations with the United States. Most promising of all, an exchange of notes between Erskine and the Madison administration in April paved the way for Congress to reopen trade with the British Empire in return for the withdrawal of the order-in-council. Americans in port cities along the Atlantic coast greeted news of the Erskine agreement with spontaneous acts of public celebration before enthusiastically resuming their trade with Great Britain.[27] It seemed that the nightmare of the Embargo was over for British subjects and American citizens alike.

But it was all too good to be true, for Erskine had completely misunderstood the intentions of his masters in Whitehall. The minister had pursued reconciliation at the expense of his instructions that had stipulated that the United States must agree to the "Rule of 1756," which closed off French colonial trade to American merchants and authorized the Royal Navy to enforce the Nonintercourse Act with France on behalf of the U.S. government. Erskine had jettisoned these requirements in pursuit of what he saw as the greater object of reopening American ports to British trade. Foreign Secretary Canning disavowed Erskine's agreement when word of the accord arrived in London in May; Whitehall recalled Erskine in July, promising to send a special envoy to Washington, D.C. That same month, the disappointing news of the British government's rejection of the Erskine agreement arrived in North America, ensuring that the Madison administration would resume the Nonintercourse Act and prohibit trade with the British Empire.[28] The Erskine incident illustrated how the geopolitical instability of the Revolutionary Atlantic World impacted trading conditions for merchants and traders in the North American West.

Astor believed that the pervasive uncertainty in British-American relations would encourage his Montreal rivals to rethink his offer. He looked on the defection of Robert Dickson from the Michilimackinac Company in the spring of 1809 as an auspicious sign. A victim of the Niagara River seizure and keen to leave Michilimackinac in the wake of a fatal duel in which he had acted as a second, Dickson spent the winter in Montreal, where he was elected a member of the prestigious Beaver Club.[29] Despite the warm reception he received there, Dickson decided that it was time "to change his situation from Canada to the American Fur Company." Moreover, Dickson told Astor that other Montreal merchants and traders were of the same mind. The New Yorker reported to Gallatin in February 1809 that "the People in Montreal are willing to sell out on more reasonable terms now than they were when I was in Canada."[30] Time and the tide of global affairs, it seemed, were on Astor's side.

Dickson's defection also provided Astor with a useful tool for courting government support for the American Fur Company. He boasted about his new recruit to Gallatin, who had become Astor's confidant and champion in the Madison cabinet. Astor lauded Dickson's long experience in the fur trade and the influence he enjoyed among Native peoples, as well as his qualities of "enterprise & Perserverance."[31] Dickson had made himself useful to the territorial government of Upper Louisiana, earning special privileges from Governor Meriwether Lewis and Secretary Frederick Bates, which allowed him access to the Indian trade of the Missouri River despite his continued loyalty to the British Crown.[32] Astor advised Gallatin to "admit a few moments conversation" with Dickson, who was the bearer of this letter, so that government could benefit "from his great knowledge &c. of the Indians as well as the trade with them." The New Yorker knew that Dickson would speak favorably of Astor's scheme as well as counseling the "great importance to the United States in case of War that the Mackina Company should be under the controul of the American Fur Compy."[33] The recruitment of the influential frontier power-broker offered tangible evidence of the ways in which the company would be an agent of American Empire.

Dickson arrived in Washington, D.C., at a moment of growing concern among U.S. policymakers about the allegiance of Native peoples in the event of war with the British Empire. A constant stream of reports from officials in the western territories blamed foreign traders for spreading disaffection among the Indian nations on both sides of the Mississippi River. In July 1808, Governor Meriwether Lewis accused the Michilimackinac Company's traders of working to "mar our best arrangements for the happiness of the Indians and the tranquility of the frontier." The following month, Lewis reported that British traders in St. Louis "were disposed in the event of war to stimulate the Saucs and Foxes who lay in their way to commence war against us."[34] While President Thomas Jefferson promised to take "effectual steps" to prevent British traders from crossing the Mississippi River, U.S. agents continued to sound alarm bells after he left the White House. In April 1809, William Clark, the superintendent of Indian affairs, passed on the reports of Nicholas Boilvin, the deputy Indian agent at Prairie du Chien, confirming his suspicions that British traders continued to interfere in "our Indian affairs in this country."³⁵ The following November, rumors circulated that two Michilimackinac Company traders, Jacques Porlier and John Bleakley, were involved in a conspiracy with the Sacs and Fox to massacre the U.S. garrison of Fort Madison on the upper Mississippi River. While an investigation in St. Louis found the "alarm without foundation," it seemed obvious to American policymakers that the influence that foreign traders enjoyed among Native peoples was to blame for the Indians' dangerous lack of attachment to the United States.³⁶

The U.S. government's security concerns focused on Tenskwatawa and his followers in the years preceding the War of 1812. In 1808, the Shawnee prophet had masterminded a move from Greenville, Ohio, to Prophetstown in Indiana Territory. He sharpened his nativist message, calling out Indian leaders who were complicit in selling land to the United States, counseling communal ownership of Native homelands, and advocating resistance to the Jeffersonian program of civilization, which meant the destruction of Native culture and the assimilation of Indians into American society through the promotion of sedentary agriculture.³⁷ In short, Tenskwatawa offered a withering criticism of American imperialism. At Prophetstown, he began to build what historian Adam Jortner has called "an Indian city-state," possessed of many of the attributes of an independent state, including diplomats, borders, and a military.³⁸ Tenskwatawa also began speaking with agents of the British Indian Department.

Despite the obvious tensions between the Shawnee prophet's determination to protect Native homelands and the United States' imperial ambitions, conflict was not inevitable. Indeed, Governor William Henry Harrison and Tenskwatawa struck up an unlikely alliance when they met at Vincennes in August 1808. The Treaty of Fort Wayne, an aggressive land-grab orchestrated by Harrison in September 1809, fractured this delicate peace. It also divided Native peoples between accommodationists and supporters of the Shawnee prophet and his brother Tecumseh. Reports from U.S. Indian agents implicated British traders and Indian agents in conspiracies to support the power of Tenskwatawa, while Native leaders friendly to the United States, such as the Miami Little Turtle, disparaged the Shawnee's followers as "British Indians."³⁹ The state-building and diplomatic enterprises of Tenskwatawa threatened the emergence of a pan-Indian nation within the territorial boundaries of the United States.

Astor argued that the American Fur Company offered the solution to the problem of meddling British traders. It would not simply remove the threat that foreigners posed to American imperialism; Astor's enterprise would transform them into agents of empire. Dickson was a case in point. He came to Washington, D.C., looking to fill the vacancy of U.S. Indian agent at Prairie du Chien, a prominent trading center on the upper Mississippi River that William Clark described as "the Grand Mart for several nations & Tribes of Indians."[40] The appointment would consummate the relationship between Astor and the Madison administration: Dickson would be an agent of both the U.S. government and the American Fur Company. This was precisely the sort of collaboration that Astor hoped for as he wrote Gallatin of his plans in the Pacific Northwest in the summer of 1809. Astor was preparing to send a ship of "300 Tons with a Cargo of Indian goods to amount of about $50000" to establish a trading post at the mouth of the Columbia River. Astor hoped that the U.S. government would look on these "many young Americans of respectable connections & of good moral character" as informal agents of empire. He solicited the recommendations of government for erecting "a Fort mounting Cannon &c.," assuring Gallatin that he would "take no Steps of any importance without the knowledge of Government."[41] If Astor's men on the Columbia River proved their influence among the region's Native peoples, it was quite likely that they could become formal agents of empire.

Despite Astor's assurances that the American Fur Company would transfer control of the Indian trade from British subjects to American citizens, he had to admit that his venture would, by necessity, have to rely on Canadian labor and experience. Many of Astor's recruits were natural-born British subjects and former employees of the Montreal companies. As with James Aird, these men's loyalty to the United States was suspect. This was certainly the case with Robert Dickson, who found himself as a second in the duel that killed John Campbell, the U.S. Indian agent at Prairie du Chien whom Dickson hoped to replace, as a consequence of a drunken argument over his shifting loyalties.[42] While Governor Harrison had appointed Dickson as a justice of the peace for St. Clair County in Indiana Territory, George Hoffman and other U.S. agents at Michilimackinac were determined that he would not replace the unfortunate Campbell. Hoffman and officers from the army garrison sent a protest to Washington, D.C., declaring Dickson to be "totally unfit" for the position and predicting that his appointment would result in "almost incalculable injury" to the United States. While they recognized that Dickson was an American citizen under the Jay Treaty, the U.S. officers argued that his true affections still lay with the British Crown and the Michilimackinac Company. There could be no doubt that Dickson would use his position as Indian agent to advance the interests of his "real sovereigns" by "prejudicing the minds of the Indians against the Americans."[43] The controversy surrounding Dickson reveals the gulf between the rhetoric of economic nationalism that Astor used when lobbying for the support of the American government and the realities of doing business in a borderlands space defined by shifting loyalties and uncertain nationality.

It turned out that Dickson's defection to the American Fur Company was not a harbinger of Montreal's decision to come to terms with Astor. In September 1809, the merchant was "much surpriz'd" to hear from the Michilimackinac Company partners that they were "not now disposed to sell out." Astor tried to make the best of this disappointing news by implicating the British government in Montreal's change of heart. Although he had no hard evidence, he opined to Gallatin that British officials had supported the Michilimackinac Company because they considered its traders to be agents of empire, extending the influence of the Crown over as many as half a million Indians. If the American Fur Company was to stand any chance of competition with Montreal, then, it would have to enjoy an equally intimate relationship with the U.S. government. Astor already had a plan in mind, suggesting to Gallatin that "perhaps the appearance of a difference between the two Countries may induce the Michilimackina. Company to sell out."[44] Recognizing the connection between Montreal's willingness to negotiate and the passage and repeal of the Embargo and Nonintercourse Acts, Astor wanted the Madison administration to direct its foreign policy to frighten his commercial rivals into a quick sale.

Astor was wrong to blame the British government for meddling in his negotiations with Montreal, but he was right about the importance of British-American diplomacy. Montreal merchants declined his proposed negotiations in the fall of 1809 because they were optimistic that the arrival of Francis James Jackson, Erskine's replacement in Washington, D.C., would herald a new diplomatic settlement between the American Republic and the British Empire. Drawing heavily on Atcheson's *American Encroachments on British Rights,* Montreal merchants sent memoranda to guide Jackson in his negotiations with President Madison and Secretary of State Robert Smith. The merchants argued that the United States had unilaterally dissolved the permanent articles of the Jay Treaty when Congress passed the Nonintercourse Act closing trade with Great Britain the previous March. This was a stroke of luck, for it meant that Jackson could negotiate new commercial articles that would protect British merchants from the "injuries" they had suffered as part of the American revenue officers' "studied plan for thwarting the rights of British subjects . . . by every vexation and impediment that could be devised."[45] By arguing that the United States had *ex parte* dissolved the Jay Treaty, the merchants tried to prod Jackson into action. They framed the new minister's arrival in Washington, D.C., as a real opportunity for change after the disappointment and damage that Montreal merchants had suffered during the decade-long inertia of British-American diplomacy.

With the Jay Treaty dead, merchants imagined that British and American diplomats could start from scratch in renegotiating the border. For the U.S. government's unilateral dissolution of the treaty's permanent articles meant that the British government ought to claim the quid pro quo of dissolving "such of the articles of the treaty of 1783, as are found to be injurious to the Nation." Jackson could undo the original sin committed by Richard Oswald in 1783 by drawing a new boundary based on "the height of land dividing the waters which have their Outlets into the Sea Coast of the States, from those which have their outlet by the Lakes and River St. Lawrence."[46] Even if the American government would not discuss altering the border of 1783, the boundary between the two countries west of the Mississippi River had yet to be drawn. The merchants saw this as an opportunity to secure guaranteed access to the trans-Mississippi West and to exclude Astor and other American citizens from trading "beyond the Rocky Mountains, and on the River Columbia." Jackson ought to insist that Madison and Smith agree to allow British traders access to the "Missouri and west side of the *Mississippi*" as a "condition in fixing a boundary line between Canada and Louisiana to the Westward and Northward of the Mississippi"; he might sweeten the deal by offering the Americans equivalent trading access to British colonies in Asia or Africa. The merchants suggested a line of rivers running west from Lake Superior that "leave the whole of the Northwest trade within British jurisdiction and be highly beneficial to it."[47]

The memoranda also suggested ways in which Jackson could modify the border of 1783 to benefit British merchants. The Jay Treaty had failed to fix duties on commodities crossing between the United States and the Canadian provinces because "the scales of duties in the States and in Canada are so widely different as to amount almost to an interdiction of entry of goods from the latter into the former." The merchants suggested that adopting the "American Scale of Duties" would correct this problem. Moreover, they argued that creating a free-trade zone was the only way of avoiding the "Vexations and Impositions" that traders had suffered at the hands of U.S. agents. Excluding American territorial claims south of the Missouri River and the domain of the Hudson's Bay Company to the north, the merchants proposed opening the entire North American continent west of the Great Lakes to traders who would pay "no duties on goods for the use of the Indians."[48] The Montreal fur trade would have no need to negotiate with Astor under such a comprehensive agreement.

There would be no diplomatic border settlement in 1809. Francis James Jackson proved a disaster for British-American relations. He arrived in Washington, D.C., in September with an entourage of eighteen servants and his "formidable" wife, a Prussian baroness. Ignoring the instructions he had received from George Canning to merely discuss a settlement for the *Chesapeake* incident, Jackson involved himself in a series of unnecessary and protracted arguments with Madison and Smith. The relationship between the British minister and the Madison administration quickly soured. In November, just two months after Jackson arrived in the Federal City, Madison requested his recall to London and refused to have anything more to do with him. Events in London also conspired against a diplomatic resolution of the Montreal merchants' complaints. The slothful and incompetent Lord Richard Colley Wellesley replaced Canning as foreign secretary in the fall of 1809. It took Wellesley over six weeks to respond to Pinkney's note requesting Jackson's recall. The foreign secretary's delay in appointing Jackson's replacement ensured that the U.S. State Department would recall Pinkney in early 1811; diplomatic protocol dictated that the United States could not maintain a minister plenipotentiary to the Court of St. James while a mere chargé d'affaires headed the British legation in Washington, D.C.[49] The British and American governments were barely able to conduct diplomatic relations in the winter of 1809–10, let alone frame new commercial articles that would redefine their shared border in North America.

Montreal was ready for a deal by 1810. The disappointing news of the breakdown of diplomatic negotiations in Washington, D.C., and Madison's reinstatement of the Nonintercourse Act against the British Empire brought the Montreal partners back to the bargaining table with Astor. But this time it was the Michilimackinac Company partners who courted Astor. John Richardson and William McGillivray arrived in New York City on Saint Valentine's Day 1810 to negotiate the "sale of Mr. Astor of the Interests of the Michilimackinac Company." "Dire necessity" had driven Richardson and McGillivray to make the journey south, for the pair did not want to abandon their trade in the United States.[50] Aside from the loss of business, Richardson hated Americans. From the late 1790s, he had willingly used his cross-border business ties to aid the British government's counterespionage efforts.[51] By February 1810, however, Astor's interest in buying out the Michilimackinac Company seemed to offer Richardson and his partners the only alternative to financial ruin. Jackson's disastrous performance meant that British merchants and traders could expect no respite from the "many impediments . . . thrown in the way of the Trade" by American revenue officers.[52] Richardson and McGillivray were desperate.

More than anything else, it was Madison's reinstatement of the Nonintercourse Act that brought McGillivray and Richardson south. The merchants had no doubt that U.S. agents would seize large quantities of their goods and furs on the border. Richardson confessed his fears to his partner, Thomas Forsyth, back in Montreal, that "if we fail with Mr. Astor, a journey to Washington will be requisite to know upon what footing we shall stand, the ensuing season." He worried that under "the existing non-intercourse act, we are prohibited ingress and egress with supplies and returns."[53]

A growing sense of crisis in Montreal followed the news that the U.S. government had reinstated the Nonintercourse Act. The venerable Montreal merchant Alexander Henry wrote John Askin in May 1809 that "the embargo is raised and for which I am very sorry, as it will hurt the Trade of this Country much."[54] Madison's suspension of the act before the British government disavowed Erskine's note caught out many merchants and traders, who dispatched goods from Montreal with the expectation that they would have no trouble crossing the border. The St. Louis merchant Manuel Lisa reported to Auguste Chouteau, his partner in the St. Louis Missouri Fur Company, that he had received "generous offers" to supply him with goods from merchants in Upper Canada, "but it is impossible to get even a needle past the embargo."[55] John Askin's son, the British collector of customs at St. Joseph's Island in the Mackinac Straits, reported the difficulties faced by

Charles Oakes Ermatinger, who traded along "Lake Superior & would have gone in the lands again had his Goods arrived here before non-intercourse Law [had] taken effect." Rather than risk seizure, Ermatinger stored his merchandise at St. Joseph's Island in the hope that the border would be open by the following spring.[56]

Richardson continued to argue that the Nonintercourse Act was "a direct infringement of the ten permanent articles of the treaty of 1794," which it seemed now was only binding on the part of the British government. While, in Richardson's opinion, the United States had unilaterally dissolved the treaty, he learned from Governor-General Sir James Craig that the Board of Trade "consider that treaty as not at an end." The merchant was "at a loss to comprehend . . . upon what principle it can be competent to one party to do away one side of a joint contract, and yet keep the other party bound."[57] With no effective representation in Washington, D.C., the *ex parte* dissolution of the Jay Treaty by the U.S. government no longer provided British merchants with hope for a new border settlement. On the contrary, it was an open invitation for American revenue officers to do their worst.

Richardson and McGillivray entered into a provisional agreement to form an international partnership with Astor that would protect their trade from entrepreneurial American agents on the border. The deal would see Astor purchase a 50 percent stake in the Michilimackinac Company in return for the Montreal partners receiving a one-third share of Astor's planned Columbia River venture. For Astor, the agreement won him half of the fur trade of the Great Lakes and the Missouri River without having to risk opposition to the established Montreal firms. For Richardson and McGillivray, Astor's status as an American citizen and, particularly, his close connections with the Madison administration promised to protect their cross-border trade from uncertainty. With Astor as a partner, there would be no repeat of the damaging seizure on the Niagara River. As Richardson and McGillivray only spoke for the Montreal partners of the Michilimackinac Company, the agreement could not be finalized until the annual meeting of the wintering partnerships at Fort William in June and July. Astor tried to force an earlier official acceptance, but given the dire alternatives to a joint venture, the agreement of the wintering partners seemed like a mere formality.[58] Alexander Henry certainly thought so, writing to John Askin in February 1810 that "the whole trade of the Country is carried on by Americans and their agents, and I expect the Indian Trade will fall into their Hands, as Mr. Astore has offrd to purchase out the Makenau Co. he has a Treaty from Congress to an exclusive right to the Indian Trade."[59]

A joint partnership between Astor and the Montreal firms did not look so much like the American Fur Company that Astor had promised to James Madison and Albert Gallatin. While he anxiously awaited news of acceptance from the wintering partners, the New York merchant began sounding out Gallatin on importing Indian trade goods into the United States from Canada "in case the none intercourse if not taking of[f]."[60] While the new British-American Michilimackinac Company would draw supplies from New York, it would also continue to rely heavily on old connections with Montreal, particularly the labor of thousands of Canadiens, and not just for the trade in the Great Lakes and the Missouri River Valley. In March 1810, Alexander McKay, Donald Mackenzie, and Duncan McDougall, all British subjects from Canada, signed provisional articles of partnership with Astor to form the Pacific Fur Company—the Columbia River division of the American Fur Company.[61] Astor had always hoped that the U.S. government would direct its diplomacy and commercial policies to pursue his ends, namely to pressure his foreign rivals to come to terms with him by restricting border crossings from Canada. Now that he was part of a joint venture with British merchants, he expected Madison and Gallatin to relax commercial restrictions.

As it happened, Astor had no need to worry about the Nonintercourse Act, for Congress's passage of Macon's Bill No. 2 lifted all commercial sanctions against both Great Britain and France. Faced by the first budget deficit in years, Madison searched for a way to coerce the European belligerents into accepting American constructions of navigation and nationality without harming American merchants. Gallatin drafted a bill, introduced into the House of Representatives by Nathaniel Macon, to allow American merchants the freedom to trade wherever they liked and the right to import both British and French goods. The measure passed the House but was amended in the Senate into the so-called Macon's Bill No. 2. The bill opened trade with both Great Britain and France, but it did so by promising to reinstate the Nonintercourse Act against whichever power failed to end its own commercial restrictions against the United States by March 3, 1811.[62] Astor and his potential partners should not have to worry about commercial restrictions on the border.

That was the rub. Richardson and McGillivray rejected their earlier agreement with Astor when they learned about Macon's Bill No. 2. With no reason to worry about large-scale seizures on the border, they had no need to give away half of their business to Astor. They no longer had any use for him and his Washington connections. Indeed, even as Richardson and McGillivray reluctantly negotiated with Astor in New York City, their agent, Nathaniel Atcheson, was busy lobbying the king's ministers in Whitehall to secure their support for the Montreal fur trade in the trans-Mississippi West and the Pacific Northwest.[63] Not all the partners of the Michilimackinac Company felt so sanguine about the future. Accepting Macon's Bill No. 2 over Astor's offer meant betting on the willingness of Whitehall to rescind the orders-in-council before Napoleon abandoned his restrictions on continental commerce. The aging James McGill and the firm of Parker, Gerrard & Ogilvy were not in a gambling mood, however. They decided to cut their losses by selling their shares in the company to the firms of Richardson and McGillivray in May 1810. McTavish, McGillivrays & Company and Forsyth, Richardson & Company renamed their reformed venture the Montreal-Michilimackinac Company, and for the first time since 1807, they looked forward to prosecuting their trade free from American commercial restrictions on British shipping and goods.[64]

They were mistaken. In a surprising shift in policy, Napoleon hinted to U.S. minister John Armstrong, Jr., that France was prepared to suspend the operation of the Berlin and Milan Decrees, which had previously prevented American merchants from trading between the British Empire and continental Europe, after November 1, 1810. While diplomatic scholars have debated the sincerity of the so-called Cadore's letter, Madison saw this offer as an opportunity to pressure the British government into rescinding its orders-in-council. The president issued a proclamation on November 2, 1810, formally recognizing that the French Empire had suspended its edicts violating America's neutral commerce. Under the terms of Macon's Bill No. 2, the British Empire had ninety days in which to remove its own restrictions on American trade or face the suspension of its commerce with the United States.[65] The Montreal-Michilimackinac Company had already submitted its order for Indian trade goods to London. Unless the British government responded to Madison's pressure, their goods would molder in storehouses for at least a year while accumulating interest in London.

Montreal merchants prepared for the worst in the winter of 1810. As copartners in the North West Company, McTavish, McGillivrays & Company sent a memorial to Francis Gore, the lieutenant-governor of Upper Canada, in support of provincial road-building projects because they expected U.S. agents to disrupt their trade on the riverine border. The North West Company continued to send the majority of its goods to the annual rendezvous at Fort William on Lake Superior via Niagara and Detroit. Moreover, they also transported flour, Indian corn, and liquor produced in Detroit and Sandwich to supply northwest traders. The transportation network of the St. Lawrence River and the Great Lakes was no longer safe. The merchants reminded Gore that their trade was "continually exposed to the vexatious interference of the American Customs House Officers." A proposed road between Kempenfelt Bay on Lake Ontario and Penetanguishene Bay on Lake Huron would alleviate the need for traders to navigate the narrow straits of the Niagara and Detroit Rivers. Thus the new road would remove the "necessity of their following the Frontier of the Americans and from passing under their Forts and guns and free them also from the very vexatious and arbitrary impositions of the American Government."[66] After years of lobbying to relocate the border, Montreal merchants now planned to alter the long-term geography of their trade, abandoning critical riverine junctions to the control of U.S. agents.

Richardson's and McGillivray's fear that the effective enforcement of the Embargo and Nonintercourse Acts could ruin them stands in marked contrast to experiences elsewhere on the northern border. U.S. officials in New York and New England appeared unable, or even unwilling, to control widespread smuggling operations in Passamaquoddy Bay, on Lake Champlain, and through the port of Oswego on Lake Erie. Trade in potash, lumber, and other commodities had increasingly tied the growing economy of upstate New York to Montreal. As the Queenston merchant Robert Hamilton had predicted a decade earlier, the St. Lawrence River captured this trade as the cheapest and easiest means of bringing new agricultural commodities to market.[67] Popular opposition to the Embargo's economic effects in New York and Vermont manifested itself not only in rampant smuggling but also in the increasing difficulty that customs collectors faced from local juries, who were unwilling to convict the smugglers even when they were caught redhanded. Such was the seriousness of the civil disobedience on Lake Champlain in April 1808 that Jefferson declared the region to be in insurrection, mobilizing the New York and Vermont state militias to little avail.[68]

Unlike their counterparts in New York and Vermont, customs agents in the Great Lakes knew when and where merchants and traders would attempt to cross the border. The Montreal fur trade was time-sensitive: goods and furs had to arrive at certain places at certain times to avoid a lost season. Consequently, the convoys of boats traveling to and from Montreal followed a fairly predictable calendar. In contrast to the dense woodland cover and numerous islands and coves that smugglers in New York and Vermont could exploit to their advantage, the geography of the Montreal fur trade was far more exposed. River-bound convoys passed through narrow, fixed channels, including the Niagara and Detroit River Valleys, often in sight of U.S. garrisons. It was easier for American agents to control these chokepoints than to police the deep forests and rugged shorelines of the eastern states.

Above all, Canada merchants viewed the Embargo and Nonintercourse Acts in light of their ongoing struggle with U.S. agents on the border. This was not some ill-advised policy on the part of the Jefferson administration that was inadvertently inflicting financial pain; these acts were part of a targeted campaign to destroy their trade. Moreover, numerous incidents from the Niagara River to the Mackinac Straits over the past several years had provided Richardson and McGillivray with ample evidence of the ability of U.S. customs officials to enforce commercial policy on the border.

Madison's proclamation convinced the Montreal-Michilimackinac Company that they needed Astor after all. William McGillivray traveled south to New York City to reopen negotiations in January 1811. McGillivray and Astor signed new articles of agreement on January 28 to form the South West Company, a five-year partnership between the Montreal-Michilimackinac Company and the American Fur Company to prosecute the "Trade to the Interior Country from Michilimackinac." The new partners organized the South West Company to remedy two problems. First, it was designed to prevent damaging opposition between two companies, which "would be productive of certain loss to both." This is what had attracted Astor to the deal. Second, the agreement would protect the movement of "People, Supplies, and Materials" between the Atlantic ports and the hunting grounds of the American interior. Under the articles, Montreal and New York would both serve as logistical centers for the fur trade, dispatching goods imported from London and receiving peltry returns from Michilimackinac. But the agreement also planned for shifting this arrangement in response to "political events."[69] In other words, the South West Company was meant to protect the Montreal partners from the Nonintercourse Act by ensuring that they would still have access to the fur trade through their American division.

Unresolved tensions lurked beneath the surface of this marriage of convenience. The two parties still remained in competition in the Pacific Northwest. While Astor's earlier offers had included cooperation between the North West Company and the Pacific Fur Company on the Columbia River, this was not part of the South West Company agreement. Rather, the articles stated that the North West Company would not trade "within the Territorial Limits of the United States," and that the agreement had "no application whatsoever to any Countries beyond the ridge of the Rockey Mountains the river Missouri nor to the North West Coast or in the Pacific Ocean."[70] In this uneasy arrangement, Astor and the firms of Richardson and McGillivray were both partners and competitors in the Indian trade.

The South West Company also stood at odds with the arguments of economic imperialism that the partners had made with their respective governments. Both the Michilimackinac Company and Astor had tried to secure state sponsorship for their commercial enterprises by arguing that it would benefit the imperial ambitions of the British or American governments. The South West Company was an international partnership that operated across the border. The Montreal merchants, at least, could claim some sort of "British" victory from an agreement that promised to maintain their traders' access to the American West. Astor had won a majority share of the fur trade for New York City, but his agreement with Montreal had clearly fallen short of the nationalistic objectives that he had outlined to Jefferson and Madison. The South West Company did not merely employ British subjects in its ranks but enabled the continued movement of people, commodities, and capital between British North America and the United States. The company satisfied no one. The geopolitical uncertainty of the Revolutionary Atlantic World had brought Astor and the Montreal merchants together in a temporary alliance in which both sides still harbored imperial ambitions for the commercial conquest of North America.

The *Tonquin* arrived off the mouth of the Columbia River on March 25, 1811. After a long, fractious voyage from New York City via Cape Horn, John Jacob Astor's agents could finally begin to bring physical form to his carefully laid plans to establish control over the fur trade of the Pacific Northwest. As the traders worked to raise the walls of Fort Astoria, Wilson Price

Hunt led an overland expedition up the Missouri River with the aid of the trader James Aird. It would be almost another year before the traders would complete their long journey to the Pacific Coast. In the meantime, Astor's son-in-law Adrian Bentzon negotiated an agreement with the Russian American Company in Saint Petersburg to supply the Russians with goods and carry their furs to Guangzhou, China.[71] The South West Company may have averted commercial warfare between Astor and Montreal in the Great Lakes and the Missouri River, but the competition between American and British merchants in the contested and unbounded region of the Pacific Northwest was heating up on the eve of the War of 1812.

The North West Company found Astor's aggressive moves on the Columbia River deeply alarming. Nathaniel Atcheson had tried to warn the British government about the challenge that Astor's proposed commercial operations would pose to Crown sovereignty in the Pacific Northwest in 1810. Meeting with Robert Jenkinson, Earl of Liverpool, at the Colonial Office and Lord Wellesley at the Foreign Office, Atcheson found sympathy but no action from Spencer Perceval's ministry, which was focused on the European conflict.[72] Atcheson once again appealed to the British political classes, authoring the pamphlet *On the Origins and Progress of the North-West Company of Canada* in 1811. He argued that the fur trade was central to the economy and security of British North America. The trade was not merely "one of the most important branches of commerce carried on between British America and the Mother Country," but it also "attaches to the British empire a race of men (Indians) which no system merely political could maintain either in subordination or fidelity."[73] Atcheson further argued that the North West Company was the only means by which the fur trade could be conducted in an orderly and profitable fashion. The company restrained cut-throat competition among traders, who would otherwise ply Indian hunters with vast quantities of liquor, bringing violence to the frontier and ruin to British merchants. In sum, the North West Company was an imperial agency, its reach extending deep into the North American continent, exceeding that of colonial governments, military posts, and the Indian Department.[74] The vitality of the North West Company, then, was essential to the well-being of the British Empire.

As an agency of empire, the North West Company required the support of the British imperial state. The company sought a Crown charter that would award it the monopoly of the fur trade in the Northwest and protect the right it had received from the East India Company to trade directly with China. But, above all, Atcheson argued that the British government needed to press its territorial claims in the Pacific Northwest where Fort Astoria threatened the survival of the North West Company. The fur trade must expand to survive. The mouth of the Columbia River was a critical chokepoint in the riverine network, not only of the Pacific Northwest but as part of "a line of inland navigation, intersecting the whole continent of America, and joining the Atlantic to the Pacific." The success of Astor's Columbia River enterprise would not depend on his business acumen or the honest labor of his traders. Rather, Atcheson pointed to the "advantages, which the people of the United States derive from the aid and patronage of their government." The survival of the North West Company, then, depended on the "timely interference of the British government."[75] Whitehall would need to level the playing field or risk losing Great Britain's territorial claims in the Pacific Northwest and the protection of the king's Indian allies in the Great Lakes.

While Astor seemed to be gaining the upper hand on the Columbia River, his partnership was failing to deliver the protection that Richardson and McGillivray had hoped for in the Great Lakes. The United States reinstated the Nonintercourse Act against the British Empire in March 1811, closing the border to trade. Astor's connections with the Madison administration were meant to exempt British traders from customs seizures at the border. But his influence in Washington, D.C., had its limits. In August 1811, Madison turned down Astor's application for a special license to import Montreal's share of the South West Company through Michilimackinac.[76] U.S. agents would prey on any traders who tried to carry goods across the border.

Samuel Abbott, the new customs collector at Michilimackinac, refused to allow entry to Indian trade merchandise in 1811. Astor's agent Henry Brevoort reported that the goods from Montreal remained at St. Joseph's Island, and "no hope is entertained that Government will grant them admission."[77] He painted a picture of desolation on the island, in which "upwards of a score of Indian Traders, who being cut off from their accustomary supplies of goods from the Company are completely set adrift upon the wide world, as desperate as so many famished wolves."[78] At St. Joseph's Island, John Askin, Jr., noted the nervous activity reflected in the "constant arrival of Canoes for some days past from Michilimackinac and Boats from Montreal."

The British customs collector predicted that the "non-importation act will effect the S. W. Furr Company much for their Goods must remain here this winter unsold." Nevertheless, the South West Company sent George Gillespie, Toussaint Pothier, and Jean Baptiste Berthelot to the island "in hopes that the Act will be repealed."[79] They would be disappointed.

The traders resorted to smuggling. John Askin, Jr., wrote to his brother Charles, a Queenston merchant, that "Mr. Robert Dickson was with us some time ago and its reported that he had got to the Mississippi with a compleat assortment of Goods." How Dickson had evaded the "Yanky Collectors," John Jr. would not say, but the trader had managed to sneak across the border from Queenston to Buffalo before traveling down the Ohio River from Fort Pitt to St. Louis. He wintered among the Sioux on the upper Mississippi River.[80] Dickson was not alone; one scholar estimates that the South West Company managed to smuggle fifty thousand dollars' worth of goods into the United States through Green Bay in 1811.[81] Dickson and other traders might have evaded American agents on the border, but they should never have had to take this risk in the first place. For the Montreal partners, the whole point of their agreement with Astor was that he was meant to use his status as an American citizen and his influence with government to protect their traders from predatory U.S. customs officers.

Astor tried again to secure an exemption from the U.S. government to import the South West Company's goods into the United States in March 1812. Madison would not help him. The president claimed that only Congress could grant an exception to the Nonintercourse Act. Astor turned next to Jefferson, hoping that the former president's enthusiasm for his imperial ambitions had not waned in retirement. Jefferson seemed as optimistic as ever about the connection between Astor's enterprise and a republican empire of liberty. He predicted that Astoria would help to people the Pacific Coast with "free and independent Americans, unconnected with us but by ties of blood & interest, and enjoying like us the rights of self-government." For all his hyperbole, though, Jefferson repeated Madison's advice: Astor must look to Congress for his salvation.[82] New York representative Samuel L. Mitchill presented a petition to the House of Representatives on behalf of the American Fur Company on March 30, seeking permission to import "sundry goods suitable for the Indian market" from British Canada. While the House referred the petition to the Committee of Commerce and Manufactures, it stood little chance of success because the majority of Republican lawmakers refused to weaken the Nonintercourse Act by granting exceptions.[83] Astor's friends in Washington had again failed him.

By March 1812, Congress was preparing for war. The arrival in Washington, D.C., of John Augustus Foster, the new British minister, in July 1811 did nothing to resolve the differences between the United States and the British Empire. Although he was a significant improvement over Francis Jackson, talks between Foster and Madison reached deadlock within weeks of his arrival.[84] The Battle of Tippecanoe added further strain to British-American relations. While the Madison administration had approved William Henry Harrison's military preparations for a strike against Prophetstown in July 1811, American politicians and policymakers blamed the British government for sponsoring the Native attack on U.S. forces on the morning of November 7, 1811. Foster's vehement renunciation of British involvement, which included the publication of letters written by Governor-General Sir James Craig ordering his agents to restrain the king's Indian allies from war, had no effect. Washington received ever more reports from its Indian agents that Great Britain was responsible for inciting frontier violence. At Fort Wayne, U.S. agent Benjamin Stickney claimed to have uncovered Shetoon, a Wyandot chief, who he accused of being in the pay of the infamous British Indian agent Matthew Elliott, in May 1812.[85] The U.S. government had no desire to relax border controls when it seemed that war with the British Empire was imminent.

Astor finally secured Madison's permission to import some of his goods into the United States on the eve of war. After Congress proved a dead end, Astor continued pestering Albert Gallatin, arguing that admitting his goods was in the interest of national security. Astor relayed accounts he had received that "the Indians are very angry in consequence of short suplys," before petulantly threatening to "quite the Business" if he could not get his goods across the border.[86] On June 16—just two days before Congress declared war on Great Britain—Gallatin informed the U.S. customs collectors at Michilimackinac and Detroit that Madison had authorized Astor to bring "a quantity of arms, ammunition and other Indian goods" across the border to ensure that they did not fall into the hands of the British Indian Department.[87] Suspecting that Astor was trying to pull a fast one by deviating from their agreed business plan, John Richardson refused to allow the goods to leave St. Joseph's Island. With war imminent, Richardson saw it as "our bounden duty as British Subjects, that not a piece or an article of any description of Goods intended for the Indian Trade, shall be placed or sold, so as to come into the possession or controul of your Government."[88] Perhaps Astor rued the irony that, after years of trying to exploit Montreal's fear of Republican commercial policy, it was his American Fur Company that found itself the victim of the border.

On June 18, 1812, John Jacob Astor was on the road to Washington, D.C., somewhere south of Baltimore when he learned that Congress had declared war on Great Britain.[89] The merchant dispatched the courier James Vosburgh to Upper Canada to warn his agents there to prevent his furs falling into the hands of the local authorities. Vosburgh arrived in Queenston on June 25, where he delivered his message to the merchant Thomas Clark. Clark, in turn, informed British general Sir Isaac Brock. Astor's panicked attempt to protect his financial interests in Upper Canada inadvertently alerted British officials at Fort George to Congress's declaration of war before their American counterparts at the neighboring Fort Niagara. Consequently, British officers arrested a number of U.S. citizens in Queenston, including one unfortunate U.S. Army lieutenant, who was unaware that he was now an enemy combatant, as well as seizing American-owned property north of the border.[90]

This incident proved deeply embarrassing to Astor. Vosburgh's subsequent arrest in Niagara for treason made public Astor's role in alerting British authorities to the outbreak of war.[91] Moreover, another of Astor's agents, a Mr. Carp, also sent expresses to both Montreal and St. Joseph's Island to warn "the pepal engaged with me in the Indian trade" of Congress's declaration of war. Astor assured Gallatin that Carp "had no other view than to take care of the property," but whatever his intentions, the damage to Astor's reputation was done.[92] Astor would continue to be dogged by allegations of treachery for years to come.

As Astor discovered to his chagrin, the outbreak of war in 1812 brought increased urgency to the problem of defining the border. The rival states were determined to use the boundary as a means of controlling political behavior during wartime in a way that had simply not been possible during the War of Independence. The idea of treason was predicated on the exclusive character of political allegiance to a nation as a territorially defined sovereign entity. The outbreak of the War of 1812 made it more important than ever for citizens to live on one side of the boundary and subjects on the other. Historian Alan Taylor is right that a "*synergy* of multiple grievances" lay behind Congress's decision to declare war.[93] Its origins cannot be understood as a zero-sum game between western causes, whether security concerns or expansionist ambitions, and eastern maritime causes. Rather, the War of 1812 was a conflict to define American nationhood as the basis for transcontinental empire. This is why Astor would continually have to defend himself against charges of treachery after the war. His trade involved border crossings by liminal figures who did not fit neatly into a world divided between American citizens and British subjects, particular in the hindsight of the postwar years. In many ways, Astor was a victim of his own rhetoric of economic nationalism. In seeking to mobilize the power of the American national state to support his commercial empire by arguing that the fur trade ought to be the exclusive preserve of Americans, Astor was helping to foster a political climate in the United States that naturalized national boundaries and rendered border crossings suspect.

6

"WHEN THE AMERICAN STRIPES ALONE PROTECT THE WESTERN HEMISPHERE"

∴
∴

The London *Morning Chronicle* broke the news of the new British-American commercial treaty in October 1815. While both governments had ratified the peace treaty concluded at Ghent on Christmas Eve 1814, the commercial convention marked the final conclusion of the broader diplomatic settlement ending the War of 1812. As the *Morning Chronicle* had feared, the British negotiators had proved no match for their American counterparts: the commercial agreement abandoned the king's Indians to "the mercy of their neighbours" and left the British Empire "on worse ground than when we began the war."[1]

Over the next two months, the *Morning Chronicle* constructed an extensive critique of the Treaty of Ghent and its related commercial convention, which the newspaper argued had dealt a devastating blow to Britain's imperial ambitions in North America. The diplomatic agreements ensured the loss of the Montreal fur trade by confirming the border of 1783 and by extinguishing the right of free movement that British subjects and Native peoples had enjoyed under the Jay Treaty. Consequently, the *Morning Chronicle* predicted, the United States would shortly amass "an immense empire," reaching westward to the Pacific Ocean and perhaps extending southward to include the "insurrectional provinces of New Spain."[2] Distracted by the negotiations held in Vienna about the future of Europe, the British government had played into the hands of American imperialists by abandoning the fur trade of the Great Lakes, the Mississippi and Missouri River Valleys, and the Pacific Northwest. "Whilst we are buried in apathy and neglect, and disregard that immense field of enterprize the efforts of Spanish America open upon us," the *Morning Chronicle* lamented, "the Government and individuals of the United States are eager to improve all the advantages to our detriment." The revolutions in Spanish America meant that empire was up for grabs, but Great Britain stood idly by as the United

States prepared for "the day when the American stripes alone protect the Western hemisphere."[3]

The *Morning Chronicle* provoked a response from the Philadelphia *Aurora General Advertiser*, which ran a series of editorials in December 1815 arguing for the exclusion of the Montreal fur trade from the territory of the United States. William Duane penned his column to assail the *Morning Chronicle*'s argument that the Native peoples residing within the borders of the United States were independent nations that ought to enjoy the right of trading with whomever they pleased. Duane denounced the "most lame and impotent effort" of British imperialists to use the fur trade to maintain their influence among the Indians.[4] To the *Aurora* and its readers, the very idea of Native independence was as an affront to American sovereignty. Moreover, the fur trade worked against the United States' paternalistic project of civilizing Native peoples by destroying their cultural practices. This Jeffersonian program sought to convert American Indians to sedentary farming practices as a way of assimilating them into U.S. society. From this point of view, the Montreal fur trade threatened to cast Native peoples into oblivion by encouraging them to resist the inevitable march of American progress.

The American Republic's recent experience of fighting a war against the British Empire and its Indian allies had made real the threat that foreign traders posed to ordinary American citizens. Indeed, Duane and the *Aurora* had played a leading role in fighting the Republican propaganda war against Federalist opponents of the conflict, printing lurid accounts of Indian "depredations" committed against wounded soldiers and unarmed women and children with the assistance, or at the very least indifference, of British officers and Indian Department agents. Duane's arguments in favor of excluding British traders were hardly novel by 1815, but the shadowy agents that menaced the antebellum frontier had taken on new, inhuman faces. Duane asked, "do not the practices of her *Dicksons* and her *Elliotts*, and other agents along our whole frontier, from Detroit to Chicago, and thence to the Mississippi, demand of the United States government, the protection of our settlers from the instigated massacres of those barbarous agencies?"[5] He could pose this rhetorical question to his readers knowing well that the names of Robert Dickson and Matthew Elliott would conjure up innumerable atrocities reported in the *Aurora*'s pages over the past few years.

The War of 1812 was the second civil war fought within the British Atlantic World. As historian Alan Taylor has argued, the conflict pivoted on the ambiguous boundary between British subjects and American citizens. While subjects and citizens would fight on both sides of the conflict, as would Native peoples, the bitter experience of fighting the war would harden lines of difference between them. The violence and devastation that both sides visited on people and property along the northern border contributed to a growing sense of American and British-Canadian nationalism. In the United States, figures like the trader Robert Dickson and the Indian agent Matthew Elliott were seen as race traitors, their decision to ally with feared and hated Indians disqualifying them as potential fellow citizens.[6] Americans no longer sympathized with the plight of Upper Canadians who labored under the yoke of monarchical oppression. Instead, they looked upon their northern neighbors as an alien people.

The *Aurora* denounced citizens of convenience as a threat to American nationhood and empire. According to Duane, the liminal figures engaged in the Montreal fur trade did not merely threaten renewed violence on the frontier but their insidious influence within the U.S. government also undermined the public good. He cited two cases of the "baleful influence which the *North West Company* obtained in our public affairs" in the years leading up to the war with Great Britain. First, David Duncan, the disgraced former collector of customs for Michilimackinac, resurfaced to accuse John Jacob Astor of abusing his influence with Treasury Secretary Albert Gallatin. Astor, who "held a great many shares in the stock of the English North West Company," managed to convince Gallatin to release contraband goods that Duncan had bravely seized from an "armed force" of British traders who were attempting to smuggle them into the United States. Second, the *Aurora* explained how Astor was responsible for alerting British authorities in Upper Canada of Congress's declaration of war nine days before the news arrived in Detroit. For Duane, the lessons of the War of 1812 were clear: The "policy of the U. States demands the greatest earnestness and constancy in interdicting an intercourse which has been productive of so many cruel calamities to our frontier people, and which could obtain such an influence in the treasury branch of the executive government."[7]

The Treaty of Ghent and the commercial convention of 1815 made it possible for the United States to close the northern border to British merchants and traders. The bitter wartime experience may have helped to mobilize the popular will in support of economic nationalism, but the peace settlement was instrumental in empowering the American national state to enforce border policies that would discriminate against foreigners. While the Treaty of Ghent usually receives short-shrift from diplomatic historians and early American scholars, the editors of both the London *Morning Chronicle* and the Philadelphia *Aurora General Advertiser* recognized the deep significance of the diplomatic settlements of 1814–15 for the future of both the British and American Empires. The American plenipotentiaries articulated more expansive claims over the actions of non-citizens, most notably Native peoples living within the republic's territorial bounds. Moreover, the war abrogated the commercial and residential privileges that non-citizens had enjoyed under the Jay Treaty to move and trade across the northern border. American diplomats ensured that neither Native peoples nor British subjects could freely pass between the British Empire and the American Republic. Despite what the Treaty of Ghent might say, it did not restore the *status quo antebellum*.

Under cover of darkness, John Askin, Jr., and 280 Odawa and Ojibwa warriors climbed into their canoes at St. Joseph's Island on July 16, 1812, to attack the American garrison at Michilimackinac. Askin, the son of the merchant John Askin, Sr., and Manette, an Odawa woman, was a long-serving British collector of customs at St. Joseph's Island and an influential figure among the Native peoples of the upper Great Lakes. He and his men formed part of an invasion force of over two hundred Canadien boatmen, forty British regulars, and two pieces of artillery. Commanded by British captain Charles Roberts, the flotilla of fifty canoes and twelve barges landed on Mackinac Island just before daybreak on July 17. While Roberts positioned his artillery on high ground overlooking the American fort, it was the king's Indian allies who would convince the U.S. garrison to surrender without firing a shot. Askin's Odawa and Ojibwa force formed the left wing of Roberts's army, while Robert Dickson commanded 103 Sioux and Winnebago warriors on the right. Askin later wrote to his father that "the Indians were like devils to Storm the place." Considering his position hopeless and fearing that Askin's and Dickson's men would massacre his troops, the U.S. commander, Captain Porter Hanks, agreed to surrender without a fight. "A happy thing," Askin wrote his father, "for had they fired & wounded any person not a soul would have been saved from the Hatchet."[8]

A month later, Captain Charles Askin, John's younger brother, witnessed the capitulation of the American garrison at Detroit. News of the sudden and unexpected surrender of Michilimackinac began a swift reversal of American fortunes in the Detroit River Valley. William Hull, the governor of the Michigan Territory, began the American invasion of Upper Canada in early July, seizing the undefended town of Sandwich. Word of Michilimackinac's surrender seriously unnerved Hull, who feared that his army would soon fall prey to an overwhelming force of Indians heading southward to massacre the Americans. Hull and his troops soon got a taste of the grizzly fate they would meet at the hands of Britain's Indian allies. The Shawnee war captain Tecumseh ambushed an American guard, killing seventeen men and mutilating their bodies. All this was too much for the unstable Hull, who ordered a hasty retreat to Detroit during the night of August 7–8.[9]

Captain Charles Askin, a volunteer in the 41st Regiment of Foot, crossed the Detroit River into Michigan Territory as part of an invasion force led by Major-General Sir Isaac Brock on August 15. In his account of the invasion, Askin noted that Brock had been careful to send his Native troops across the river first.[10] Aware of the Americans' deep-seated fear of Indians, Brock convinced Hull to surrender rather than expose his men—and more importantly himself—to what they saw as the barbarous violence of Indian warfare.[11] Hull's unilateral decision was bitterly resented by his junior officers. Askin, who witnessed the American troops file out of Fort Detroit, recorded that they "did not march with the honors of War though I am told they were allowed to do it by the Capitulation" because "the Officers of the Am. Army were so mortified that they had to surrender without fighting that they were indifferent about it or anything else." For Askin and the combined force of Canadian militia, British regulars, and Indian warriors, though, the capture of Detroit was a source of great pride that helped to erase the recent memory of the mass desertions that had followed Hull's ill-fated invasion of Upper Canada. Askin confided to his diary that "I never felt so proud, as I did just then. As soon as we were in the Fort, the American Colours were taken down and ours hoisted. Three Cheers were given as they were hoisted by the Militia and others outside the Fort & the Indians when the Salute with the Cannon was given gave an Indian yell every shot."[12]

The opening weeks of the war revealed much about the overall character of the conflict. President James Madison's decision to focus U.S. military operations on invading Upper Canada meant that the war on land would largely be fought along the border. Indeed, only a few weeks after witnessing the capitulation of Detroit, Charles Askin fought in the Battle of Queenston

Heights on the Niagara peninsula, helping to repel an eastern invasion force led by U.S. general Stephen Van Rensselaer.[13] The early stages of the conflict also showed how quickly military action could change the border. In the space of a couple of weeks, the capture of Michilimackinac and Detroit by British forces redrew the political map of North America, sweeping aside the agreement that Richard Oswald and the American commissioners had framed in Paris thirty years before.

The conflict played out in the communities that straddled the border, dividing families and friends. Four of John Askin's sons and at least one of his grandsons served with either the British Army or the Canadian militia. His son-in-law Elijah Brush, however, was an American officer in the Wayne County militia defending Detroit.[14] The capitulation of Detroit saved the Askin family from tragedy. Many other families and friends in border communities would not be spared from visiting violence on one another in the years to come.

Hull's dramatic reversal in fortune, from leading an invasion of Upper Canada to his surrender on American soil, also demonstrates the volatility of allegiance in the border conflict. Hull was unquestionably a poor leader who was unequal to his command, but his proclamation to the Western District, which promised to liberate Canadians from colonial tyranny, hit the mark by provoking mass desertions in the Upper Canada militia. When the British commander Isaac Brock arrived in the Western District a few weeks later, many deserters returned to the king's colors and willingly participated in the capture of Detroit.[15] The change of heart that the returning militiamen experienced speaks less to their calculating character in backing the side that appeared to hold the upper hand than it does to their political agnosticism. Even after seemingly casting his lot with the British Empire by participating in the capture of Michilimackinac, Robert Dickson assured John Jacob Astor in October 1812 that he had done "every thing in his Power to keep the Indians at Peace untill the war was Declared when it became out his Power." Indeed, Dickson was so bold as to ask Astor to push his claim for five thousand dollars for supplies that he had issued to the local Indians on behalf of the U.S. government.[16] Neither the United States nor the British Empire could take for granted the loyalty of the people who resided within their respective territories.

The War of 1812 would change this. In September 1812, John Askin could happily write that his son-in-law Elijah Brush had "acquitted himself as a brave man" in the service of the United States.[17] But over the next few years, the bitter wartime experiences of residents of border communities meant that Americans and Canadians increasingly looked on one another with hostility. The beginning of this shift, too, was present in the first weeks of the war. Both armies looted border communities, destroying property and laying waste to crop fields. Hull's men looted homes in Sandwich, while Brock's troops reaped their revenge in the Detroit River Valley. The conflict would only become more destructive. Alan Taylor calculates that the military campaign on the Niagara peninsula in 1813 dispossessed 12,000 inhabitants, depopulating a region of 160 square miles.[18] The American fear and loathing of Indians as murderous "savages," which had proved such a potent weapon in Brock's arsenal during Hull's disastrous campaign, also aroused resentment toward their British sponsors. Brock was certainly not alone in appreciating the psychological advantage that Indian warriors gave the British forces in battle. British commanders valued Native troops for the fear that they spread in the American ranks, and they would continue to employ Indian warriors to this effect throughout the war. While the United States would eventually recruit its own Indian allies from among the Iroquois peoples of New York, the conflict more deeply entrenched the American racial hatred of Native peoples and encouraged their darkest fantasies of exterminating Indians.[19] In sponsoring Indian violence, Canadians marked themselves as an alien people in the eyes of most Americans.

The growing sense of nationalism in the United States and Upper Canada presented a new kind of challenge for citizens of convenience. It was not just policymakers and government agents who found the ambiguous borders of nationality troubling: popular feeling increasingly looked on liminal figures as disloyal and a threat to the public good. This was particularly true for Indian traders in the United States. Kinship ties and the close connections between trade and diplomacy in Native political culture meant that traders played a key role in brokering and maintaining the military alliance between the British Crown and Indian nations during the war. This role made it particularly difficult for traders to claim the rights of American citizenship once the war ended. They were twice traitors: once by taking up arms against the government of the United States, and a second time by fighting with Indians against their own race.

The association of the North West Company with Indian warfare meant that American forces would target its merchants and traders when they got the chance. When U.S. forces occupied Queenston in November 1813, the company's local agent, Thomas Dickson, was "Plundered of Every thing even the very... Boots he had on." American soldiers arrested Dickson and he was "carried off Prisoner to the States."[20] In August 1814, the American flotilla tasked with recapturing Michilimackinac first attacked the North West Company's facilities at St. Joseph's Island and on the St. Marys River. The trader Ramsey Crooks, John Jacob Astor's leading western agent, witnessed the capture of the company's schooner *Mink*, "laden with Two Hundred and thirty Barrels of Flour." Crooks wrote Astor that U.S. Major Andrew Holmes led "a Company of Regulars [and] some Sailors" to the St. Marys River, where "the company's Store houses were burned, there fine Schooner Perservance destroyed and a quantity of dry goods sugars and spirits said to belong to a Mr. Johnson taken and brought to the fleet."[21] The American raid dealt a serious blow to the precarious operations of the North West Company, destroying over four thousand pounds sterling worth of equipment and supplies that were extremely difficult for the company to replace in wartime.[22]

The shifting tide of the war dictated the political maneuvering of the American and Canadian partners of the South West Company. The conflict on the border brought chaos to the commercial activities of the company, but it did remain in business throughout the war. Astor and his Montreal partners maintained a surprisingly regular correspondence in which both parties tried to adapt their peacetime commercial agreement to the unpredictable and dangerous circumstances of war. At the same time, it was obvious to both the American and Canadian partners that the outcome of the war would have revolutionary consequences for the future of the fur trade. New York and Montreal responded to news of the changing fortunes of war by positioning their agents to take advantage of the new postwar order in North America and the Atlantic World.

The fall of both Michilimackinac and Detroit to British forces during the first weeks of the war strengthened Montreal's claim to control the future of the Indian trade. Finding himself largely dependent on the goodwill of his Montreal partners, Astor managed to secure a passport from the British governor-general Sir George Prevost to travel to Montreal, where he received Prevost's permission to remove his share of the peltries at Michilimackinac. Astor also managed to channel some of his furs in British territory through Plattsburgh on Lake Champlain.[23]

American victories in 1813 shifted the advantage to Astor. U.S. Commodore Oliver Hazard Perry defeated a British fleet at the Battle of Lake Erie in September, securing American naval control of the Great Lakes. William Henry Harrison exploited Perry's success, recapturing Detroit and leading a successful invasion of Upper Canada that culminated with an American victory at the Battle of Moraviantown in October. The death of the influential Shawnee war captain Tecumseh struck a major blow to Indian unity and summed up the changing fortunes of the war in the West.[24] The North West Company feared that American control of the Great Lakes spelled the end of their trade. They begged Governor-General Prevost to use his influence in London to solicit the Hudson's Bay Company's permission to open a northern supply route to the West. The Montrealers explained that "by the fatal and ever to be deplored disaster which has befallen His Majesty's Fleet on Lake Erie there is every reason to apprehend that the Americans will get possession of Michilimackinac and the command of Lake Huron." The loss of Michilimackinac and American control of Lake Erie and Lake Huron would "completely cut off" communication between Montreal and the Northwest, making it impossible for the company's agents to transport Indian goods and furs between the Atlantic entrepôt and the western hunting grounds.[25] In November 1813, the North West Company partners found themselves in the humiliating position of begging for help from the rival Hudson's Bay Company for their very survival.

Astor scented blood. Hopeful that the American invasion force led by General James Wilkinson would soon capture Montreal, Astor sent his nephew George Astor and fellow New York merchant John Day northward. He charged the pair with recovering more of his South West Company furs and purchasing all the Indian trade goods and West India produce they could lay their hands on "should our people have possession of Montreal." Moreover, Astor also ordered Day to meet with his Montreal partners "to sound them of how they would like to sell me their Interest in the Indian Country."[26] As George Astor and John Day made their way across Lake Champlain, John Jacob Astor ordered his principal western agent, Ramsey Crooks, to accompany the American expedition to recapture Michilimackinac. Should the island fall, Crooks was to immediately purchase upwards of $100,000 of furs to ship to Buffalo, New York, and make arrangements to send Indian trade goods to St. Louis the following spring.[27] Barely a month after Perry's victory at the Battle of Lake Erie, Astor had put into action an imperial scheme to exploit the recent run of American victories and defeat his commercial rivals in Montreal.

American arms would not deliver a decisive blow to the British Empire in 1813. Crooks informed Astor that the United States had suspended all operations against Michilimackinac, deeming them "totally impracticable." He tried to reassure his master that there were "but very few Skins" at Michilimackinac because fighting in the West had made it impossible to carry on the fur trade. Moreover, he was confident that "the merchants on the British side have not any and on the american [side] my sole dependence will be on what small parcels the inhabitants in their distracted state last year had the good fortune to conceal." He, however, remained hopeful that U.S. forces would soon capture Montreal. The anticipated victory would mean that "the upper Posts must fall, a universal pacification of course take place between the United States and North Western Indians; and the commerce of the South west and part of the north become the patrimony of American Adventurers."[28] The postponement of the American attack on Michilimackinac was disappointing news. Astor wondered, "surely our people know not the importance of Michilimackinac & St. Joseph, I was sure they had done & taken it." Nevertheless, he shared Crooks's optimism that the fall of Montreal was imminent.[29] Astor would again be disappointed. Although outnumbering their foes almost two to one, the disastrous expedition that General James Wilkinson led up the St. Lawrence River in November 1813 suffered a series of humiliating defeats before settling into disease-riddled winter quarters.[30] The war would soon enter its third campaign year with no end in sight.

On the other side of the continent, the loss of Fort Astoria on the Columbia River in October 1813 threw into doubt Astor's imperial ambitions. When news of the outbreak of war arrived at Astoria in January 1813, the leading traders Duncan McDougall and Donald Mackenzie decided to abandon the fort and lead an overland expedition to St. Louis once their fellow traders had come in from the interior forts. In the meantime, traders from the North West Company arrived at Astoria and the two rival factions shared a common life there while dividing up the trade. The North West Company bought out Astor's agents in October, only a few weeks before the British warship H.M.S. *Raccoon* arrived at the Columbia River. Captain William Black took possession of the fort on behalf of the Crown on December 12, renaming it Fort George.[31] Wartime conquests redrew the political map of North America, but there was no clear victor—in Washington or London, New York or Montreal—after two years of war.

The Canada merchants had been thinking about peace since the day the war began. Years of failed British-American diplomacy had done little to prevent entrepreneurial U.S. agents from preying on the Montreal fur trade in violation of the Jay Treaty. The outbreak of war meant that the British and American governments would eventually have to make peace, and the Canada merchants intended to make sure that the ensuing treaty would protect their commercial interests. The merchants of Upper and Lower Canada sent a joint memorial to Governor-General Prevost laying out their expectations for a peace settlement only a few months after the outbreak of war. By voiding the Treaty of Paris, the merchants believed that the War of 1812 had finally "placed within reach of the British government, the reparation of a most gross and extraordinary error in the negociation and treaty, at the close of the American war": the cession of the trans-Appalachian West. They proposed a simple solution. The British government must insist that the United States accept a new border as a *sine qua non* for peace. The new boundary would protect Native homelands, rendering them "independent of the United States." Alongside ensuring that the British Empire would maintain its naval supremacy on the Great Lakes, the protection of Native homelands would guarantee the security of British North America from future invasion. They proposed a boundary running from Sandusky on Lake Erie to the source of the Missouri River, via the Ohio and Mississippi. The new border would mean removing American citizens from the northwest corner of the state of Ohio, and from the Indiana, Illinois, and Michigan Territories, as well as establishing the Rocky Mountains as the western boundary of the United States.[32]

It is too easy to dismiss such a radical redrawing of the British-American boundary as so much pie in the sky. The idea of removing thousands of American colonists from much of the present-day Midwest seems fanciful, if not altogether delusional. But in the wake of the early British victories at Michilimackinac and Detroit, it seemed as if anything might be possible. Diplomacy in the Revolutionary Atlantic World frequently redrew territorial boundaries much older than the border of 1783 and transferred sovereignty over populations much larger than the American colonists occupying the U.S. territories north of the Ohio River. One need look no further than the Franco-American Treaty of 1803, which transferred the vast territory and population of Louisiana to the United States. If the American Republic could extend its boundaries through diplomacy, the reverse was also true. To be sure, the strategic situation in North America changed a great deal over the next two years, but it was not unreasonable for the merchants to continue to expect that the British-American peace treaty would frame a new border settlement.

Allied victories in Europe against Napoleonic France raised hopes in Montreal and New York that 1814 might bring peace to the Atlantic World. Astor and his Canadian partners in the South West Company had once believed that the war could award them control of the North American Indian trade, but by 1814 the conflict seemed to be locked in a stalemate, with both British and American forces squandering promising military gains. In the meantime, the war had spread chaos throughout the Great Lakes, bringing trade to a virtual standstill. Frustrated by the disappointments of 1813, Astor wrote Crooks in February 1814 that "unless we have Peace we can not do anything in the Indian trade."[33] Far away in Michilimackinac, British trader Frederick Oliver shared Astor's dire assessment. The North West Company had no merchandise for Oliver, who pinned his hopes on "a General peace" in Europe and North America, which would restore his fortunes.[34]

It was an article of common faith among Canada merchants on both sides of the Atlantic that the British government's complete ignorance of the commercial geography of North America was responsible for the disastrous border settlement of 1783. In the telling and retelling of the tragedy in Paris, the British peace commissioner Richard Oswald was less a villain than the victim of his own incompetence. The meeting between Canada merchants and Oswald in February 1783 represented the final act in this comedy of errors. So the story went, Oswald "literally burst into tears" when he realized the mistake he had just made in handing over the trans-Appalachian West to the United States. He confessed "his complete ignorance" of the existence of the western posts and "the country being given away being an object worth of notice in any respect."[35] Oswald's death in 1784 ensured that the Canada merchants could tell their story without fear of contradiction. The folklore of Oswald's tearful confession was really a cautionary tale:

the future prosperity of the Britain Empire depended on merchants educating Whitehall about the commercial and political realities on the ground in North America. If ignorance had led to disaster in 1782–83, then knowledge could pave the way for triumph in 1814.

The transatlantic lobbying apparatus of the merchants "interested in the Trade, Navigation, and Fisheries of the British North American Colonies" swung into action in early 1814. London merchants John Inglis and John Bainbridge sent memorials from merchant committees in Lower Canada, Nova Scotia, and London to the prime minister, Lord Liverpool, before peace talks began. The London merchants demanded that a "new Boundary shall be established for the Indian Country and the independance of the Indians guaranteed by Great Britain." In essence, Inglis and Bainbridge resurrected the old idea of a neutral Indian barrier state, which Montreal merchants had suggested to John Graves Simcoe in the early 1790s. They explained that the United States should be prohibited from building forts, collecting revenue, or exercising "any territorial or other Jurisdiction" in the Indian state. Alongside the negotiation of a new boundary, which would also resolve the territorial dispute between northeastern Massachusetts (the present-day state of Maine) and New Brunswick, the merchants called for the exclusion of American shipping from Britain's North American and Caribbean colonies; the acquisition of the islands of Saint Pierre and Miquelon, south of Newfoundland; and "an Indemnification" from the American government for the Michilimackinac Company's losses from the seizure of their property on the Niagara River in 1808. Inglis and Bainbridge saw these core points as "absolutely essential" for the future prosperity and protection of British North America.[36]

The Canada merchants' trusted pamphleteer Nathaniel Atcheson began mobilizing British public opinion in support of renegotiating the border. Published in March 1814, *A Compressed View of the Points to Be Discussed in Treating with the United States of America* argued that the interests of Canada, rather than the defense of maritime rights, ought to be foremost in the minds of British diplomats. Given the due attention and "parental protection" of the British government, Atcheson predicted that the growing prosperity of Canada would "establish an influence on the continent of North America, spreading even in time to the Pacific, and trading from the shore of that ocean with the rich regions of the East." All that stood between

Britain's North American colonies and this glorious future was "one grand point, the necessity of the establishment of *a new line of boundary,* between the British and American possessions."[37]

According to Atcheson, the history of the border since 1783 was the story of continued American encroachments on the rights of British traders and, increasingly, of the United States' "unrelenting and systematic plan" for removing Native peoples with a "determined zeal" that had convinced the king's Indian allies that "their extermination was the real object of that government and its rapacious land-jobbers." Atcheson argued that the peace treaty must offer "security and permanency, not only to our boundary line, but to that of our faithful Indian allies." Reasoning that "mountains separate, but rivers approximate mankind," he proposed that diplomats ought to use watersheds to fix a new border protecting "the natural patrimony of the Canadas." This boundary line would follow the same path laid out in the Canada merchants' 1812 memorial to Governor-General Prevost. It would transfer control of the Great Lakes and Lake Champlain to Great Britain, expel American colonists from lands extorted from the western Indian nations since the Treaty of Greenville, and invalidate American territorial claims to the Pacific Northwest coast. Neither Britain nor the United States would be allowed to build forts within the boundaries of the new Indian state, but the British government would serve as the sole guarantor of Native rights and territory. Atcheson admonished Whitehall for acting as "a silent spectator of wrongs and injustice" committed by the United States against Britain's Indian allies, which he chronicled for his readers' perusal in the pamphlet's appendix.[38] The vigilance of the British public in ensuring that their government would promote Canadian interests at the peace table would be rewarded not just with treasure but with the moral satisfaction of knowing that they had played their part in fulfilling the empire's paternal obligations to its Indian allies.

Rumors that peace negotiations were about to begin encouraged the London merchants to file yet another petition with the British government in May 1814. John Inglis and his business partner, Edward Ellice, reminded Foreign Secretary Henry Bathurst, Earl Bathurst, of how their trade cemented the crucial alliance between the British Empire and the "Indian Nations of North America." The specter of unchecked American imperialism, however, threatened the independence of the Native peoples, the survival of the British-Indian alliance, and the security of Canada. The merchants warned

Bathurst that the king's Indian allies would face the "extermination of their race" if British diplomats declined to honor the Crown's promise to defend Native homelands from predatory Americans.[39] Inglis and Ellice deployed the same potent rhetorical combination of imperial interest and moral rectitude used by Nathaniel Atcheson to argue for renegotiating the border.

The London merchants suggested several different boundaries, ranging from the Ohio River, which, they bitterly reminded Bathurst, "should have been the boundary between Canada and the United States in the treaties of 1783 and 1796 [sic]," to the maintenance of the present border devoid of customs barriers and open to traders of all nations "without being subject to taxes or duties."[40] The aggressive imperial expansion of the United States had shown that treaties proclaiming the independence of Native peoples were "proverbially useless." U.S. agents on the border had preyed on British traders with impunity, despite the promises of the Jay Treaty to protect the freedom of Native peoples to trade with whom they pleased. Only a peace treaty establishing a new border by ceding U.S. territory to the British Empire or the Indian nations could secure the property of Indian trade merchants from arbitrary confiscation by the American national state. Only a new border could prevent the Canada merchants from abandoning a trade that, they assured Bathurst, would yield an annual return of £250,000 when freed from American harassment, alongside its incalculable value to the British-Indian alliance that underpinned the security of British North America.[41]

By the time peace negotiations between the United States and Great Britain finally began in August 1814, the Canada merchants on both sides of the Atlantic Ocean had spent months trying to exorcise the ghost of Richard Oswald. The transatlantic lobbying network of the Montreal fur trade had worked hard to ensure that the Liverpool ministry in London and the British peace commissioners in Ghent were fully aware of the stakes involved in renegotiating the border with the United States. In doing so, the merchants had developed a sophisticated argument that bound together realist calculations of Britain's imperial ambitions with an idealist appeal to the paternalistic obligations of the Crown to protect the Native peoples who had shed blood for the British Empire. Taken as a whole, the Canada merchants' arguments in favor of renegotiating the border with the United States represented a compelling rejection of American imperialism by supporting the sovereignty of Native peoples and promoting the creation of an Indian state under the protection of the British Empire.

The British government agreed. The creation of an Indian barrier state between the territories of the British Empire and the American Republic was the only *sine qua non* that Foreign Secretary Robert Stewart, Viscount Castlereagh, issued in his instructions to the plenipotentiaries bound for Ghent. While Castlereagh anticipated that the negotiations with the United States would address maritime issues, border regulations, and the Newfoundland fisheries, he made it clear to Admiral James Gambier, Baron Gambier; William Adams; and Henry Goulburn, who formed the British commission, that unless the United States' representatives were prepared to include the king's Native allies in the peace treaty and agree to "a full and express Recognition of their limits," they were to break off the negotiations and return to London. An Indian state was not simply about providing justice for the western nations who had fought for the Crown; the British government believed that it was the only means of securing an enduring peace with the United States. The Indian state would serve "as a useful barrier" between the British Empire and the American Republic that would "prevent collision" and make sure that both governments would "render these people, as far as possible, peaceful neighbors to both States."[42]

The British government presented the Indian state as a mutually beneficial proposal, but privately the Liverpool ministry saw it as a means to resist American imperialism. A memorandum "respecting the Indian boundary" in possession of the British plenipotentiaries explained how the United States' imperial program of constructing towns, forts, and customs houses had undermined British subjects' Indian trade under the Jay Treaty before the war. By securing the "line of communication" at important junctions including Michilimackinac and Chicago, U.S. agents had nearly succeeded in destroying the trade by subjecting it to taxes and other impediments.[43] The new boundaries of an independent Indian state would roll back the apparatus of American imperialism and strengthen commercial and diplomatic ties between the Indian nations and the British Empire.

The proposal came as a shock to the American plenipotentiaries. They met with their British counterparts for the first formal meeting on August 8, expecting to discuss the Royal Navy's impressment of American sailors, Britain's maritime blockade of trade with its enemies, and disputes about the location of the border from the St. Lawrence River to the Lake of the Woods.[44] Instead, Adams, Gambier, and Goulburn explained that they expected to negotiate an Indian state and the resolution of American claims to the Newfoundland fisheries alongside maritime and boundary regulations. The next day, John Quincy Adams, Jonathan Bayard, Henry Clay, Albert Gallatin, and Jonathan Russell, the U.S. commissioners, responded that they had received no instructions from their government on Indian affairs or fisheries.[45] Moreover, they argued that the British government's *sine qua non* was unprecedented in international law: they claimed that no treaties between the two countries, or with any other European colonial power, had ever defined the boundaries of Native homelands. The British plenipotentiaries countered that the United States' treaties with Indians indicated that their government "must in some sort" consider them to be independent peoples. The American commissioners pointed out the "obvious" difference between the treaties concluded between the government and Native peoples living in their claimed territory and the proposed treaty with a foreign power. Thinking it likely that the British government had "received erroneous impressions" from Canadian traders, the American commissioners waxed lyrical about the "liberal and humane" treatment that Native peoples received from the United States, engaged, as it was, in a civilizing mission that protected the lives and properties of Indians from violence and fraud. If not for the humanity and justice of the United States' treatment of Native peoples, the American commissioners reasoned, how could anyone account for the unprecedented sixteen years of peace that had followed the Treaty of Greenville?[46]

The British delegation was unmoved. They insisted that including the Indians in the peace and defining the boundaries of their homelands were both a *sine qua non*, and they explained that the Indian state would form a barrier between British and American domains in which neither government would be authorized to purchase land. This was not what the American plenipotentiaries wanted to hear. Reporting back to Secretary of State James Monroe, they explained how the British proposals amounted to "nothing less than a demand of the absolute cession of the rights both of sovereignty and of soil" over a vast swathe of American territory. With instructions from Washington not to agree to make any land cessions, the American commissioners would not budge. And neither would the British commissioners, who explained that unless they could provisionally agree to create an Indian state, there would be no point in continuing the negotiations. To prevent a complete rupture of the peace talks, both parties agreed to suspend their meetings until the British plenipotentiaries could explain the current impasse to the Liverpool ministry.⁴⁷ It seemed that the peace talks might fail after only two days of discussion.

The two sides seemed further apart when negotiations resumed ten days later. The British commissioners spoke with Castlereagh as he passed through Ghent on his way to Vienna, the main European diplomatic event in the summer of 1814. They explained to the Americans that while the British government would accept a provisional article, the *sine qua non* stood.⁴⁸ The men further proposed that "the lines of the Greenville treaty" would provide a "proper basis" for establishing an Indian state as a "permanent barrier" between Britain's Canadian colonies and the United States. The American commissioners estimated that as many as 100,000 U.S. citizens already inhabited this territory. They asked the British delegation what their government planned to do about these colonists? Under whose government would they fall? The British commissioners replied that this was open to discussion, but, ultimately, the colonists would have to "make their own arrangements, and provide for themselves."⁴⁹ In other words, American citizens would have to leave the territory.

In addition to the provisional article creating an Indian state, the British delegation also outlined their proposed revision of the northern border. Arguing that joint control of the Great Lakes would inevitably lead to future conflict, Great Britain, as the weaker regional power, claimed the sole right to maintain a military establishment on the lakes; the United States would have to disarm. They also proposed relocating the border to allow direct communication between the British provinces of New Brunswick and Lower Canada in the northeast, and Upper Canada and the Mississippi River west of Lake Superior. Finally, the British commissioners warned their American counterparts that if the Americans walked away from the current negotiations without requesting further instructions from the Madison administration, the British government would not be bound by the current terms that it now offered. If the war took a bad turn for the Americans, which seemed quite likely given that peace in Europe had freed up British military resources for redeployment in North America, the British government would drive an even harder bargain.⁵⁰

The American commissioners recognized that the Indian state proposal was a direct challenge to American nationhood and empire. They believed that the British demands amounted to an acceptance of "foreign interference in their domestic concerns" and the abandonment of the United States' "natural rights on their own shores and in their own waters." They continued to argue that the Indian state was an unprecedented proposal that violated the "maxim of public law," which prohibited the "interposition of a foreign Power in the relations between the acknowledged sovereign of the territory and the Indians situated upon it." But their objections to the Indian state were not based solely on legal abstractions. The British proposals, the U.S. commissioners argued, would "inflict the most vital injury on the United States," dismembering its territory, stunting its economic and demographic growth, and exposing the republic to invasion. A peace treaty framed along these lines, then, would be little more than an armistice, and the commissioners refused to send the British proposals to Washington, declaring them to be only "a fit subject for deliberation when it becomes necessary to decide upon the expediency of our absolute surrender of national independence."[51] Henry Goulburn, who had become the Liverpool ministry's lead man in Ghent, warned Lord Castlereagh that the negotiations had reached a breaking point.[52]

But Castlereagh was not ready to bring the British delegation home. He advised Goulburn to wait for instructions from London before replying to the American commissioners. Lord Bathurst, the secretary of war and the colonies, cautioned Goulburn not to break off the negotiations. Together with Prime Minister Lord Liverpool and Castlereagh, Bathurst authored a reply that cast the British Empire as the victims of American imperial ambition. The conquest of Native homelands, the acquisition of Louisiana, the attempted annexation of the Spanish Floridas, and the repeated invasions of Upper and Lower Canada all spoke to an American "system of acquisition and aggrandizement" that had grown to the extent of "annexing entire Provinces to their Dominions." Under these circumstances, the British government argued, the creation of an Indian state and American demilitarization on the Great Lakes were reasonable measures that would protect Britain's North American colonies and promote peace with the United States.[53] The American ministers denied that their government harbored any ambitions to seize British territory. Rather, they argued that the "undue interference of traders" was the sole source of controversy between the United States and Britain's North American colonies, which, the commissioners pointed out, could be easily solved by both countries agreeing to reserve the Indian trade in their respective territories to their own nationals. The American commissioners concluded their protest of the Liverpool ministry's accusations by declaring inadmissible any treaty including an Indian state and American disarmament on the Great Lakes.[54]

The British government dropped its insistence on an Indian state. Bathurst informed Goulburn that the government wanted to make peace now. Napoleon's defeat and (temporary) exile had changed the political climate on the European continent and at home. European powers opposed the Royal Navy's blockade of the United States, while the British electorate was ready for peace after decades of war. Bathurst explained that the British Empire could do without an Indian state so long as Crown forces continued to hold Niagara and Michilimackinac, especially if its diplomats could renew the commercial clauses of the Jay Treaty that ensured an open commercial border for Native peoples and traders.[55] Liverpool informed Goulburn of the change of policy toward the king's Indian allies, which made "*including them in the Treaty* and the *restoring them to all the Rights and Privileges which they enjoyed in 1811* a sine qua non."[56] Everything else was open for debate. While both sides agreed that peace should restore Native peoples to their prewar situation, the American commissioners steadfastly refused to include Indians in the treaty in any way that would recognize them as independent nations and effectively place them under the protection of the British Empire.[57]

Accepting an Indian state would have meant rolling back American Empire on the ground. But including Native peoples in the peace treaty would have still raised fundamental questions about the character of American sovereignty, undermining the United States' claim to imperial dominion in North America and nationhood in the Atlantic World. The American commissioners explained to their counterparts that the United States claimed "the entire sovereignty over the whole territory and the persons embraced within the boundaries of their dominions." The British Empire could make no claims on behalf of its Indian allies, who formed, according to the ministers, "only parts of the dominions of the United States, and it is altogether immaterial, whether or how far, under their political institutions and policy, these communities or persons are independent States, allies or subjects." Rather, Indian nations were "parts of a whole of which the United States are the sole and absolute sovereigns."[58] The American commissioners claimed that the British government was behaving as if the western Indian nations were its subjects, not just its allies. The United States could not allow the British Empire to negotiate on behalf of Native peoples residing in U.S. territory without compromising American sovereignty and renouncing the United States' transcontinental imperial ambitions.

The fate of the negotiations finally came to a head in October. Lord Bathurst penned a new Indian article that required both the United States and the British Empire to conclude peace with the belligerent Indian nations on the basis of restoring their prewar status. Bathurst explained to Goulburn that if the American commissioners refused to accept this provisional article, the British commissioners should suspend their negotiations and return home.[59] The two sides continued their sparring over the legal status of Native peoples, but the American commissioners accepted the new article because it supported the United States' claim of an exclusive jurisdiction over all the peoples inhabiting its territories.[60] As an imperial power acting within its domain, the American Republic would make its own peace with the western Indian nations without the interference of the Crown.

The negotiations had confirmed that the United States would exercise sovereignty over the peoples living within its bounds, but the negotiators had yet to determine where the northern border lay in 1814. Bathurst instructed the British commissioners to negotiate on the basis of *uti possidetis*—each party would retain the territory it possessed at the close of hostilities. In particular, London urged its plenipotentiaries to be "*inflexible* in insisting on the retention of Fort Niagara & Fort Michilimackinac," which in the case of the former would require the cession of no less than five miles of surrounding territory, and in the case of the latter, Mackinac Island and its fortifications. Bathurst recognized that some horse-trading would be necessary, suggesting that Great Britain would exchange Fort Castine and Fort Machias, east of the Penobscot River in present-day Maine, for Fort Amherstburg and Fort Erie in Upper Canada.[61] The proposed bartering would mean that the British Empire would control the critical junctions of inland communication and commerce in the Great Lakes, from the Niagara River in the East to the Mackinac Straits in the Northwest.

The boundary negotiations quickly descended into stalemate. The American commissioners rejected the British proposal, explaining that they were not authorized to cede any territory. On the contrary, they were only prepared to discuss the mutual restoration of the ground captured during the war.[62] The British government decided to play for time. Liverpool advised Goulburn to apprise the Americans of their desperate situation should the war continue: the United States faced economic ruin with no prospect of relief from war-ravaged Europe.⁶³ But, it was the British government, not the American commissioners, who cracked. Bathurst instructed the plenipotentiaries to abandon *uti possidetis* and accept the American offer to restore the border to its course through the middle of the lakes and rivers.⁶⁴ He explained that the government could only maintain *uti possidetis* as long as the war wore a favorable appearance. Governor-General Prevost's defeat at the Battle of Plattsburgh in September 1814 meant that this was no longer the case.

The cabinet was determined to make peace with America. Chaos ruled in Europe. In France, Bathurst feared the rise of a new revolutionary government, keen to renew war with Great Britain. In Vienna, Tsar Alexander I was proving "irritable" toward Britain's Polish policy. Moreover, Britain's great military genius Sir Arthur Wellesley, the duke of Wellington, advised the government to bring the American conflict to a swift conclusion. Bathurst sought to sooth the ministers, noting that "altho' our Peace will not be very creditable compared with our Overture, yet it will be the best thing which can happen, particularly if soon concluded." A swift peace, he counseled, "may prevent much mischief in Europe."⁶⁵ The British government sacrificed the border with the United States to broader geopolitical concerns about the post-Napoleonic world.

The peace treaty signed in Ghent on Christmas Eve 1814 seems to offer little grist for the scholarly mill. Almost five months of negotiations resulted in just eleven articles, four of which largely focus on the mechanisms of halting hostilities on land and sea. Of the remaining seven, five articles established a series of joint British-American commissions to resolve outstanding disputes about the location of the border, one promised British-American cooperation in combating the evils of the transatlantic slave trade, and another promised that the two parties would negotiate peace with the Indians and restore the various nations to the rights, privileges, and possessions that they had enjoyed in 1811.⁶⁶ Judged by the treaty's text, it was little more than a temporary armistice that restored the *status quo antebellum*.⁶⁷

There is more to the Treaty of Ghent than meets the eye, however. What was said during the five months of negotiations mattered: the American commissioners articulated an imperial theory of expansive sovereignty that extended the exclusive authority of the American national state over all the peoples inhabiting the vast territories of the United States, regardless of their formal relationship to the U.S. government. This was not a new idea in itself. American policymakers had long recognized that monopolizing Indian relations was an important part of their imperial schemes. The American peace commissioners had struggled to prevent British agents from participating in their negotiations with the Indian confederates in the 1790s, for example. But the British delegation at Ghent recognized that there was something different about the American rhetoric in 1814. They noted that "the American Government has now, for the first time, in effect declared that all Indian Nations within its line of demarcation are its subjects."[68] The British government chose to accept this argument when it abandoned both its attempts to broker peace on behalf of the western Indian nations and its commitment to an Indian state. The United States asserted its exclusive right to treat with Native peoples residing within its imperial domain. As such, the Ghent negotiations were an important moment in the evolution and articulation of an American imperial doctrine.

The silences of the treaty are also significant. The agreement did not renew the Jay Treaty rights of British subjects and Native peoples that had been abrogated with the outbreak of war in 1812. While the Ghent commissioners postponed commercial negotiations until 1815, the peace process up until that point suggested that the United States would try to extend the same sovereign claims over other groups of non-citizens residing within its borders.

In the spring of 1815, two Montreal merchants and the new British commander-in-chief conspired against fulfilling the terms of the Treaty of Ghent. The merchants, William McGillivray and John Richardson, believed that the Indian trade was "upon the point of annihilation by the late Treaty," jeopardizing the security of Britain's North American colonies. Consequently, they tried to convince Sir Gordon Drummond to "re-consider the question of the delivery of the Post at Michilimc. to the Americans." They argued that Drummond should stick to a strict construction of his instructions and not order the evacuation of Michilimackinac unless it was mentioned specifically "by name." The merchants had scoured the new treaty, looking for loopholes or ambiguous clauses that would allow them to maintain their commercial access to the Indian trade of the United States. And the pair thought they had found a contradiction in the accord that would allow Drummond to hold on to the fort, at least for now. Richardson and McGillivray pointed out that while the treaty's first article agreed to restore

Michilimackinac to the United States as a territorial spoil of war, the sixth article provided for continued British occupation of Mackinac Island as one of the disputed islands in Lake Huron whose future would be determined by a joint boundary commission. In this contradiction, the merchants found an opportunity for British officials to delay handing over Michilimackinac pending the decision of the joint boundary commission. In the meantime, McGillivray and Richardson urged Drummond to deny American customs officials access to the island.[69]

The merchants only half-convinced Drummond. He was not prepared to accept their argument that Michilimackinac was one of the disputed islands that fell under the remit of the boundary commission, but he did agree not to order the evacuation of the post. Drummond thought the delay justified because it was evidently in the interest of the North West Company, which he considered "to be intimately connected with those of the Indian tribes friendly to Great Britain and consequently closely blended with the interests of these Provinces and of the Empire." He promised McGillivray and Richardson that he "would cause an intimation to be made" to the post's commander to postpone the evacuation of the British garrison until he received further instructions from Whitehall.[70] Drummond, who replaced Sir George Prevost as governor-general in April 1815, wrote Lord Bathurst that both he and his predecessor advised exercising "much procrastination" over returning Michilimackinac to the United States, which he would not do until he received explicit orders from the British government.[71] Drummond's policy of delay mirrored that adopted by Sir Frederick Haldimand in 1783 when he delayed the evacuation of the western posts. In that case, it had taken thirteen years for U.S. troops to occupy the border forts.

But 1815 was not 1783. The United States held the British forts of Amherstburg and Fort Erie, and Secretary of State James Monroe was not receptive to any proposals to delay the mutual restoration of territory. He protested the delay to the British chargé d'affaires Anthony St. John Baker and instructed the U.S. commander of Detroit not to remove the American garrison from Amherstburg until he had received notice of the British evacuation of Michilimackinac.[72] The hard line that Monroe took over the return of Fort Amherstburg spooked Drummond, who immediately sent orders to Lieutenant-Colonel James McDonnell to evacuate Michilimackinac. For good measure Drummond sent a copy of his order to Baker in Washington, D.C., as well as reassuring Bathurst that he had no intention of provoking the United States, particularly as he had received the "extraordinary Intelligence" of Napoleon's escape from exile on the Island of Elba, which reignited the war in Europe.[73] With the exception of Fort Astoria on the Columbia River, the British Empire and the American Republic completed the restoration of territory captured during the war in the summer of 1815.

While British and American officials arranged the transfer of captured posts in North America, diplomats in London finalized a British-American commercial convention that helped to determine how the border would function. The American commissioners in Ghent sent their proposals for a commercial convention to the British ministers just two days after signing the peace treaty. They proposed renewing many of the expired or abrogated terms from the Jay Treaty, including restoring the two countries to the status of most favored nation and reestablishing an open border in North America for British subjects and American citizens to trade freely with one another on equal terms.[74] The British commissioners, however, were preparing to leave Ghent. Their powers as plenipotentiaries had expired when they signed the peace treaty, and the commercial negotiations would have to wait.[75] Henry Clay and Albert Gallatin left Ghent for Great Britain, where they met with Lord Castlereagh in April 1815. The foreign secretary suggested that the Americans speak informally with Henry Goulburn, William Adams, and Frederick Robinson (the vice-president of the Board of Trade) as a precursor to opening formal negotiations.[76] Weeks went by in silence; Clay and Gallatin prepared to leave London in early May without a commercial agreement in hand.[77] The situation of the American commissioners in 1815 again appeared to mirror that faced by John Adams, John Jay, and Benjamin Franklin in 1783 and 1784, when Great Britain refused to negotiate a commercial treaty with the United States.

But 1815 was not 1783. Clay's and Gallatin's threat to leave London spurred the Liverpool ministry into action. The American commissioners met with Adams, Goulburn, and Robinson at the Board of Trade on May 11 and 16 for informal discussions that set out a framework for formal negotiations. The British representatives invited Clay and Gallatin to lay out their proposals. The Americans wanted to negotiate regulations to cover trade in both peace and war. For regular peacetime trade, they proposed that the two countries place one another on the footing of most favored nation and abandon discriminatory duties on trade between the United States and the British Isles. Clay and Gallatin also suggested framing permanent regulations for trade between the United States and Britain's colonies in North America, the West Indies, and South Asia. For regulating trade in wartime, the commissioners wanted to discuss rules for impressment, U.S. trade with the colonies of Britain's enemies, and the regulation of privateers and prizes. After consulting with Liverpool's cabinet, the British representatives indicated that their government was prepared to treat on the basis of most favored nation status, and that they would also be authorized to discuss American trade with Britain's colonies in North America and Asia. But they would not discuss any change in policy concerning American trade with the British West Indies. Adams, Goulburn, and Robinson also explained that the British government was willing to discuss wartime trade regulations though they thought an agreement unlikely.[78] These points of difference aside, both parties felt confident that they could negotiate a new commercial arrangement.

The British-American commercial convention, however, did not include any agreement on the Indian trade. This dealt a serious blow to the Canada merchants' hopes of securing expanded commercial access to the United States after the disappointment of the Treaty of Ghent's confirming the border of 1783. William McGillivray advised Governor-General Prevost in March 1815 that an article permitting British subjects to trade in the Mississippi and Missouri River Valleys through Michilimackinac would protect the Montreal fur trade.[79] London merchant Edward Ellice forwarded reports from Michilimackinac traders of their "most serious alarm having just heard of the Peace" to Henry Goulburn as negotiations got underway. Ellice's correspondent expressed his disbelief that "the Indians had been a second time betrayed in our negociations." He dismissed the Treaty of Ghent's Indian article as "a mere mockery" that did nothing to protect Native peoples from "military posts & custom-house duties."[80]

The British representatives hoped to gain access to the Indian trade in the United States by tying it to the question of American trading rights in the East Indies. During the informal conversations at the Board of Trade, Frederick Robinson argued that the United States would have to offer Great Britain some kind of commercial concession if American merchants were to enjoy trading rights in British ports in South Asia. He suggested that the North American fur trade would be a suitable equivalent. Clay and Gallatin emphatically rejected Robinson's suggestion, explaining that Washington had "positively instructed" them not to agree to the "renewal of the trade between British subjects and the Indians within our territories."[81] Undeterred, the British plenipotentiaries continued to push the American delegation to permit British subjects access to the Indian trade of the United States in return for allowing American merchants to undertake indirect voyages to the British East Indies when formal negotiations began in June. The Americans refused. Robinson again asked whether they might find some "middle course" that would allow British subjects access to the Indian trade "without interfering with those political motives" that had informed the Americans' instructions from the Madison administration.[82] There was no middle ground, and the British plenipotentiaries reluctantly dropped their proposal.

As with the Treaty of Ghent, the British-American commercial convention signed in London on July 3, 1815, is a thin document. Embracing a scant five articles, the convention merely arranged trade between the United States and the British Isles, and allowed American merchants limited access to British ports in India.[83] Much remained undecided. The plenipotentiaries agreed to lay aside their negotiations on wartime trade and the commerce between the United States and Britain's colonies in North America and the Caribbean. The convention followed the tradition of many commercial treaties between European powers, which distinguished the freedoms that their subjects would enjoy in the trade between their respective home nations from the far more restricted access that their merchants might gain within overseas European imperial possessions. In this case, the commercial convention made arrangements between the United States and Great Britain, but it explicitly excluded their respective imperial domains in North America from the agreement. The accord welcomed the United States into the commercial community of European nations by agreeing that trade between Great Britain and American Republic would be on the footing of most favored nation. But both nations recognized their respective imperial domains in North America by omitting their colonies from the convention.

In this way, the exclusion of North America from the commercial convention was significant to American nationhood and empire. The fact that the convention denied the rights of British subjects and Native peoples to move and trade across the northern border had real meaning for people on the ground. The War of 1812 had abrogated the third permanent article of the Jay Treaty, which had permitted American citizens, British subjects, and Native peoples to freely cross between the territory of the British Empire and the American Republic to carry on trade with one another. The commercial convention did not renew or replace it. As with the peace treaty, the silences in the commercial convention are more important than the text itself.

The day after Albert Gallatin signed the Treaty of Ghent, he turned his hand to composing a lengthy defense of the agreement. With the American plenipotentiaries in the dark about proceedings at the great European Congress in Vienna, and hearing rumors of the potential secession of the New England states at the Hartford Convention, he tried to reassure James Monroe that the treaty was "as favorable as could be expected under existing circumstances."[84] Gallatin could have saved himself the hand-wringing for the treaty met with popular applause. Anthony Baker, who had carried the treaty and notice of its ratification by the prince regent to Washington, D.C., reported to his masters in London that "the intelligence of the Peace appears to have been compleatly unexpected and has occasioned the greatest rejoicing throughout the Country."[85] Coinciding with news of Andrew Jackson's lopsided victory over British forces at the Battle of New Orleans, Americans welcomed peace because it promised to save the republic from political disunion and financial ruin. The public was less concerned with scrutinizing the terms of the treaty than in celebrating their deliverance from evil.

The terms of the Treaty of Ghent and the commercial convention did matter, however, for they represented a break with the past, not the affirmation of the prewar status quo. In Ghent, the American plenipotentiaries refused to allow the British government to negotiate on behalf of its Indian allies, arguing that the Crown was trying to usurp the U.S. government's sovereign authority over all the peoples residing within its territorial domain. In London, the United States' commissioners would not permit Native peoples residing within U.S. territory to trade with British subjects. The right of the United States to exclude British subjects from the fur trade was an important part of subordinating Native peoples to the authority of the U.S. government. The Jay Treaty had protected commercial and diplomatic intercourse between the western Indian nations and the British Empire. The war freed the United States from its diplomatic obligation to honor the rights of British subjects and Native peoples to trade with one another, while the Treaty of Ghent and commercial convention ensured that these rights were not renewed.

The diplomatic settlement ending the War of 1812 advanced the American imperial project by isolating Native peoples from rival foreign powers in ways that had not been possible before the war. The bitter experience of fighting the Civil War of 1812 promoted separate strains of nationalism in the United States and Britain's Canadian provinces, but the Treaty of Ghent and the commercial convention made it possible for the U.S. government to manifest this growing sense of difference on the border. The treaty and convention, then, articulated an imperial logic that extended the United States' authority over non-citizens and rejected the interference of foreign powers in the American Empire. It did not take long for U.S. agents to put this logic into practice. Andrew Jackson's unauthorized invasion of Spanish Florida in 1816 aimed at asserting control over Choctaw and Seminole peoples by isolating them from foreign agents.[86] The diplomatic settlement of 1814–15 provided a foundation for the United States to stake out an imperial domain in North America by rejecting British interference with the Native peoples residing in its borders. The success of this scheme, however, ultimately depended on the capacity of the American national state to distinguish its own citizens from foreigners.

7

"BRITISH SUBJECTS ARE ALWAYS BLACK SHEEP"

⋯

In the winter of 1818, John Lawe poured his desperation into a letter to fellow trader Thomas Anderson. Reflecting on his declining fortunes and health, Lawe wrote, "This is three years nearly Dear Tommy since peace has been made and I have been in Hell ever since." Constantly harassed by the American government's "Hell Hounds," Lawe lamented the loss of his youthful vigor, replaced by graying hair, a worn body, and an "agitated" mind—and all for being a British subject. Lawe estimated that U.S. agents at Green Bay had cost him at least two thousand pounds by throwing "every Obstacle" in the way of his trade "since these doodles has taken possession of this place." The future looked bleak. U.S. agents had denied his application for a fur trade license for 1819, and he bitterly reflected that the king's ministers "have not made a better provision for his poor straggling & faithful Subjects he has in these wild woods."[1] Lawe's misery was not short of company. His neighbor Louis Grignon complained to Robert Dickson in February 1819 that "British Subjects are always black Sheep."[2]

The winter of discontent in Green Bay reflected the new political landscape of the northern border after the War of 1812. The peace settlement of 1814–15 cleared the way for American imperial expansion in the Great Lakes and beyond. A growing network of U.S. agents at places like Green Bay sought to control the local population through fur trade regulations that discriminated against foreigners and restricted the cross-border movement of Indians. U.S. customs officials and Indian agents saw the trading operations of British subjects like Lawe and Grignon as a violation of American sovereignty. They blamed British traders for sponsoring frontier violence and asserting Native independence from American rule. The ability of U.S. agents to exclude foreign nationals from the fur trade was an important part of the American imperial project.

British officials were reluctant to accept the reality of American Empire. They hoped that the Treaty of Ghent and the commercial convention had turned the clock back to 1811. In March 1815, Governor-General Sir George

Prevost tried to reassure the king's Indian allies that their "Father" had remembered them in the peace and that "every thing should be put on the same footing as before the War." He urged them to return to their lands, plant their corn, and hunt deer, and he promised that "traders will bring your Supplies as formerly."[3] But Indians attempting to return to their homelands south of the Great Lakes found their path blocked in the Detroit River Valley. U.S. Colonel Anthony Butler had fortified the island of Bois Blanc and refused entry to the United States to any warrior who had fought for the Crown. British Indian agent William Caldwell reported that the Indians gathered at Sandwich in June 1815 "are not permitted to go across the River to hunt as formerly."[4] While James Monroe ordered Butler to remove his garrison from the island in the Detroit River, American troops engaged in an extensive scheme of fort-building to control critical junctions of trade and communication in the Great Lakes.[5] British chargé d'affaires Anthony Baker warned Foreign Secretary Lord Castlereagh that U.S. troops were deploying throughout the West, reestablishing garrisons at Chicago and Prairie du Chien, and raising a new fort at Green Bay "in the heart of the Country of the Winnebago and Falsowine Indians, who distinguished themselves by their exertions in our favour during the late war." British General Sir Gordon Drummond warned that the network of forts would place "the Western Indians completely in the power of the United States." Drummond urged the British government to issue a "firm remonstrance" for what he considered to be a violation of the Treaty of Ghent's provision to restore the prewar status quo in Indian country.[6]

Despite what they heard from British officials, it was clear to many of the king's Indian allies that the peace was not what they had been promised. Black Hawk, a principal war captain of the Sacs, reminded British Indian agents that Robert Dickson had promised him "that all Your Red Children would be included in that Peace" and that "you gave us hopes that the Ohio would be the future boundary of the Americans." But now, Black Hawk reported that "the Americans according to their stories are the Masters of us and our Lands." For now, the Sac leader was prepared to accept the British account of the treaty "and remain quiet," but the Crown's agents recognized the damage that the peace had done to their alliances.[7] Lieutenant-Colonel James McDonnell, the British commander of Michilimackinac, reported that local Indians were "bitterly disappointed" by the peace. He was furious that "instead of the flattering promises, which I was so lately instructed to make to them, being realized, the Whole Country is given up." He warned his superiors that "a breach of faith, is with them an utter abomination, & never forgotten." Indeed, the British officer pointed out that the Indians "often alluded to the destruction of their fathers by Genl. Wayne in 1795, under the very guns of our Fort on the Miami River."[8] The postwar settlement in the Great Lakes did not seem like a return to 1811 for either Black Hawk or McDonnell.

The Canada merchants also continued to hope that they might find a way to continue their trade as if the war had never happened. The London firm of Inglis, Ellice & Company wrote to Henry Goulburn on behalf of their Montreal correspondents in July 1815 to discover whether they should believe alarming reports that the commercial convention had prohibited the trade between British subjects and the Indian nations residing within U.S. territory. The merchants hoped that the "stipulations so honorably made by this Country in the negociation of Ghent, relative to the rights & independence of the Indian tribes of North America" would allow them to rely on "the protection of His Majesty's government in the trade heretofore carried on from Canada, with the Indians resident in the territories of the United States."[9] Goulburn, who had helped to negotiate both the peace treaty and the commercial convention, knew that the answer was an unequivocal no. The terms of the commercial convention rightly alarmed Montreal merchants. The news arrived at Michilimackinac in March 1816, where a shocked Jean Baptiste Berthelot declared, "I do not know what to think of this."[10] The Montreal firm of Forsyth, Richardson & Company wrote the Green Bay trader Jacques Porlier that "we shall forever regret that at the late Treaty of peace more favorable terms had not been procured for the Indians." Nevertheless, the merchants continued to hope for the best, noting that the U.S. government had yet to pass new regulations for the fur trade.[11]

While Congress had not yet taken legislative action, the situation on the ground should have been clear to Montreal merchants by the summer of 1816. American officials strongly urged the government to exclude British subjects from the fur trade. Benjamin Stickney, the U.S. Indian agent at Fort Wayne, warned James Monroe in April 1815 that local British agents were "acting over the same part they did after the Treaty of 1783" by encouraging Indians from the north to launch an attack on Vincennes.[12] Lewis Cass, the governor of Michigan Territory, traced the source of the difficulties that the United States faced in conducting Indian diplomacy to British traders, who, he cautioned Treasury Secretary Alexander James Dallas, were about to renew their activities with "increased exertion" under the sponsorship of the British Indian Department.[13] News of the commercial convention encouraged local U.S. officials, like Benjamin Stickney, who believed that the exclusion of British subjects from the Indian trade "will produce a vast change in our relations." Stickney expressed his relief to Governor Cass that the British government had not been "fully aware of how much it put it in their power to annex us through the medium of their traders," and had foolishly "given up the point" in the commercial negotiations.[14]

U.S. agents began trying to stop Indians from crossing the border between the American Republic and the British Empire. In a council held at Drummond Island in June 1816, representatives of the Sioux, Winnebagos, Menominees, Odawas, and Ojibwas reflected bitterly on the different ways in which the United States was seeking to control them. The Sioux leader Wabasha explained to British Indian Department superintendent William McKay that "an omission appears to have been made at the Treaty made between the Big Knives and English, for since the Hatchet has been buried, the Big Knives threaten to erect Forts upon your Childrens Lands, which they cannot suffer, the Land is their only Support." Moreover, U.S. officials were refusing to allow Indians to cross the border, denying them "the pleasure of seeing you" and leaving them "totally deprived of the Benefit of having English Traders amongst them." Wabasha lamented that "there is a Barrier unexpectedly placed between us and you." Little Corbeau, another Sioux leader, agreed, noting that "when my ancestors formerly used to visit you there were no obstacles in their way; they did not meet any difficulty in coming to you or returning home." Now it was a different story. "At present," he explained, "that is not the case; I have met with much difficulty on my route here."[15] After the Treaty of Ghent, Indians no longer enjoyed the right to travel between the United States and the British Empire as they had formerly done under the protection of the Jay Treaty.

With no formal instructions from Washington, D.C., to target foreign traders, U.S. agents on the border quickly took matters into their own hands. At Michilimackinac, Major William H. Puthuff, the U.S. Indian agent, and Lieutenant Colonel Talbott Chambers, commander of the U.S. garrison, began preying on British merchants and traders in the late summer of 1815. Puthuff believed that British traders were agents of the Crown who intended to "alienate the Indians from the American Government and people, [and] to attach them to the British Interests by every and by any the most insidious means." Moreover, as a veteran of the War of 1812, he believed these "blood thirsty assissin[s]" "openly encourag'd the waste of Blood" by Indians, handing them rewards for the "the scalp fresh torn, alike from the hapless Father, defenceless tender and affectionate Mother, or innocent unoffending Babe."[16] An Odawa woman, Elizabeth Mitchell, was one of Puthuff's first victims. The wife of Dr. David Mitchell, a British Army surgeon, Elizabeth had stayed behind on Mackinac Island to attend to the couples' farm and modest trade when her husband joined the new British garrison at Drummond Island. Puthuff accused Mitchell of trading illegally in liquor before uncovering what he believed to be her role in calling a secret Odawa council with hostile intentions toward the United States. The Indian agent issued a public order prohibiting Mitchell from holding any intercourse with Native peoples. Mitchell paid the order no heed and only avoided arrest by fleeing to Drummond Island.[17] The British commander of Drummond Island saw Puthuff's pursuit of Elizabeth Mitchell as part of a broader scheme to "extinguish" the British Empire's influence among Native peoples south of the border.[18] Lieutenant-Colonel James McDonnell described Chambers as "a most illiberal Democrat, who sanctions the persecution of everyone connected with us," while he reported to his superiors that Puthuff "actually out Herods Herod, with his frantic violence, with an equal mixture of impudence and falsehood."[19] If McDonnell's warmth of feeling is any indication, Chambers and Puthuff were proving themselves formidable opponents of British subjects seeking to infiltrate the United States.

Puthuff began assembling an extensive network of spies throughout the Great Lakes when he learned that Congress had passed the Indian Intercourse Act excluding foreign nationals from the fur trade in April 1816.[20] By offering his informants a half-share of seizures, he proved remarkably successful at intercepting illegal traders. In a matter of weeks, Puthuff managed to seize upwards of fifteen thousand dollars' worth of furs and goods bound for Drummond Island.[21] While the Madison administration had been forced to allow exceptions to their initial comprehensive ban of foreign nationals because there simply were not enough American citizens to supply the necessary manpower, Puthuff was supremely confident that he would apprehend all the British traders who had entered the United States without a license issued by him. He maintained four boats "almost constantly manned" to cruise the approaches to Michilimackinac, while his network of spies had supplied him with detailed information on "every Trader who has thus gone into the Country," including the "probable time that they may be expected at the Foot of Lake Michigan."²² Puthuff sat back and waited for his unsuspecting victims to fall into his trap.

The success of Puthuff's operations shocked merchants and traders. Pierre Rocheblave, the Montreal agent of the South West Company, warned the Green Bay trader Jacques Porlier not to come to Michilimackinac. "As soon as people arrive here they are seized," Rocheblave wrote in June 1816. "I believe it almost impossible that you should Save your Packs . . . the avenues being too well guarded." He advised Porlier and his fellow Green Bay traders Louis and Pierre Grignon to sit tight and hide their furs in case U.S. agents searched their homes.²³ When Ramsey Crooks, John Jacob Astor's agent, arrived at Michilimackinac the following month, he discovered a distraught Rocheblave, who complained that Puthuff's "prohibitory system" had spread panic among his traders. They would not "risk a dollar's worth of Goods in the trade." Crooks reported back to Astor that it was impossible to approach the island without being intercepted by a detachment of troops from the U.S. garrison. Indeed, he noted sarcastically that this "*laudable zeal*" had carried a party of soldiers "no less than Seventy five Miles from Mackinac" to capture a party of traders.²⁴ While Crooks did convince Governor Cass to allow Astor to employ some foreign nationals of "fair Character," this did not help the majority of British traders, like Jacques Porlier, who spent a dispiriting winter in St. Charles, across the Missouri River from St. Louis.²⁵ Porlier complained to Rocheblave that a "tribunal of mercantile inquisition" had denied him a license to trade among the Sauks because he was "not clothed with the spotless robes, without which one could not be admitted to the number of the privileged ones." In an effort to avoid disaster, Porlier rented a second-floor store in St. Charles where he tried, largely in vain, to hawk his trade goods.²⁶ The Montreal firms of Forsyth, Richardson & Company and McTavish, McGillivrays & Company had no desire to share in Porlier's ruin. Puthuff's campaign had provided ample evidence of the U.S. government's ability to control cross-border trade, and with the North West Company engaged in a violent competition with Thomas Douglas, the earl of Selkirk's settlers on the Red River in present-day Manitoba, the merchants agreed to sell Astor their remaining interest in the South West Company in early 1817.[27] The American Fur Company now controlled the fur trade of the United States.

The fur trade may have been run out of New York City, rather than Montreal, but the U.S. government could not rely on the American Fur Company to ensure that only U.S. citizens participated in the trade. While Astor had always been careful to align his private ambitions with the national interest, the American Fur Company could not thrive without traders, boatmen, and *voyageurs* from Lower Canada. There were simply not enough American citizens who had sufficient knowledge of the fur trade and were also willing to put up with the back-breaking labor of portaging and rowing canoes to replace the manpower provided by British subjects. The realities of doing business clashed with the determination of President James Monroe to put an end to the involvement of foreigners in the Indian trade. Monroe did relax the total exclusion of British subjects from the fur trade, allowing American traders to employ "foreign boatmen & interpreters," but he did so by putting in place a strict regulatory system designed to identify "foreigners who are odious to our citizens, on account of their activity or cruelty in the late war." American traders obtaining licenses for foreign interpreters had also to pay for an American apprentice to learn Native languages. As soon as U.S. citizens could supply the necessary manpower for the Indian trade, Monroe meant to exclude all foreigners without exception.[28] A license Puthuff issued to the American Fur Company traders Robert Stuart and William H. Wallace in August 1818 illustrates the ways in which U.S. agents tried to control the participation of non-citizens in the Indian trade after the War of 1812. The license authorized Stuart and Wallace, who were both American citizens, to trade in the Wabash River Valley. The traders also employed Alexis Luc Reaume as an interpreter and four boatmen, all of whom were British subjects. Puthuff annexed the descriptions of the five foreigners to the license, recording that the interpreter Alexis Reaume was "about 5 feet 6½ inches, fair complexion, brown eyes, blk: hair," while the boatman Joseph Maçon was a "stout" "half breed" of five foot four inches, with a blue-inked tattoo on his wrist.[29] In an age before photography, these physical descriptions offered the only means of trying to validate individual identity. The ability of the American government to isolate Native peoples from the commercial and political networks of the United States' imperial rivals depended on the capacity of U.S. agents to control citizens and non-citizens alike, and, more particularly, to be able to tell them apart.

Citizens of convenience were at the center of this imperial challenge. Few traders were natural-born citizens of the United States, while many could claim residency at the western posts at the time of the American occupation in 1796. Even Puthuff, whose cold efficiency in controlling trade in the Mackinac Straits had struck fear into the hearts of merchants and traders, expressed his doubts about who were the "proper subjects for the rights of Citizenship." The vast majority of the inhabitants of Michilimackinac were Canadiens or *métis* who had sworn allegiance to Great Britain during the British occupation of the island in the War of 1812. Local traders claimed that British officers had compelled them to swear their loyalty to the Crown. While some traders felt bound by their oath, others claimed that they had not forsaken their rights of American citizenship by swearing allegiance to a foreign prince under duress.[30]

John Bowyer, the U.S. Indian agent at Green Bay, faced a different challenge: the local inhabitants "without exception" declared themselves to be British subjects, living under the protection of the Jay Treaty. Bowyer worried that the traders and *voyageurs* of John Lawe, Jacques Porlier, and Louis and Pierre Grignon "will always be tools for those who employ them, and through them the British influence will be kept up with the Indians in this quarter."[31] Ninian Edwards, the governor of Illinois Territory, doubted whether the U.S. government could exclude British subjects from the fur trade as long as they could be "naturalized, at any moment upon application to the competent Tribunal" under the terms of the Jay Treaty. Edwards believed that switching nationality was merely a strategy which would allow traders to "carry on the same trade, and practise the same machinations in the character of American citizens."[32] Controlling non-citizens was no simple matter.

The attempts of British traders to claim American citizenship after the War of 1812 actually worked to codify a process of naturalization that would solve the challenge that citizens of convenience posed to American imperial expansion, and in doing so, help to define the American people as a distinct nation. The new fur trade regulations had forced many Green Bay traders into a change of heart. While they had proudly proclaimed themselves British subjects in 1818, John Lawe, Jacques Porlier, and Augustin,

Charles, Louis, and Pierre Grignon all applied for American citizenship in the summer of 1819 under the second article of the Jay Treaty. Local U.S. officials could not agree on what to do about these applications. Louis Grignon appealed to Governor Cass to "be recognized as a Citizen" after his petition was rejected, while Adam Stewart, the collector of customs at Michilimackinac, believed that John Lawe and Augustin, Charles, and Pierre Grignon were already American citizens "under Jay's Treaty of 1796." He only administered oaths of allegiance and naturalization to the traders at the insistence of Green Bay Indian agent John Bowyer, who believed that they were British subjects.[33] The U.S. government had issued instructions for regulating the involvement of foreign nationals in the fur trade, but it had not established a system for deciding who was an American citizen and who was not under the ambiguous terms of the Jay Treaty.

Jacques Porlier would inadvertently help to change that. Porlier had applied for a fur trade license from John Bowyer as an American citizen, but he acknowledged that he had fought against the United States during the War of 1812. Porlier claimed that the British commander of Michilimackinac had forced him to bear arms against his will. While Bowyer expressed doubts about Porlier's citizenship, William Puthuff wrote on his behalf to Lewis Cass in August 1818.[34] In Cass's absence, the territorial secretary William Woodbridge was responsible for deciding Porlier's fate. Porlier provided Woodbridge with corroborating testimony that he had resided within the limits of the United States since 1787 and had not availed himself of the opportunity to declare himself a British subject under the Jay Treaty during 1797. In consultation with the local U.S. district attorney, Woodbridge decided that Porlier was an American citizen, and he ordered Bowyer to issue him a fur trade license.[35] Woodbridge's decision was not the end of the matter, however, and Porlier's case ended up on the desk of Secretary of War John C. Calhoun in September 1819. Calhoun referred the question of the trader's legal status to the U.S. attorney general, William Wirt. Wirt decided that Porlier was "not yet" an American citizen. He interpreted the wording of the second article of the Jay Treaty to imply that anyone who did not declare themselves a British subject in 1797 should be considered as "having *elected to become* [American] Citizens," which, the attorney general determined, left it up to the U.S. government to decide "the manner and terms of their admission." Wirt advised Calhoun that Porlier could apply for naturalization under the Alien Act of 1795, which allowed resident aliens the right to apply for citizenship after two years.³⁶ The Jay Treaty, then, did not allow individuals to claim American citizenship; it merely allowed them to apply for naturalization under the same terms and subject to the same process as any other resident alien.

Wirt's decision became government policy. Calhoun informed Cass that the attorney general had reversed Secretary Woodbridge's decision and revoked Porlier's license.³⁷ Cass instructed the Indian agents at Chicago, Fort Wayne, Green Bay, Michilimackinac, and Piqua, Ohio, not to grant any licenses to traders who claimed American citizenship under the Jay Treaty unless they had also been naturalized "agreeably to the acts of Congress." He further ordered them to revoke all the existing licenses they had issued contrary to these new regulations.³⁸ The decision to revoke fur trade licenses already issued by U.S. agents came as a nasty surprise to American Fur Company traders who had already purchased goods and extended credit to Native hunters but now learned that the U.S. government would not allow them to travel to the wintering grounds. The trader Robert Stuart was "extremely Surprised" that Bowyer had revoked the license of Bernard Grignon; he could not understand how the attorney general's opinion on the Jay Treaty could be "in Any respect legal; for it is a well known fact, that the provisions of National Treaties are paramount to any Statute, or local regulations." He promised to find out how Grignon could become a citizen "by next spring."³⁹ Stuart asked Cass to provide clear instructions about the naturalization process, explaining that their absence was burdening traders with "severe losses, and very serious inconveniences."⁴⁰ Cass expressed his regret about the case of Porlier and the other traders that Stuart represented, but he explained that they had no choice but to apply for naturalization if they were to receive fur trade licenses. Porlier and the Grignons could apply "without delay" to the county court at Michilimackinac under a provision in the Naturalization Act of 1802 that allowed aliens who were living in the United States before July 1795 the opportunity to be naturalized after only two further years of residence.⁴¹

Stuart explained to Jacques Porlier in May 1820 that the U.S. government would not consider him to be a citizen "until he obtain a certificate of the Same, from a Court, according to the prescribed course pointed out by the acts of Congress." Stuart thought that this was no hardship. He explained that the required oath was unobjectionable, "for its spirit is simple, that whilst a person continues a Citizen, he abjures all allegiance to every other

Potentate & country; and will obey & support the Laws of the U.States." In Stuart's opinion, "any man who cannot without repugnance take such an oath, ought not, I think, either to have, or claim the rights of a Citizen."[42] It seemed only fair to Stuart that individuals like Porlier should declare their exclusive allegiance to the United States as the price of citizenship.

Jacques Porlier agreed. At some point during the summer of 1820, he became a naturalized citizen of the United States.[43] We can never look into the heart of Porlier, or his fellow traders, to see whether his decision to become an American citizen was one of convenience or of principle or of some combination of the two. Indeed, beyond determining whether a candidate for naturalization was of "good moral character, attached to the constitution of the United States, and well disposed to the good order and happiness of the same," the judges who administered the oaths of allegiance to traders in 1820 did not subject prospective citizens to political tests as part of a quest for ideological purity.[44] Ultimately it did not matter whether Porlier chose citizenship out of convenience or conviction because his decision was now part of a regular process of naturalization and a matter of public record. Where Robert Dickson and James Aird had shifted between American citizenship and British subjecthood, depending on which side of the border they were doing business on, Porlier no longer had that option. The U.S. regulation of the Indian trade, which was an important part of the American imperial project after the War of 1812, had forced individuals like Porlier to make a firm choice in the knowledge that to remain an alien in the territories was to submit to the authority of the United States without enjoying the rights of full citizens. The American people were born of American Empire.

Epilogue
"THE GALLANT CHAMPIONS OF BRITISH INFLUENCE"

⁘

Samuel R. Thurston, the delegate from Oregon Territory, presented a memorial of fifty-six U.S. colonists to the U.S. House of Representatives on December 26, 1850, praying that Congress would confirm their land titles in Oregon City. The Donation Land Claim Act passed by Congress the previous September had set aside portions of Oregon City to help provide revenue to establish a university in the territory. The memorial's subscribers had all purchased lots in Oregon City before Congress had reserved them for the use of the territorial legislature, and they were naturally worried that they would lose their homes and investments.

Thurston, however, believed that sinister forces meant to manipulate this memorial to further the imperial ambitions of the British Hudson's Bay Company. More specifically, he accused the "chief fugleman," Dr. John McLoughlin, and his "pimps," Jesse Quinn Thornton and Aaron E. Waite, of forming a "paltry British clique" to "reinstate the supremacy of the Hudson's Bay Company, and bring Oregon again into bondage." These "gallant champions of British influence," Thurston claimed, had manipulated the meaning of the memorial from providing relief for U.S. citizens holding lands in Oregon City to confirming the vast land claims of McLoughlin, who was in cahoots with the Hudson's Bay Company and the British government.[1]

McLoughlin was a force to be reckoned with. Standing over six feet four inches tall, and with a shock of long white hair, he was a physically imposing figure who had largely governed the Columbia River Valley as a personal fiefdom for over forty years. Born in the province of Quebec in 1784 of Irish and Canadien parents, McLoughlin entered the service of the North West Company, which merged with the Hudson's Bay Company in 1821. He arrived in the Columbia River Valley in 1824, overseeing the move of Hudson's Bay Company's main trading post from Fort George to Fort Vancouver in 1825. McLoughlin served as the company's chief factor in the Columbia Department until 1846. His early biographer Frederick V. Holman wrote that McLoughlin "lived and ruled in the manner befitting that of an old English Baron in feudal times."² The Oregon City memorialists of 1850 had all bought land from McLoughlin, who possessed vast claims in the territory, which Thurston believed the former chief factor meant to hand over to the Hudson's Bay Company. While the delegate welcomed relief for U.S. citizens who had "innocently purchased" land in Oregon City, Thurston was determined to ensure that Congress should deny the claims of McLoughlin, whom Thurston denounced as "a British subject, who *never was* invited to the country, who is a possessor of a princely fortune, and who has striven to prevent the settlement of the country and to procure the whole of it for the British monarchy!"³

The public battle between Thurston and McLoughlin that played out in territorial and national politics in the 1850s took place because of ambiguities in the border settlement framed by the Oregon Treaty of 1846. The election of the aggressive imperialist James K. Polk as president of the United States in 1844 threatened to ignite long-simmering British-American tensions over the "Oregon Question" into open warfare. Unable to agree on their overlapping territorial claims west of the Rocky Mountains, the British and American governments had reached a compromise in 1818 to allow the joint occupation of Oregon Territory by British subjects and American citizens. Dissatisfied with the status quo, Polk reaffirmed American sovereign claims over the entirety of the territory, while Congress moved to abrogate the most recent joint occupancy agreement with the British Empire.⁴ Riding into office on a wave of public enthusiasm for American imperial expansion, Polk's audacious claims in Oregon threatened to bring the British and American Empires to blows. Despite Polk's belligerent campaign slogan of "Fifty-four Forty or fight," alluding to the line of latitude which he intended to force the British government to accept as the U.S.-Canadian border, he had no desire to fight the British Empire at the same time as American forces were invading Mexico. U.S. secretary of state James Buchanan and British minister Richard Packenham managed to reach a compromise in June 1846 that established the westward running of the U.S.-Canadian border along the 49th parallel, with the exception of Vancouver Island, which became a wholly British possession. The treaty's second article promised that the navigation of the Columbia River would be "free and open" to British subjects, while the third article protected the property of British subjects south of the 49th parallel.⁵ The agreement made no provision for determining the

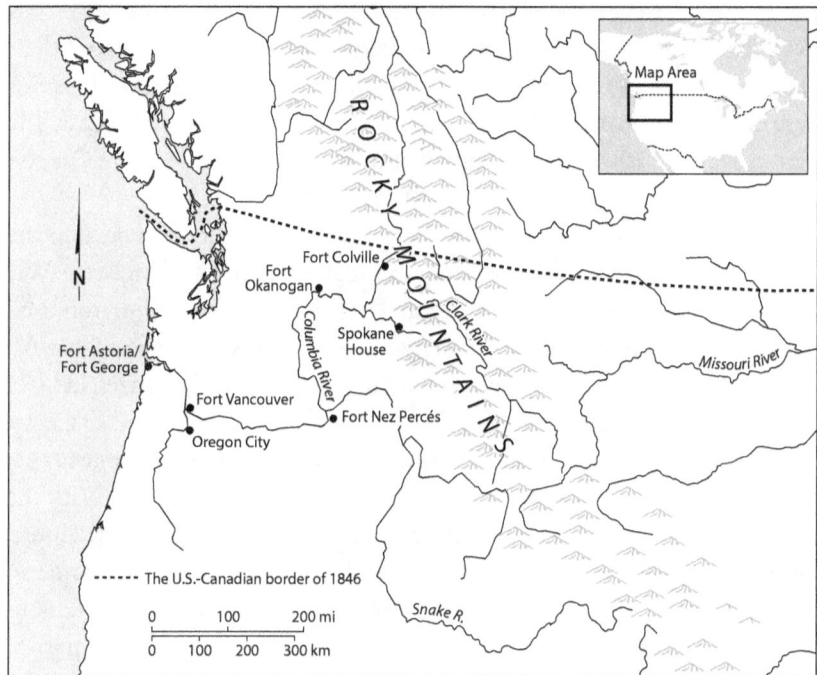

The Columbia River and the border of 1846. (Map by Bill Nelson)

nationality of individual colonists on either side of the new boundary in the Pacific Northwest.

At first glance, there appears to be a parallel between the rights that British subjects enjoyed under the Oregon Treaty in the 1840s and those that they had enjoyed under the Jay Treaty prior to the War of 1812. Under the Jay Treaty, British subjects enjoyed free movement back and forth across the northern border of the United States, while the Oregon Treaty protected the right of the king's subjects to cross the newly defined U.S.-Canadian boundary through their free navigation of the Columbia River. Unlike the Jay Treaty, however, the Oregon Treaty did not exempt British subjects resident in Oregon from the regular process of naturalization. Still, there was a tradition of cooperation between American citizens and British subjects in the territory, which suggests that the latter might have continued to enjoy some political rights after 1846. Early electoral laws in Oregon defined the franchise by race, class, gender, and residence rather than by nationality. British subjects voted and held office in both the territorial legislature and executive before 1846.⁶ Moreover, the law establishing Oregon as a U.S. territory in August 1848 enfranchised foreign nationals who indicated their intention to become American citizens without establishing a time limit for these individuals to either begin or complete the naturalization process. The utterance of an oath, then, was sufficient to allow British subjects in Oregon to exercise the same political rights as U.S. citizens.

Where ambiguity over individual claims to nationality had created the conditions for citizens of convenience in the American West before the War of 1812, the reverse was true in Oregon Territory after 1848. Thurston used McLoughlin's uncertain status to deny his land claims in Oregon City. Although McLoughlin acknowledged that he was not yet a U.S. citizen in 1850, he had registered his intent to become naturalized with George L. Curry, a clerk of the Provisional Circuit Court of Clackamas County, on May 30, 1849, and voted against Thurston in the first territorial elections.⁷ With the support of the former chief justice of the Oregon Territory Supreme Court, Thurston argued that McLoughlin had not filed his intention to become an American citizen in accordance with Oregon's organic laws and U.S. naturalization laws because Curry represented a defunct court that was part of the provisional government of Oregon, rather than a territorial court under the jurisdiction of the United States. Despite living in Oregon for more than forty years, McLoughlin was an alien who could claim none of the privileges of U.S. citizenship, including land rights under the Donation Land Claim Act.⁸ His dilemma was summed up in a letter to the *Oregon Spectator* by the mysterious "Z," who explained that foreign colonists like McLoughlin, "by the cunning and artifice of the delegate," could neither claim land as U.S. citizens nor as British subjects, having "forfeited all claims to protection to their possessory rights from the British Government" by taking an oath to uphold the U.S. Constitution.⁹ In 1850s Oregon, there was nothing convenient about being a foreigner in a familiar land.

John McLoughlin became a U.S. citizen in 1851 and continued to fight for his land claims until his death in 1857; the Oregon state legislature finally confirmed his claims to his heirs in 1862.¹⁰ The following year the Hudson's Bay Company and the U.S. government resolved their longstanding conflict over the rights that the company enjoyed in Washington Territory and the state of Oregon.¹¹

Despite its popular representation as the longest undefended border in the world, the U.S.-Canadian boundary has always been a site of controversy. This did not end with the Oregon Treaty. From the so-called Pig War of 1859, a territorial dispute between Britain and the United States over the San Juan Islands, to more recent clashes between Canada and the United States over fishing rights in both the Pacific and Atlantic Oceans, border crossings remain a sporadic source of tension between Canada and the United States.[12] As close economic and geopolitical partners, the movement of peoples, capital, and commodities between the two countries is important to the mutual well-being of Canada and the United States. At the same time, the border continues to function as a means of differentiating nationals from non-nationals. While twenty-first-century surveillance technology would amaze David Duncan or William Puthuff, their successors in the U.S. Border Patrol monitor a border that is a historical artifact of the empire they helped to build.

NOTES

ABBREVIATIONS

ASPFR : Lowrie et al., *American State Papers: Documents, Legislative and Executive, of the Congress of the United States, Foreign Relations Series*
BHC : Burton Historical Collection, Detroit Public Library
BLN : Notes from Foreign Legations, Great Britain, Record Group 59, General Records of the Department of State, National Archives of the United States
CO : Colonial Office Papers, National Archives of the United Kingdom
FO : Foreign Office Papers, National Archives of the United Kingdom
LAC : Library and Archives of Canada
MPHC : *Historical Collections of the Michigan Pioneer and Historical Society*
PAG : Albert Gallatin Papers, New-York Historical Society
PJA : Quaife, ed., *The John Askin Papers*
PJGS : Cruikshank, ed., *The Correspondence of Lieut. Governor John Graves Simcoe*
PPR : Cruikshank and Hunter, eds., *The Correspondence of the Honourable Peter Russell*
PWS : Winthrop Sargent Papers, Massachusetts Historical Society
Stat : U.S. Government, *The Public Statutes at Large of the United States of America*
TPUS : Carter, ed., *Territorial Papers of the United States*
WHC : Thwaites et al., eds., *Collections of the State Historical Society of Wisconsin*
WLC : William L. Clements Library, University of Michigan

INTRODUCTION

1. *Morning Herald, and Daily Advertiser,* January 29, 1783. The London newspapers reported the conclusion of the preliminary peace treaty between Great Britain and the United States on November 4, 1782. Thomas Townshend, home secretary in the Shelburne cabinet, did not inform Parliament of the particular articles of the American treaty until after the conclusion of peace preliminaries with France and Spain, and the cessation of hostilities with the United Provinces.

2. "Representation of the Merchants Trading to the Province of Quebec," January 31, 1783, Shelburne Papers, 72:461, WLC.

3. *Morning Herald, and Daily Advertiser,* February 5, 1783.

4. "Sundry Observations on ye. American Treaty, by Richard Oswald," February 6, 1783, Shelburne Papers, 87, part 2:216.

5. Ibid.

6. Andrew Jackson O'Shaughnessy, *An Empire Divided: The American Revolution and the British Caribbean* (Philadelphia: University of Pennsylvania Press, 2000), xi.

7. Maya Jasanoff, *Liberty's Exiles: American Loyalists in the Revolutionary World* (New York: Vintage Books, 2012), 8–9.

8. Alan Taylor, *The Civil War of 1812: American Citizens, British Subjects, Irish Rebels and Indian Allies* (New York: Vintage Books, 2010), 4–8.

9. Peter S. Onuf, *The Mind of Thomas Jefferson* (Charlottesville: University of Virginia Press, 2007), 66.

10. John Torpey, *The Invention of the Passport: Surveillance, Citizenship, and the State* (Cambridge: Cambridge University Press, 2000), 1, 4–17.

11. James H. Kettner, *The Development of American Citizenship, 1608–1870* (Chapel Hill: University of North Carolina Press, 1978); Benedict Anderson, *Imagined Communities: Reflections on the Origin and Spread of Nationalism* (New York: Verso, 1983).

12. The political scientist Rogers M. Smith argues that lawmakers throughout U.S. history have structured American citizenship according to ascriptive inequalities based on hierarchies of race, ethnicity, and gender. Smith, *Civic Ideals: Conflicting Visions of Citizenship in U.S. History* (New Haven, Conn.: Yale University Press, 1997), 1–12.

13. For the indeterminate nature of political forms in the late eighteenth century, see J. G. A. Pocock, "States, Republics, and Empires: The American Founding in Early Modern Perspective," in Terence Bell and J. G. A. Pocock, eds., *Conceptual Change and the Constitution* (Lawrence: University Press of Kansas, 1988), 55–77; Peter Onuf and Nicholas Onuf, *Federal Union, Modern World: The Law of Nations in an Age of Revolutions, 1776–1814* (Madison, Wis.: Madison House, 1993); and David C. Hendrickson, *Peace Pact: The Lost World of the American Founding* (Lawrence: University Press of Kansas, 2003).

14. Leonard J. Sadosky, *Revolutionary Negotiations: Indians, Empires, and Diplomats in the Founding of America* (Charlottesville: University of Virginia Press, 2009); Eliga H. Gould, *Among the Powers of the Earth: The American Revolution and the Making of a New World Empire* (Cambridge, Mass.: Harvard University Press, 2012).

15. For arguments emphasizing the overarching importance of Thomas Jefferson's ideological commitment to idealist principles in U.S. foreign relations, see Robert W. Tucker and David C. Hendrickson, *Empire of Liberty: The Statecraft of Thomas Jefferson* (Cambridge: Cambridge University Press, 1990); Bradford Perkins, *The Creation of a Republican Empire, 1776–1865* (Cambridge: Cambridge University Press, 1993); and Doron Ben-Atar, *The Origins of Jeffersonian Commercial Policy and Diplomacy* (New York: St. Martin's Press, 1993). For a recent study that attempts to move beyond the realist-idealist dichotomy in interpreting Jeffersonian foreign policy, see Francis D. Cogliano, *Emperor of Liberty: Thomas Jefferson's Foreign Policy* (New Haven, Conn.: Yale University Press, 2014).

16. For the difficulty of applying the law of nations to North America in the eighteenth century, see Gould, *Among the Powers of the Earth*, 26–27.

17. "The Treaty of Navigation and Commerce," April 11, 1713, in George Chalmers, ed., *A Collection of Treaties between Great Britain and Other Powers* (London, 1790), 1:391–92.

18. Adrian J. Pearce, *British Trade with Spanish America, 1763–1808* (Liverpool: Liverpool University Press, 2007), 18–21; "The Peace of Utrecht, 1713," July 13, 1713, in Chalmers, ed., *A Collection of Treaties*, 2:81–82, 85–86.

19. For a discussion of mercantilism, see John J. McCusker and Russell R. Menard, *The Economy of British America, 1607–1789* (Chapel Hill: University of North Carolina Press, 1985), 35–47.

20. For the privileges enjoyed by diasporic merchant communities in West Africa, see Ray A. Kea, *Settlements, Trade, and Polities in the Seventeenth-Century Gold Coast* (Baltimore: Johns Hopkins University Press, 1982), 206–47, and George E. Brooks, Jr., *Eurafricans in Western Africa: Commerce, Social Status, Gender, and Religious Observance from the Sixteenth to the Eighteenth Century* (Athens: Ohio University Press, 2003), 68–121. For the Mediterranean world and Ottoman Empire, see Bruce Masters, *The Origins of Western Economic Dominance in the Middle East: Mercantilism and the Islamic Economy in Aleppo, 1600–1750* (New York: New York University Press, 1988), 72–109; Edhem Eldem, Daniel Goffman, and Bruce Masters, eds., *The Ottoman City between East and West: Aleppo, Izmir, and Istanbul* (Cambridge: Cambridge University Press, 1999); Maurits H. Van Den Boogert, *The Capitulations and the Ottoman Legal System: Qadis, Consuls and Beratlıs in the 18th Century* (Leiden: Brill, 2005); Edhem Eldem, "Capitulations and Western Trade," in Suraiya N. Faroqhi, ed., *The Cambridge History of Turkey*, vol. 3, *The Later Ottoman Empire, 1603–1839* (Cambridge: Cambridge University Press, 2006), 283–325; and James Mather, *Pashas: Traders and Travellers in the Islamic World* (New Haven, Conn.: Yale University Press, 2009). For the Mughal Empire, see Susil Chaudhuri, *Trade and Commercial Organization in Bengal, 1650–1720* (Calcutta: Firma K. L. Mukhopadhyay, 1975); K. N. Chaudhari, *The Trading World of Asia and the English East India Company, 1660–1760* (Cambridge: Cambridge University Press, 1978); and Ashin Das Gupta, *India and the Indian Ocean World: Trade and Politics* (Oxford: Oxford University Press, 2004).

21. Elizabeth Mancke, "Polity Formation and Atlantic Political Narratives," in Nicholas Canny and Philip Morgan, eds., *The Oxford Handbook of the Atlantic World, c. 1450–c. 1850* (Oxford: Oxford University Press, 2011), 383; Philip D. Curtin, *Cross-Cultural Trade in World History* (Cambridge: Cambridge University Press, 1984), 3.

22. Hugo Grotius, *The Freedom of the Seas; or, The Right Which Belongs to the Dutch to Take Part in the East Indian Trade*, trans. Ralph Van Deman Magoffin (Oxford: Oxford University Press, 1916), 7–8.

23. Mancke, "Polity Formation and Atlantic Political Narratives," 394–95.

24. For the importance of intersectional commerce and the Atlantic marketplace to the American Union, see Peter S. Onuf, *Statehood and Union: A History of the North-*

west Ordinance (Bloomington: Indiana University Press, 1987), 1–20, and Cogliano, *Emperor of Liberty*, 5–6. For the volatility of allegiance among western colonists, see Peter S. Onuf, "The Expanding Union," in David Thomas Konig, ed., *Devising Liberty: Preserving and Creating Freedom in the New American Republic* (Stanford, Cal.: Stanford University Press, 1995), 50–80; James E. Lewis, Jr., *The American Union and the Problem of Neighborhood: The United States and the Collapse of the Spanish Empire, 1783–1829* (Chapel Hill: University of North Carolina Press, 1998), 12–40; Peter J. Kastor, *The Nation's Crucible: The Louisiana Purchase and the Creation of America* (New Haven, Conn.: Yale University Press, 2004), 36–42; and John Craig Hammond, *Slavery, Freedom and Expansion in the Early American West* (Charlottesville: University of Virginia Press, 2007). For Jefferson's and Madison's suspicion of the loyalty of merchants, see Peter S. Onuf, *Jefferson's Empire: The Language of American Nationhood* (Charlottesville: University Press of Virginia, 2000), 90–92, and Onuf, *The Mind of Thomas Jefferson*, 110–11.

25. For the importance of the St. Lawrence River in shaping the economic and political development of Canada, see Donald Creighton, *The Empire of the St. Lawrence* (Toronto: Macmillan, 1956).

26. "Schedule of Applications for Fur Trade Licences," 1785–90, Civil and Provincial Secretaries Fonds, RG 4, B 28, 115:2322, LAC.

27. Jay Gitlin, *The Bourgeois Frontier: French Towns, French Traders, and American Expansion* (New Haven, Conn.: Yale University Press, 2010), 8–10.

28. William Earl Weeks, *The New Cambridge History of American Foreign Relations*, vol. 1, *Dimensions of the Early American Empire, 1754–1865* (Cambridge: Cambridge University Press, 2013), xviii–xix.

29. For an excellent discussion of the socioeconomic and cultural dimensions of American Empire, see Bethel Saler, *The Settlers' Empire: Colonialism and State Formation in America's Old Northwest* (Philadelphia: University of Pennsylvania Press, 2015). For recent scholarship emphasizing the similarity, rather than the exceptionalism, of American Empire compared with European forms, see Cogliano, *Emperor of Liberty*; Gould, *Among the Powers of the Earth*; Jay Sexton, *The Monroe Doctrine: Empire and Nation in Nineteenth-Century America* (New York: Hill and Wang, 2011); and Weeks, *Dimensions of the Early American Empire*.

30. François Furstenburg, "The Significance of the Trans-Appalachian West in Atlantic History," *American Historical Review*, 113 (June 2008): 647–77.

31. Elizabeth F. Cohen, *Semi-Citizenship in Democratic Politics* (Cambridge: Cambridge University Press, 2009), 15.

32. Sadosky, *Revolutionary Negotiations*, 200–201; Gould, *Among the Powers of the Earth*, 12.

33. Kastor defines local diplomacy as a "system in which international relations on the borderlands ran parallel to, but were never entirely distinct from, the elite negotia-

tions that are the familiar stuff of diplomatic history." Kastor, *The Nation's Crucible*, 112–15.

34. The Jay Treaty remains to this day an important document in international law for governing the movement of indigenous peoples across the U.S.-Canadian border.

1. "YOU DAMN YANKEE WHAT BROUGHT YOU HERE?"

1. Brig. Allan Maclean to Governor Frederick Haldimand, August 1, 1783, in *MPHC*, 20:158.

2. Ibid., 20:158–59.

3. Brig. Allan Maclean to Governor Frederick Haldimand, August 1, 1783, in *MPHC*, 20:160.

4. Governor Frederick Haldimand to Gen. George Washington, August 11, 1783, in *MPHC*, 20:165; Governor Frederick Haldimand to Maj. Gen. Friedrich Wilhelm von Steuben, August 12, 1783, in ibid., 20:167.

5. Reginald Horsman, *Expansion and American Indian Policy, 1783–1812* (Norman: University of Oklahoma Press, 1967), 4.

6. Isabel Thompson Kelsay, *Joseph Brant, 1743–1807: Man of Two Worlds* (Syracuse, N.Y.: Syracuse University Press, 1984), 402–3.

7. Isaac Weld, *Travels through the States of North America and the Provinces of Upper and Lower Canada during the Years 1795, 1796 and 1797*, 4th edition (London, 1800), 276.

8. Marjorie Wilkins Campbell, *McGillivray: Lord of the Northwest* (Toronto: Clarke, Irwin, 1962), 146.

9. "Rules of the Beaver Club," February 1807, Beaver Club Minute Book, 1807–27, McCord Museum, Montreal. Alexander Henry was the first British merchant to winter in Indian Country in 1761. Marjorie Wilkins Campbell, *The North West Company* (New York: St. Martin's Press, 1957), 164; Robert Englebert, "Merchant Representatives and the French River World, 1763–1803," *Michigan Historical Review*, 34 (Spring 2008): 63–82.

10. For the persistence of French communities in North America after 1763, see Englebert, "Merchant Representatives and the French River World," and Gitlin, *Bourgeois Frontier*. For the connection between kinship networks and commercial opportunities in the Great Lakes, see Susan Sleeper-Smith, *Indian Women and French Men: Rethinking Cultural Encounter on the Great Lakes* (Amherst: University of Massachusetts Press, 2001), and Heather Devine, *People Who Own Themselves: Aboriginal Ethnogenesis in a Canadian Family, 1660–1900* (Calgary: University of Calgary Press, 2004).

11. "Representation of the Merchants Trading to the Province of Quebec," January 31, 1783, Shelburne Papers, 72:460.

12. Henry Callender, Alexander Ellice, John Fraser, Robert Hunter, Charles Pat-

man, Robert Rashleigh, James Strachan, and Philip Sansom. "Representation of the Merchants Trading to the Province of Quebec," January 31, 1783, Shelburne Papers, 72:460; "Canada Merchants to Lord Shelburne," February 6, 1783, Shelburne Papers, 72:456.

13. R. H. Fleming, "Phyn, Ellice and Company of Schenectady," *Contributions to Canadian Economics*, 4 (1932): 9–14, 18, 30, 34–38; Bruce G. Wilson, *The Enterprises of Robert Hamilton: A Study of Wealth and Influence in Early Upper Canada, 1776–1812* (Ottawa: Carleton Press, 1983), 59.

14. Gordon Charles Davidson, *The North West Company* (Berkeley: University of California Press, 1918), 271–72.

15. Fleming, "Phyn, Ellice and Company of Schenectady," 18.

16. Joseph Hadfield, *An Englishman in America, 1785*, ed. Douglas S. Robertson (Toronto: Hunter-Rose, 1933), 43, 46.

17. Weld, *Travels through the States of North America*, 225.

18. F. Murray Greenwood, *Legacies of Fear: Law and Politics in Quebec in the Era of the French Revolution* (Toronto: University of Toronto Press, 1993), 3–4.

19. "Memorial of Merchants of Montreal," c. September 21, 1782, in *MPHC*, 20:59. Representatives of twenty-five different merchant houses signed the memorial complaining about transportation problems on the Great Lakes.

20. Englebert, "Merchant Representatives and the French River World," 63–82.

21. Gitlin, *Bourgeois Frontier*, 8–10.

22. Sleeper-Smith, *Indian Women and French Men*.

23. John Cooper, *James McGill of Montreal: Citizen of the Atlantic World* (Ottawa: Borealis Press, 2003), 57–58, 67–68.

24. Englebert, "Merchant Representatives and the French River World," 63–82.

25. Campbell, *The North West Company*, 19–20.

26. Ibid., 70; Campbell, *McGillivray*, 86, 129–30.

27. "Schedule of Applications for Fur Trade Licences," 1783, Civil and Provincial Secretaries Fonds, RG 4, B 28, 115:2322.

28. "Peltries Exported from Quebec, 1784," Shelburne Papers, 87:358.

29. "Schedule of Applications for Fur Trade Licences," 1785–90, Civil and Provincial Secretaries Fonds, RG 4, B 28, 115:2322.

30. Carolyn Podruchny, *Making the Voyageur World: Travelers and Traders in the North American Fur Trade* (Lincoln: University of Nebraska Press, 2006), xi, 11–14, 86.

31. "Representation of the Merchants Trading to the Province of Quebec," January 31, 1783, Shelburne Papers, 72:459.

32. Wilson, *Enterprises of Robert Hamilton*, 4.

33. Weld, *Travels through the States of North America*, 359.

34. Wilson, *Enterprises of Robert Hamilton*, 4, 17–19, 24, 69.

35. Donna Valley Russell, ed., *Michigan Censuses, 1710–1830, under the French, British, and Americans* (Detroit: Detroit Society for Genealogical Research, 1982), 49.

36. "The Petition of the Merchants of Detroit," July 16, 1785, in *MPHC*, 11:461. Representatives of twenty-one different fur trade businesses signed the petition complaining about transportation problems on the Great Lakes.

37. Karen Marrero, "On the Edge of the West: The Roots and Routes of Detroit's Urban Eighteenth Century," in Jay Gitlin, Barbara Berglund, and Adam Arenson, eds., *Frontier Cities: Encounters at the Crossroads of Empire* (Philadelphia: University of Pennsylvania Press, 2013), 67–86.

38. "Introduction," in *PJA*, 1:5–7.

39. Ibid, 1:12–13.

40. John Askin to Jean Baptiste Barthe, June 8, 1778, in ibid., 1:115–20.

41. Catherine Cangany, *Frontier Seaport: Detroit's Transformation into an Atlantic Entrepôt* (Chicago: University of Chicago Press, 2014), 30.

42. Jasanoff, *Liberty's Exiles*, 180; Taylor, *Civil War of 1812*, 23.

43. Greenwood, *Legacies of Fear*, 3–7.

44. Campbell, *The North West Company*, 119–24.

45. "John Askin & Co. in Account Current with Todd & McGill," January 23, 1783, John Askin Papers, LMS folder 1782–84, BHC. Figures are in sterling.

46. "Invoice of Goods Shipped by Phyn Ellices & Inglis on Board the Everetta Capn. George Featonby for Montreal," March 10, 1788, John Askin Papers, LMS folder 1787–91; Cory Willmott, "From Stroud to Strouds: The Hidden History of a British Fur Trade Textile," *Textile History*, 36 (November 2005): 210.

47. "Account Sale of Two Bales of Deer Skins Received per the Everetta Captn Featonby from Montreal from Messers Todd & McGill," March 20, 1784, John Askin Papers, box 1, folder 1784; "Account Sale of 47 Bales of Skins Received pr. the Everetta & Beaver à Montreal from Messrs Todd & McGill," April 15, 1784, John Askin Papers, box 1, folder 1784; "Account of Sale of 34 Bales of Furrs & Skins Received pr. the Everetta & Beaver á Montreal from Messrs Todd & McGill," April 25, 1784, John Askin Papers, box 1, folder 1784; "Account of Sale of 53 Bales of Furrs & Skins Received pr. the Everetta & Beaver from Mess Todd & McGill," May 25, 1784, John Askin Papers, box 1, folder 1784; "Sale of Peltries," Todd & McGill to John Askin, October 11, 1784, in *PJA*, 1:201. Figures are in sterling.

48. "Partnership to Build a Windmill and a Ship," November 30, 1792, in *PJA*, 1:449–51.

49. "Misconduct of Joseph Reah," November 24, 1786, in ibid., 1:272n64.

50. John Askin to Francis Vigo, March 15, 1786, in ibid., 1:226–27, 227n19; "Contract between Gabriel Hunot and the Miamis Company," September 13, 1787, in ibid., 1:294–96.

51. Richard White, *The Middle Ground: Indians, Empires, and Republics in the*

Great Lakes Region, 1650–1815 (Cambridge: Cambridge University Press, 1991), 94–101.

52. Daniel K. Richter, *The Ordeal of the Longhouse: The Peoples of the Iroquois League in the Era of European Colonization* (Chapel Hill: University of North Carolina Press, 1992), 21–22, 79.

53. Miami Company Journal (1786–87), John Askin Papers.

54. Helen Hornbeck Tanner, ed., *Atlas of Great Lakes Indian History* (Norman: University of Oklahoma Press, 1987), 6; Keith R. Widder, "After the Conquest: Michilimackinac, a Borderlands in Transition, 1760–63," *Michigan Historical Review*, 34 (Spring 2008): 43–61.

55. Davidson, *North West Company*, 10–12.

56. Nathaniel Atcheson, *On the Origins and Progress of the North-West Company of Canada* (London, 1811), 7–8.

57. John Pownall to Lord Shelburne, February 2, 1783, Shelburne Papers, 72:487–96.

58. Alan Taylor, *The Divided Ground: Indians, Settlers, and the Northern Borderland of the American Revolution* (New York: Knopf, 2006), 117.

59. Gordon S. Wood, *Empire of Liberty: A History of the Early American Republic, 1789–1815* (Oxford: Oxford University Press, 2009), 191.

60. Onuf and Onuf, *Federal Union, Modern World*, 93–122; Drew R. McCoy, *The Elusive Republic: Political Economy in Jeffersonian America* (Chapel Hill: University of North Carolina Press, 1980), 76–104; Ben-Atar, *Origins of Jeffersonian Commercial Policy*, 76–91.

61. "Memorandum to Mr. Oswald in Conversation," April 20, 1782, Shelburne Papers, 71:25; Richard Oswald to Lord Shelburne, July 10, 1782, Shelburne Papers, 70:44; Lord Shelburne to Richard Oswald, July 27, 1782, Shelburne Papers, 71:66.

62. Onuf, *Jefferson's Empire*, 53–79.

63. McCusker and Menard, *Economy of British America*, 35–47.

64. Vincent T. Harlow, *The Founding of the Second British Empire, 1763–1793* (New York: Longmans, Green, 1952), 1:452–53.

65. John Baker-Holroyd (Lord Sheffield), *Observations on the Commerce of the United States*, 2nd edition (Dublin, 1784), 3–5, 134, 187–91.

66. Henry Laurens to Benjamin Franklin, April 4, 1783, in Leonard Woods Labaree et al., eds., *The Papers of Benjamin Franklin* (New Haven, Conn.: Yale University Press, 1959–), 39:432.

67. Harlow, *Founding of the Second British Empire*, 1:461.

68. Charles James Fox to David Hartley, April 10, 1783, in Mary A. Giunta et al., eds., *The Emerging Nation: A Documentary History of the Foreign Relations of the United States under the Articles of Confederation, 1780–1789* (Washington, D.C.: National Historical Publications and Records Commission, 1996), 2:86.

69. "Regulations Proposed by the Quebec Merchants, 1783," FO 4/1/11.

70. Charles James Fox to David Hartley, April 10, 1783, FO 4/1/9.

71. David Hartley to Charles James Fox, April 29, 1783, in Giunta et al., eds., *Emerging Nation*, 2:100.

72. Charles James Fox to David Hartley, May 15, 1783; David Hartley to Charles James Fox, May 20, 1783; Charles James Fox to David Hartley, June 10, 1783, all in ibid., 2:119–20, 123, 147.

73. "David Hartley to the American Peace Commissioners: Propositions of the Definitive Treaty," June 19, 1783, in Labaree et al., eds., *Papers of Benjamin Franklin*, 40:196–97.

74. David Hartley to Charles James Fox, June 20, 1783, in Giunta et al., eds., *Emerging Nation*, 2:165.

75. "The American Peace Commissioners to David Hartley: Answers to Propositions," June 29, 1783, in Labaree et al., eds., *Papers of Benjamin Franklin*, 40:254–55.

76. "Draft Definitive Treaty of Peace between the United States and Great Britain," c. August 6, 1783, in Giunta et al., eds., *Emerging Nation*, 1:909–12.

77. Henry Laurens to the American Peace Commissioners, June 17, 1783, in Labaree et al., eds., *Papers of Benjamin Franklin*, 40:187.

78. David Hartley to Charles James Fox, July 17, 1783; David Hartley to Charles James Fox, August 2, 1783, in Giunta et al., eds., *Emerging Nation*, 2:196–97, 217.

79. Charles James Fox to David Hartley, August 9, 1783, in ibid., 1:915–16.

80. David Hartley to Charles James Fox, August 13, 1783, in ibid., 1:919.

81. Benjamin Franklin to Henry Laurens, August 21, 1783, in Labaree et al., eds., *Papers of Benjamin Franklin*, 40:494.

82. American Peace Commissioners to Elias Boudinot, September 10, 1783, in ibid., 40:600–605.

83. Harlow, *Founding of the Second British Empire*, 1:487–88.

84. Ibid., 1:488; "Memorandum of the American Commissioners in Europe," September 22, 1784, in Giunta et al., eds., *Emerging Nation*, 2:441.

85. Kelsay, *Joseph Brant*, 339; Taylor, *Divided Ground*, 112.

86. Colin G. Calloway, *The American Revolution in Indian Country: Crisis and Diversity in Native American Communities* (Cambridge: Cambridge University Press, 1995), 26–64.

87. Brig. Allan Maclean to Governor Frederick Haldimand, May 18, 1783, in *MPHC*, 20:118–19.

88. Ibid., 20:118–19.

89. Ibid.

90. Francis Jennings, *The Invasion of America: Indians, Colonialism, and the Cant of Conquest* (New York: Norton, 1976), 118.

91. Brig. Allan Maclean to Governor Frederick Haldimand, May 18, 1783, in *MPHC*, 20:120.

92. Taylor, *Divided Ground*, 7–8.

93. Jeremy Adelman and Stephen Aron, "From Borderlands to Borders: Empires, Nation-States, and the Peoples in between in North American History," *American Historical Review*, 104 (June 1999): 814–41.

94. Robert S. Allen, *His Majesty's Indian Allies: British-Indian Policy in the Defence of Canada, 1774–1815* (Toronto: Dundurn Press, 1992).

95. Gregory Evans Dowd, *War under Heaven: Pontiac, the Indian Nations and the British Empire* (Baltimore: Johns Hopkins University Press, 2004).

96. Governor Frederick Haldimand to Sir John Johnson, May 26, 1783, in *MPHC*, 20:124.

97. Taylor, *Divided Ground*, 115.

98. Kelsay, *Joseph Brant*, 344.

99. Jasanoff, *Liberty's Exiles*, 39.

100. "Transactions with Indians at Sandusky," August 26–September 8, 1783, in *MPHC*, 20:174–83; Taylor, *Divided Ground*, 116.

101. Horsman, *Expansion and American Indian Policy*, 5–6.

102. Taylor, *Divided Ground*, 117–18; Horsman, *Expansion and American Indian Policy*, 10–12.

103. Horsman, *Expansion and American Indian Policy*, 22; John Sugden, *Blue Jacket: Warrior of the Shawnees* (Lincoln: University of Nebraska Press, 2000), 69–71.

104. White, *Middle Ground*, 407; John Mack Faragher, *Daniel Boone: The Life and Legend of an American Pioneer* (New York: Henry Holt, 1992), 221–22.

105. Kelsay, *Joseph Brant*, 397–99; Sugden, *Blue Jacket*, 73–74.

106. Sugden, *Blue Jacket*, 74–75.

107. Kelsay, *Joseph Brant*, 402–3.

108. "Indian Speech to the Congress of the United States," December 18, 1786, in *MPHC*, 11:468–69.

109. Benjamin Frobisher to Adam Mabane, April 19, 1784, in *MPHC*, 20:219–21.

110. "Regulations Proposed by the Merchants Interested in the Trade to the Province of Quebec," February 6, 1783, Shelburne Papers, 71:459–61; Brig. Allan Maclean to Governor Frederick Haldimand, May 18, 1783, in *MPHC*, 20:118.

111. William Frank Zornow, "The Tariff Policies of Virginia, 1775–1789," *Virginia Magazine of History and Biography*, 62 (July 1954): 306–19.

2. "IT SHALL AT ALL TIMES BE FREE TO HIS MAJESTY'S SUBJECTS"

1. Sugden, *Blue Jacket*, 122–27.

2. Max M. Edling, *A Revolution in Favor of Government: Origins of the U.S. Constitution and the Making of the American State* (Oxford: Oxford University Press, 2003).

3. Robert Hamilton to John Graves Simcoe, January 4, 1792, in *PJGS*, 1:98–99.

4. "The Jay Treaty," November 19, 1794, in Hunter Miller, ed., *Treaties and Other International Acts of the United States of America* (Washington, D.C.: Government Printing Office, 1931–48), 2:246–48.

5. For the significance of the Jay Treaty to the expansion of the American national state, see White, *Middle Ground*, 472; Horsman, *Expansion and American Indian Policy*, 103; Adelman and Aron, "From Borderlands to Borders," 823; Taylor, *Divided Ground*, 294; and Patrick Griffin, *American Leviathan: Empire, Nation, and Revolutionary Frontier* (New York: Hill and Wang, 2007), 250. The author David Lavender is a notable exception. Lavender argued that the Jay Treaty benefited British traders in the West, and claimed that "the very name of the treaty came to be spoken on the frontier, like an oath." Lavender, *The Fist in the Wilderness* (New York: Doubleday, 1964), 41.

6. Stanley Elkins and Eric McKitrick, *The Age of Federalism: The Early Republic, 1788–1800* (Oxford: Oxford University Press, 1993), 439, 408.

7. Cogliano, *Emperor of Liberty*, 6.

8. "Observations on the Posts on the Lakes," John Graves Simcoe to Henry Dundas, August 26, 1791, in *PJGS*, 1:53.

9. Joseph Frobisher to Simon McTavish, December 8, 1791, North West Company Papers, F3/1, 31–32, Provincial Archives of Manitoba, Winnipeg; Merchants of Montreal to John Graves Simcoe, December 9, 1791, in *PJGS*, 1:92 (quotation).

10. Lord Dorchester to Lord Sydney, April 10, 1787, in Douglas Brymner, ed., *Report on Canadian Archives, 1890* (Ottawa, 1891), 97.

11. Paul David Nelson, *General Sir Guy Carleton Lord Dorchester: Soldier-Statesman of Early British Canada* (London: Associated University Presses, 2000), 196; Ordinances of May 10, 1787; April 17, 1788; April 12, 1790, all in Arthur G. Doughty, ed., *Report of the Work of the Public Archives for the Years 1914 and 1915* (Ottawa: King's Printer, 1916), C 196, C 203–4, C 235.

12. "Desultory Reflexions by a Gentleman of Kentucky," c. April 11, 1789, in Brymner, ed., *Report on Canadian Archives*, 107–8.

13. Lord Dorchester to Lord Sydney, June 7, 1789, in ibid., 108–9.

14. Pearce, *British Trade with Spanish America*, 86.

15. Elkins and McKitrick, *Age of Federalism*, 379–80.

16. George Washington to James Madison, November 5, 1786, in John C. Fitzpatrick, ed., *The Writings of George Washington* (Washington, D.C.: Government Printing Office, 1931–44), 29:52.

17. Edling, *A Revolution in Favor of Government*.

18. Griffin, *American Leviathan*, 152–53; William Bergmann, *The American National State and the Early West* (Cambridge: Cambridge University Press, 2012), 23–24.

19. Onuf, *Statehood and Union*, 21–42.

20. Ibid., 238–39.

21. Horsman, *Expansion and American Indian Policy*, 47–48, 84–85.
22. Sugden, *Blue Jacket*, 81, 88–89, 93–95.
23. Horsman, *Expansion and American Indian Policy*, 86–87; Sugden, *Blue Jacket*, 99–103.
24. Henry Dundas to Lord Dorchester, September 16, 1791, in *PJGS*, 1:66–67.
25. White, *Middle Ground*, 53, 142.
26. Lord Dorchester to Sir John Johnson, February 10, 1791, CO 42/73/69; Lord Dorchester to Lord Grenville, February 19, 1791, CO 42/73/63; Henry Dundas to Lord Dorchester, September 16, 1791, in *PJGS*, 1:66–67.
27. Lord Grenville to George Hammond, September 2, 1791, in Bernard Mayo, ed., *Instructions to the British Ministers to the United States, 1791–1812* (New York: Da Capo Press, 1971), 15.
28. Merchants of Montreal to John Graves Simcoe, December 9, 1791, in *PJGS*, 1:92–93.
29. Charles Stevenson to Evan Nepean, January 11, 1792; Charles Stevenson to George Hammond, March 6, 1792, in ibid., 1:102, 117.
30. William Robertson to John Askin, March 26, 1792, in *PJA*, 1:408.
31. Lord Dorchester to Henry Dundas, March 23, 1792, in *MPHC*, 24:386–87; Lord Grenville to George Hammond, March 17, 1792, in Mayo, ed., *Instructions to the British Ministers*, 25.
32. George Hammond to John Graves Simcoe, April 21, 1792, in *PJGS*, 1:130.
33. Taylor, *Divided Ground*, 267.
34. Sugden, *Blue Jacket*, 142; Horsman, *Expansion and American Indian Policy*, 89–95.
35. George Hammond to Lord Grenville, July 3, 1792, FO 4/16/16.
36. Merchants of Montreal to John Graves Simcoe, April 23, 1792, in *PJGS*, 1:133, 135.
37. George Hammond to John Graves Simcoe, July 11, 1792, in ibid., 1:176–77.
38. John Graves Simcoe to Alexander McKee, August 30, 1792, in ibid., 1:207–8.
39. Sugden, *Blue Jacket*, 128–30.
40. Ibid., 134–38.
41. "Indian Council at the Glaize," October 9, 1792, in *PJGS*, 1:229.
42. Kelsay, *Joseph Brant*, 481, 487.
43. Taylor, *Divided Ground*, 277; Sugden, *Blue Jacket*, 142.
44. John Graves Simcoe to Alexander McKee, January 23, 1793, in *PJGS*, 1:278; John Graves Simcoe to Alured Clarke, January 27, 1793, Colonial Office Papers "Q" Series, MG 11, 62:147, LAC.
45. John Graves Simcoe to John Butler and Alexander McKee, June 22, 1793, in *PJGS*, 1:365–66.

46. Kelsay, *Joseph Brant*, 501.
47. Sugden, *Blue Jacket*, 145.
48. Kelsay, *Joseph Brant*, 493–94; Larry L. Nelson, *A Man of Distinction among Them: Alexander McKee and the Ohio Country Frontier, 1754–1799* (Kent, Ohio: Kent State University Press, 1999), 165–66.
49. Taylor, *Divided Ground*, 278–79.
50. Kelsay, *Joseph Brant*, 494–97.
51. Ibid., 498–500.
52. Ibid., 503–4.
53. Taylor, *Divided Ground*, 286.
54. John Graves Simcoe to Alured Clarke, April 5, 1793, in *PJGS*, 1:310.
55. John Graves Simcoe to George Hammond, August 24, 1793, in ibid., 2:44.
56. Lord Dorchester to Henry Dundas, February 26, 1794, in ibid., 2:163.
57. "Lord Dorchester to the Seven Nations of Lower Canada," February 10, 1794, in ibid., 2:149–50.
58. Alexander McKee to John Butler, May 8, 1794, in *MPHC*, 20:351.
59. Henry Dundas to Lord Dorchester, July 5, 1794, Colonial Office Papers "Q" Series, MG 11, 67:177; Taylor, *Divided Ground*, 284.
60. Griffin, *American Leviathan*, 246.
61. Elkins and McKitrick, *Age of Federalism*, 404.
62. Ibid., 335, 338–39, 342–50.
63. Ibid., 389–92.
64. Ibid., 392–94.
65. "Instructions to Mr. Jay," May 6, 1794, in *ASPFR*, 1:472–74.
66. William Doyle, *The Oxford History of the French Revolution* (Oxford: Oxford University Press, 2002), 206–9.
67. Elkins and McKitrick, *Age of Federalism*, 402–4.
68. James McGill to John Askin, January 10, 1794, in *PJA*, 1:488.
69. Isaac Todd to John Askin, April 6, 1794, in ibid., 1:502.
70. Merchants of Montreal to John Graves Simcoe, April 23, 1792, in *PJGS*, 1:134.
71. "Conversation with George Hammond," April 30–July 3, 1792, in Harold C. Syrett et al., eds., *The Papers of Alexander Hamilton* (New York: Columbia University Press, 1961–87), 11:347.
72. "Outline of a Treaty," August 6, 1794, FO 95/512/127–28.
73. "Projet of Heads of Proposals to Be Made to Mr. Jay," FO 95/512/141–43; Lord Grenville to John Jay, August 30, 1794, FO 95/512/186; "Projet," FO 95/512/161.
74. "Copy of Paper Communicated by Mr. Jay," September 6, 1794, FO 95/512/217; Lord Grenville to John Jay, October 31, 1794, FO 95/512/270; John Jay to Lord Grenville, November 1, 1794, FO 95/512/272.

75. "Copy of Paper Communicated by Mr. Jay," September 6, 1794, FO 95/512/217.

76. "Observations," in Lord Grenville to John Jay, September 7, 1794, FO 95/512/228.

77. "John Jay's Draft of the Treaty of Amity and Commerce," September 30, 1794, FO 95/412/242–43.

78. Ibid.; Elkins and McKitrick, *Age of Federalism*, 410.

79. "The Jay Treaty," November 19, 1794, in Miller, ed., *Treaties*, 2:246–48.

80. Mather, *Pashas*, 29; Masters, *The Origins of Western Economic Dominance in the Middle East*, 76–78; Chaudhuri, *The Trading World of Asia*, 121–24.

81. Chaudhuri, *The Trading World of Asia*, 121–24; H. E. S. Fisher, "Lisbon, Its English Merchant Community, and the Mediterranean in the Eighteenth Century," in P. L. Cottrell and D. H. Aldcroft, eds., *Shipping, Trade and Commerce: Essays in Memory of Ralph Davis* (Leicester: Leicester University Press, 1981), 23–24.

82. Pearce, *British Trade with Spanish America*, 86–87.

83. Elizabeth F. Cohen identifies residence and movement as the fundamental rights associated with the "legal/territorial" definition of nationality. Cohen, *Semi-Citizenship in Democratic Politics*, 144.

84. Emer de Vattel, *The Law of Nations; or, The Principles of Natural Law Applied to the Conduct and Affairs of Nations and Sovereigns* (Philadelphia, 1829), book 1, 19:160; book 2, 7:233–36.

85. Cohen, *Semi-Citizenship in Democratic Politics*, 5, 146.

86. For a detailed historiographical discussion of the Jay Treaty, see Lawrence B. A. Hatter, "The Jay Charter: Rethinking the American National State in the West, 1796–1919," *Diplomatic History*, 37 (September 2013): 693n1.

87. Douglas Bradburn, *The Citizenship Revolution: Politics and the Creation of the American Union, 1774–1804* (Charlottesville: University of Virginia Press, 2009), 131–37.

88. Jerald A. Combs, *The Jay Treaty: Political Battleground of the Founding Fathers* (Berkeley: University of California Press, 1970); Todd Estes, *The Jay Treaty Debate, Public Opinion, and the Evolution of Early American Political Culture* (Amherst: University of Massachusetts Press, 2006); Jeffrey L. Pasley, *The First Presidential Contest: 1796 and the Founding of American Democracy* (Lawrence: University Press of Kansas, 2013), 101–31.

89. Speech of James Madison, House of Representatives, April 15, 1796; Speech of Albert Gallatin, House of Representatives, April 26, 1796, in Joseph Gales et al., eds. *The Debates and Proceedings in the Congress of the United States: With an Appendix Containing Important State Papers and Public Documents* (Washington, D.C., 1834–56), 4th Cong., 1st sess., 978–79, 1186.

90. Speech of Benjamin Goodhue, House of Representatives, April 18, 1796; Wil-

liam Cooper, House of Representatives, April 20, 1796, in ibid., 4th Cong., 1st sess., 1053–54, 1095, 1097.

91. Lord Dorchester to Col. Alexander McKee, April 23, 1796, in *MPHC*, 25:116.

92. "Explanatory Article to Article 3 of the Jay Treaty," May 4, 1796, in Miller, ed., *Treaties*, 2:346–48; Phineas Bond to Timothy Pickering, April 9, 1796, BLN, vol. 2; Lord Dorchester to the Duke of Portland, May 28, 1796, in *MPHC*, 25:119; "Treaty with the Wyandot, etc., 1795," August 3, 1795, in Charles J. Kappler, ed., *Indian Affairs: Laws and Treaties* (Washington, D.C.: Government Printing Office, 1903–), 2:42–43; Alfred Leroy Burt, *The United States, Great Britain and British North America: From the Revolution to the Establishment of Peace after the War of 1812* (New York: Russell and Russell, 1961), 160.

93. William Hull to Henry Dearborn, November 1807, in *MPHC*, 40:249.

94. Lord Dorchester to the Duke of Portland, June 18, 1796, in ibid., 25:125.

95. Kelsay, *Joseph Brant*, 519.

3. "TO GUARD THE NATIONAL INTEREST AGAINST THE MACHINATIONS OF ITS ENEMIES"

1. "By James Wilkinson Brigadier General and Commander in Chief of the Troops of the United States, A Proclamation," July 12, 1797, BLN, vol. 2; "Machinations against the United States Government," July 12, 1797, in *PJA*, 2:112–13.

2. The population of Detroit and the surrounding farms was 2,215 in 1796. The town of Cincinnati had a population of 950 in 1805. Andrew Morrison, *The Industries of Cincinnati: Her Relations as a Center of Trade; Manufacturing Establishments and Business Houses* (Cincinnati, 1886), 18.

3. "The Jay Treaty," November 19, 1794, in Miller, ed., *Treaties*, 2:246–48.

4. Chaudhuri, *The Trading World of Asia*, 121–24; Fisher, "Lisbon, Its English Merchant Community," 23–44; L. M. E. Shaw, *Trade, Inquisition and the English Nation in Portugal, 1650–1690* (Aldershot, Eng.: Carcarnet Press, 1989), 52–65.

5. Mancke, "Polity Formation and Atlantic Political Narratives," 383.

6. The political theorist Elizabeth F. Cohen identifies the rights of individuals or groups to enter, remain, or leave the sovereign borders of a state as the basic definition of nationality. Cohen, *Semi-Citizenship in Democratic Politics*, 143–44.

7. "A Proclamation," July 12, 1797, BLN, vol. 2; James Wilkinson to the Justices of the Peace of the Western District of Upper Canada, July 16, 1797, in *PJA*, 2:116.

8. "Machinations against the United States Government," July 12, 1797, in *PJA*, 2:112–13.

9. Cohen, *Semi-Citizenship in Democratic Politics*, 15, 150.

10. John Clarke, *Land, Power, and Economics on the Frontier of Upper Canada* (Montreal and Kingston: McGill–Queen's University Press, 2001), 64–66.

11. "Departure of Colonel England from Detroit," July 10, 1796, in *PJA*, 2:46–47.

12. George Sharp to Peter Audrain, May 20, 1797, Hershel Whitaker Papers, BHC. The declaration contained 113 signatures or marks. A further five individuals, whose names are absent from the declaration registered by George Sharp, signed a letter to James Wilkinson as British subjects, expressing their concern at his declaration of martial law. "The Petition of Sundry British Magistrates, Merchants and Others Holding Property Residing in and Resorting to the Town of Detroit," July 24, 1797, BLN, vol. 2. The U.S. government undertook three censuses of Detroit and its environs in July and August 1796 that divided the greater Detroit and Wayne County region into nine categories of which "the city" was one. According to the combined census, 653 men above the age of sixteen lived in Detroit and Wayne County, at least 118 of whom (18%) elected to remain British subjects. From the same census, 106 men above the age of sixteen resided in the city of Detroit, of whom 36 (34%) elected to remain British subjects. Russell, ed., *Michigan Censuses, 1710–1830*, 59, 60–62, 74.

13. Fifty individuals with French names signed or attested Sharp's declaration. George Sharp to Peter Audrain, May 20, 1797, Hershel Whitaker Papers.

14. Cangany, *Frontier Seaport*, 30.

15. John Askin to D. W. Smith, August 26, 1797, in *PJA*, 2:120–21.

16. Peter Audrain to Winthrop Sargent, June 28, 1797, PWS, 4:321.

17. "Machinations against the United States Government," July 12, 1797, in *PJA*, 2:112–13.

18. George Sharp to Peter Audrain, May 20, 1797, Hershel Whitaker Papers. Among the merchants of Detroit who elected to remain British subjects were George Sharp, John Askin, John Askin, Jr., Alexander Duff, James Leith, George Leith, William Hands, Angus Mackintosh, James Mackintosh, Jean Baptiste Barthe, William Park, John McGregor, Robert Gouie, Richard Donovan, Robert Innis, Richard Pattinson, Jonathan Schieffelin, and William Forsyth.

19. Fisher, "Lisbon, Its English Merchant Community," 23–44; Pearce, *British Trade with Spanish America*, 9.

20. "The Grand Jury of Wayne County upon Their Oaths," March 9, 1797, Wayne County, Northwest Territory Papers, C 835, Q2, BHC; "Machinations against the United States Government," July 12, 1797, in *PJA*, 2:112–13.

21. Patrick McNiff to Winthrop Sargent, July 12, 1797, PWS, 4:333–35.

22. Chalbert Joncaire to Winthrop Sargent, December 6, 1796, PWS, 4:211; "Machinations against the United States Government," July 12, 1797, in *PJA*, 2:112–13.

23. James Wilkinson to the Justices of the Peace of the Western District of Upper Canada, July 16, 1797, in *PJA*, 2:116–17.

24. Taylor, *Civil War of 1812*, 106–10.

25. James Wilkinson to the Justices of the Peace of the Western District of Upper Canada, July 16, 1797, in *PJA*, 2:115–17.

26. James McHenry to Arthur St. Clair, May 24, 1796, James McHenry Papers, WLC.

27. Anthony Wayne to James McHenry, September 30, 1796, James McHenry Papers.

28. Robert Liston to Timothy Pickering, July 2, 1797, BLN, vol. 2; Bradford Perkins, *The First Rapprochement: England and the United States, 1795–1805* (Berkeley: University of California Press, 1967), 99–100.

29. James Wilkinson to Winthrop Sargent, May 28, 1797, PWS, 4:302.

30. Robert Liston to Timothy Pickering, June 29, 1797, BLN, vol. 2; Gerald H. Clarfield, *Timothy Pickering and American Diplomacy, 1795–1800* (Columbia: University of Missouri Press, 1969), 120–24.

31. James Wilkinson to Winthrop Sargent, May 28, 1797, PWS, 4:302–3.

32. Ibid., 4:303.

33. Patrick McNiff to Winthrop Sargent, July 12, 1797, PWS, 4:334–35.

34. "The Petition of Sundry British Magistrates, Merchants and Others Holding Property Residing in and Resorting to the Town of Detroit," July 24, 1797, BLN, vol. 2.

35. "James Wilkinson to the British Magistrates, Merchants, and Others Holding Property, Residing in and Resorting to the Town of Detroit," n.d., BLN, vol. 2.

36. Matthew Ernest to James Wilkinson, March 3, 1798, PWS, 4:557; Peter Audrain to Winthrop Sargent, January 20, 1798, PWS, 4:522–23.

37. Peter Audrain to Winthrop Sargent, March 1, 1798, PWS, 4:542.

38. David Strong to Winthrop Sargent, March 4, 1798, PWS, 4:547.

39. Peter Audrain to Winthrop Sargent, January 20, 1798, PWS, 4:523.

40. Ibid., 4:522.

41. Ibid., 4:523–24.

42. Peter Audrain to Winthrop Sargent, October 12, 1797, PWS, 4:446–47.

43. British merchants elsewhere often interpreted the commercial privileges they enjoyed under treaties in a similar way. According to scholar L. M. E. Shaw, British merchants in Portugal saw the Anglo-Portuguese Treaty of 1654 as a "magna carta" that protected their commercial privileges. Shaw, *Trade, Inquisition and the English Nation in Portugal*, 65.

44. "Petition of Leith Shepherd and Duff to Jas. Wilkinson," c. 1797, in *PPR*, 1:304.

45. James Wilkinson to Leith, Shepherd & Duff, October 15, 1797, in ibid., 1:304–5.

46. Ibid.

47. "The Jay Treaty," November 19, 1794, in Miller, ed., *Treaties*, 2:246–48.

48. Ibid.; "Treaty with the Wyandot, etc., 1795," August 3, 1795, in Kappler, ed., *Indian Affairs*, 2:42–43; Act of May 19, 1796, ch. 30, 1 *Stat.* 471; Phineas Bond to Timothy Pickering, April 9, 1796, BLN, vol. 2; "Explanatory Article to Article 3 of the Jay Treaty," May 4, 1796, in Miller, ed., *Treaties*, 2:346–48; Burt, *United States, Great Britain and British North America*, 160.

49. "Communicated to Congress," January 18, 1803, in U.S. Government, *American State Papers, Documents, Legislative and Executive, of the Congress of the United States, Indian Affairs Series* (Washington, D.C.), 1:684; Bergmann, *American National State and the Early West,* 183–84.

50. Stephen J. Rockwell, *Indian Affairs and the Administrative State in the Nineteenth Century* (Cambridge: Cambridge University Press, 2010), 61.

51. Sadosky, *Revolutionary Negotiations,* 8.

52. "Communicated to Congress," January 18, 1803, in U.S. Government, *American State Papers: Indian Affairs,* 1:684.

53. "Speech of Capt. Joseph Brant," 1802, in *MPHC,* 23:19.

54. Sugden, *Blue Jacket,* 189–93, 209–12.

55. Bergmann, *American National State and the Early West,* 219–20.

56. British Indian agent Thomas Duggan reported that the Crown's Indian friends "appear to be as much attached to us as ever" in July 1797. Thomas Duggan to Joseph Chew, July 9, 1797, in *MPHC,* 20:522.

57. James Wilkinson to Winthrop Sargent, November 17, 1797, PWS, 4:475–77.

58. "Evidences of Foreign Interference to Excite Indian Hostility," c. October 26, 1797, James McHenry Papers.

59. Kelsay, *Joseph Brant,* 575–82, 585. Desperate to "conciliate" the Mohawks, Upper Canada's Executive Council upheld the legality of Brant's land sales in 1797.

60. "Petition of Leith, Shepherd, and Duff and Others to Peter Russell," October 27, 1797, in *PPR,* 1:307–8.

61. Elkins and McKitrick, *Age of Federalism,* 582; Clarfield, *Timothy Pickering and American Diplomacy,* 22–26.

62. Leith, Duff & Shepherd to Peter Russell, July 9, 1798, Executive Council Fonds, RG 1, L 3, vol. 285, L 4/19, LAC; Governor Robert Prescott to Robert Liston, May 14, 1798, in *MPHC,* 25:169.

63. Peter Audrain to Winthrop Sargent, March 28, 1797, PWS, 4:254–55.

64. Wayne County Court of Common Pleas Records, 1796–1804, Michigan Supreme Court Records, 1796–1857, series 1, boxes 1–6, Bentley Historical Library, University of Michigan, Ann Arbor; Court of Common Pleas Records, 1801–2, Wayne County, Northwest Territory Papers, C 835, C 7, Q2. The fifteen merchants, with the number of suits in parentheses, are George Meldrum and William Park (50); John Askin (36); Richard Pattinson, trading under Atkinson & Richard Pattinson and Thomas McCrae & Co. (32); Robert Gouie (24); John and James McGregor (23); Robert Forsyth and William Smith (21); George Leith (the firm of Leith, Shepherd & Duff later included his son James, who was also a British resident), William Shepherd and Alexander Duff (17); Angus Mackintosh (15); Richard Donovan (13); and John Askin, Jr. (10). New district courts replaced the Wayne County Court of Common Pleas in 1805, the records of which are incomplete.

65. "Partnership Agreement between John Askin and John Anderson," September 24, 1796; "Goods Ordered for Indian Trade," September 20, 1796, in *PJA*, 2:62–63, 66.

66. Angus Mackintosh to Antoine Lafond, July 2, 1800, Angus Mackintosh Fonds, MG 19, A 31, vol. 2, LAC.

67. "Merchandise Dr. Sundries, for Goods & Liquors Imported This Year," November 8, 1797; "Sundries Dr. to Profit & Loss," April 10, 1798; "Merchandise Dr. Sundries, for Goods & Liquors Imported This Year," September 21, 1798; "Merchandise Dr. Sundries, for Goods & Liquors Imported This Year," August 29, 1799; "Sundries Dr. to Profit & Loss," April 10, 1799; and "Sundries Dr. to Profit & Loss," April 10, 1800, all Journal of James and Andrew McGill, James McGill Papers, 69, 133, 194, 347, 303, 463, McGill University Archives, Montreal. The journal only provides detailed accounts for 1797 to 1800.

68. Angus Mackintosh to McTavish, Frobisher & Co., November 5, 1798, Angus Mackintosh Fonds, vol. 2; "Goods Ordered for Indian Trade," September 20, 1796, in *PJA*, 2:66.

69. "Memorandum on Trade and Commerce by Robert Hamilton," September 24, 1798, in *PPR*, 2:266. "No. 1 Note of Merchandize and Rum from Montreal Which Passes the Niagara Portage in 1797 Consigned to Merchants Residing on the American Side of the River at Detroit"; "No. 2 Value of Returns in Peltries from the American Territory for the Year"; and "No. 3 Packs from Detroit Transported over the Niagara Portage," all in ibid., 2:267–68. Hamilton's figures were in the provincial currency of Upper Canada, which was valued at approximately 75% of sterling. Hamilton reported that 43,000 gallons of liquor, 1,000 minots of salt, and £50,000 of merchandise crossed the portage from Montreal to Detroit in 1797.

70. "Memorandum on Trade and Commerce by Robert Hamilton," September 24, 1798, in ibid., 2:266.

71. Ibid., 2:266–68.

72. Alexander Henry to John Askin, January 27, 1798, Askin Family Fonds, MG 19, A 3, 20:6743, LAC.

73. "Memorandum on Trade and Commerce by Robert Hamilton," September 24, 1798, in *PPR*, 2:268.

74. Kenneth Wiggins Porter, *John Jacob Astor: Business Man* (Cambridge, Mass.: Harvard University Press, 1931), 1:50.

75. William Hallowell to Simon McTavish, August 21, 1794, North West Company Papers, F3/1, 185. The North West Company had evidently sent an American ship to China in 1793. Campbell, *McGillivray*, 97–98.

76. Clarence M. Burton et al., eds., *The City of Detroit Michigan, 1701–1922* (Detroit and Chicago: S. J. Clarke, 1922), 1:268.

77. "Notice of Contest of Election of Jonathan Schieffelin," October 18, 1800, in *MPHC*, 8:517–18.

78. Peter Audrain to Governor Arthur St. Clair, October 20, 1800, in William Henry Smith, ed., *The St. Clair Papers: The Life and Public Services of Arthur St. Clair, Soldier of the Revolutionary War; President of the Continental Congress; and Governor of the North-Western Territory, with His Correspondence and Other Papers* (Cincinnati, 1882), 2:500.

79. Burton et al, eds., *The City of Detroit*, 2: 269; *Journal of the House of Representatives of the Territory of the United States, North West of the Ohio, at the First Session of the Second General Assembly, A.D. 1801* (Chillicothe, 1801), 11 (November 23, 1801).

80. Peter Audrain to Winthrop Sargent, January 20, 1798, PWS, 4:523.

81. James Wilkinson to Henry Burbeck, July 13, 1797, Wilkinson-Burbeck Papers, WLC.

82. John Askin to Mathew Ernest, c. December 9, 1798, in *PJA*, 2:163–64.

83. Peter Audrain to Winthrop Sargent, January 26, 1798, PWS, 4:527–28.

84. Lavender, *Fist in the Wilderness*, 41.

85. Patrick McNiff to Albert Gallatin, October 22, 1801, PAG, 3:248.

86. Angus Mackintosh to Alexander Macomb, September 5, 1799, Angus Mackintosh Fonds, MG 19, A 31, vol. 2; John Askin to Robert Hamilton, April 8, 1802, in *PJA*, 2:373.

87. Peter Audrain to John Cleves Symmes, December 15, 1802, PAG, 3:6.

4. "THE EQUIVOCAL ATTRIBUTES OF AMERICAN CITIZEN AND BRITISH SUBJECT"

1. "Memorial and Petition to His Excellency Peter Hunter," February 25, 1803, in *MPHC*, 23:425–26. Forsyth, Richardson & Co. and Parker, Gerrard, Ogilvy & Co. were copartners in the New North West Company. Its colloquial name came from the marks it used to distinguish its bales from those of the North West Company.

2. "Memorial and Petition to His Excellency Peter Hunter," February 25, 1803, in *MPHC*, 23:426–27.

3. Burt, *United States, Great Britain and British North America*, 200; Campbell, *McGillivray*, 91, 96, 153. Kaministiquia (Fort William) is the present-day site of Thunder Bay, Ontario.

4. "Memorial and Petition to His Excellency Peter Hunter," February 25, 1803, in *MPHC*, 23:426.

5. Forsyth, Richardson & Co. to Maj. James Green, April 18, 1803; "Memorial and Petition to His Excellency Peter Hunter, February 25, 1803," in *MPHC*, 23:431, 427.

6. Campbell, *McGillivray*, 132.

7. The House of Representatives approved Senate amendments on "An Act to Regulate the Collection of Duties on Imports and Tonnage" on February 18, 1799. U.S. Government, *Journal of the United States House of Representatives*, 5th Cong., 3rd sess., February 18, 1799, 480; Act of March 2, 1799, ch. 22, 1 *Stat.* 627–704.

8. James Wilkinson to Henry Dearborn, September 8, 1805, in *TPUS*, 13:198.

9. Alan Taylor notes the ways in which "the frontier inverted the American and British positions on freedom of movement" before the War of 1812. Taylor, *Civil War of 1812*, 126. The British government's sponsorship of fluidity along the border did not apply only to their Native allies but also to British merchants and traders.

10. For the evolution of the Royal Navy's policy of impressment, see Denver Brunsman, *The Evil Necessity: British Naval Impressment in the Eighteenth-Century Atlantic World* (Charlottesville: University of Virginia Press, 2013).

11. Forsyth, Richardson & Co. to Phineas Bond, February 3, 1804, FO 5/41/254.

12. "The Jay Treaty," November 19, 1794, in Miller, ed., *Treaties*, 2:246–48.

13. Forsyth, Richardson & Co. to Phineas Bond, February 3, 1804, FO 5/41/254.

14. Patrick McNiff to Albert Gallatin, October 22, 1801, PAG, 3:248.

15. Angus Mackintosh to McTavish, Frobisher & Co., October 16, 1800, Angus Mackintosh Fonds, vol. 2.

16. Angus Mackintosh to McTavish, Frobisher & Co., January 31, 1801; Angus Mackintosh to James Henry, February 11, 1801; Angus Mackintosh to McTavish, Frobisher & Co., June 18, 1802, all Angus Mackintosh Fonds, vol. 2.

17. "Upper Canada Licenses, 1806," Upper Canada Sundries, RG 5, B 9, vol. 53, file 1, LAC.

18. Matthew Ernest to John Steele, August 1, 1801; Albert Gallatin to John Steele, July 7, 1802, in *TPUS*, 7:31, 59 (quotations).

19. Peter Hunter to the Duke of Portland, August 20, 1800, CO 42/325/196; "An Act for Granting to His Majesty, His Heirs and Successors, to and for the Use of This Province, the Like Duties on Goods and Merchandise Brought into This Province from the United States of America, as Are Now Paid on Goods and Merchandise Imported from Great Britain and Other Place," in Upper Canada, *The Provincial Statutes of Upper-Canada, Revised, Corrected, and Republished* (York, Ont., 1818), 136. The act created ports of entry and clearance at Cornwall, Johnstown, Newcastle, York, Kingston, Niagara, Queenston, Fort Erie Passage, Turkey Point, Amherstburg, and Sandwich.

20. "To Peter Hunter—The Memorial of Simon McTavish, John Gregory, William McGillivray, Duncan McGillivray, William Hallowell and Roderick McKenzie of the City of Montreal in the Province of Lower Canada, Merchants and Copartners in Trade under the Name of Firm of McTavish Frobisher and Company," May 15, 1802, Executive Council Fonds, RG 1, E 3, 48:20–21.

21. Lieutenant-Governor Hunter referred the memorial to the Court of the King's Bench for Upper Canada in 1802. Attorney-General Thomas Scott upheld their complaint while requiring merchants to pay a security bond to ensure that the tobacco was not sold in Upper Canada. McTavish, Frobisher & Co. to James Green, November 29, 1802, in *MPHC*, 23:425; Thomas Scott to John McGill, July 9, 1803, and Thomas

Dickson to John McGill, September 10, 1803, both Department of National Revenue Fonds, RG 16, A 1, vol. 297, LAC.

22. "Act of March 2, 1799, ch. 22, 1 *Stat.* 706 & 708.

23. "Establishment of U.S. Customs Service," in Matthew Ernest to John Askin, May 2, 1800, in *PJA,* 2:287.

24. Gabriel Duval to Stanley Griswold, November 21, 1806, William Woodbridge Papers, box 3 (1805–6), BHC; "Statement of the Accounts of the Collector of Customs," January 20, 1806, in *MPHC,* 8:553–54; Albert Gallatin to Thomas Jefferson, January 22, 1806, in *TPUS,* 10:35–36.

25. Peter Audrain to Albert Gallatin, July 6, 1808, in *TPUS,* 10:231.

26. "Extra Official Communication with Regard to the Canada Trade," n.d., in *ASPFR,* 3:153.

27. "Observations on Messrs. Forsyth and Richardson's Letter," April 5, 1804, FO 5/41/256–58.

28. Perkins, *The First Rapprochement,* 172–81.

29. Anthony Merry to Lord Hawkesbury, April 10, 1804, FO 5/41/252–53.

30. "Answer and Claim of Northwest Company," in William Wirt Blume, ed., *Transactions of the Supreme Court of the Territory of Michigan, 1805–1814* (Ann Arbor: University of Michigan Press, 1935), 2:36–37. The North West Company constructed the portage to the northwest trade as an alternative to Grand Portage, which lay inside the boundary of the United States.

31. Ibid.

32. "Copy of a Letter Addressed to Captain Duncan the Collector of the Port of Michilimackinac, by the Agents of the North West Company after his Seizure of the Two Boats," June 13, 1805; "The Collector's Answer," June 14, 1805, both BLN, vol. 3.

33. "Memorial of Montreal Merchants," November 8, 1805, in *MPHC,* 25:219–20; "Proclamation by Governor Wilkinson," August 26, 1805, in *TPUS,* 13:203.

34. William E. Foley and C. David Rice, *The First Chouteaus: River Barons of Early St. Louis* (Urbana: University of Illinois Press, 1982), 91–92.

35. Ibid. Although St. Louis was technically part of the Spanish Empire when the town was founded in 1764, Spanish officials did not arrive to take possession of it from France until 1767. With no French official present, Stoddard stood in for the French government in the ceremony to mark the retrocession of Louisiana from Spain to France on March 9, 1804, before performing a transfer ceremony from France to the United States on March 10.

36. Stephen Aron, *American Confluence: The Missouri Frontier from Borderland to Border State* (Bloomington: Indiana University Press, 2006), 1; Gitlin, *Bourgeois Frontier,* 14–15.

37. Foley and Rice, *The First Chouteaus,* 94; Gitlin, *Bourgeois Frontier,* 15–17, 49–52.

38. Aron, *American Confluence,* 86; Foley and Rice, *The First Chouteaus,* 72.

39. "Report of Governor St. Clair to the Secretary of State," February 10, 1791, in *TPUS*, 2:331.

40. Foley and Rice, *The First Chouteaus*, 75, 81. Chouteau continued to do business with James McGill into the 1800s.

41. George Gillespie to Auguste Chouteau, August 19, 1803, Chouteau Family Papers, box 5, Missouri History Museum Archives, St. Louis.

42. George Gillespie & Company continued to handle the importation of trade goods and the consignment of furs for Auguste Chouteau until he became a partner in the St. Louis Missouri Fur Company in 1809. The company's articles of association prevented its partners from trading on their own account outside of the company. George Gillespie & Co. to Auguste Chouteau, May 1, 1809; "Articles of Association of the St. Louis Missouri Fur Company," March 7, 1809, both Chouteau Family Papers, box 10.

43. Foley and Rice, *The First Chouteaus*, 94.

44. Aron, *American Confluence*, 94–95; Pierre Chouteau to Henry Dearborn, Pierre Chouteau Letter Book (1804–19), Chouteau Family Papers, box 7, 7–8.

45. Impost Book (1802–65), U.S. Customs District of Michilimackinac Records, Bentley Historical Library. Goods imported by the Montreal fur trade through Michilimackinac were bound for the Illinois country and the Louisiana Territory. The opening of the Kaministiquia portage in 1803 meant that goods destined for the northwest trade no longer passed through the United States. While U.S. customs duties remained the same, revenue at Michilimackinac increased from $19,361 in 1803 to $33,545 in 1804.

46. Aron, *American Confluence*, 91–92, 110, 137; Anthony F. C. Wallace, *Jefferson and the Indians: The Tragic Fate of the First Americans* (Cambridge, Mass.: Belknap Press of Harvard University Press, 1999), 224–25.

47. James Wilkinson to Henry Dearborn, September 8, 1805, in *TPUS*, 13:196–97.

48. Wallace, *Jefferson and the Indians*, 221–22.

49. James Wilkinson to Henry Dearborn, September 8, 1805, in *TPUS*, 13:196–98.

50. Bradburn, *The Citizenship Revolution*, 286.

51. James Wilkinson to Henry Dearborn, September 8, 1805, in *TPUS*, 13:196–98.

52. "Memorial of Montreal Merchants," November 8, 1805, in *MPHC*, 25:218–20; Thomas Dunn to Anthony Merry, November 15, 1805, and Thomas Dunn to Anthony Merry, November 25, 1805, both Governor-General's Office Fonds, RG 7, G 15a, 2:11–12, 19–20, LAC.

53. Anthony Merry to James Madison, January 7, 1806, no. 1, BLN, vol. 3.

54. Anthony Merry to James Madison, January 8, 1806, BLN, vol. 3.

55. Thomas Jefferson to William Henry Harrison, January 16, 1806, in Logan Easrey, ed., *Messages and Letters of William Henry Harrison* (Indianapolis: Indiana Historical Commission, 1922), 1:186.

56. Perkins, *The First Rapprochement,* 177–81; Donald R. Hickey, "The Monroe-Pinkney Treaty of 1806: A Reappraisal," *William and Mary Quarterly,* 3rd series, 44 (January 1987): 72.

57. Adam Jortner, *The Gods of Prophetstown: The Battle of Tippecanoe and the Holy War for the American Frontier* (Oxford: Oxford University Press, 2012), 3–4.

58. James Wilkinson to Henry Dearborn, December 10, 1805, in *TPUS,* 14:299.

59. James Madison to Anthony Merry, January 29, 1806, Governor-General's Office Fonds, RG 7, G 15b, 1:16–22.

60. James Madison to Anthony Merry, May 21, 1806, FO 5/49/90; John Breckinridge to James Madison, March 22, 1806, FO 5/49/91–92.

61. Anthony Merry to Lord Mulgrave, January 31, 1806, FO 5/48/27–28.

62. Thomas Blackwood to James and Andrew McGill, June 8, 1806, MS 430/2, Thomas Blackwood Papers, McGill University Special Collections, Montreal.

63. Anthony Merry to James Madison, September 20, 1806, BLN, vol. 3.

64. Albert Gallatin to James Madison, October 28, 1806, BLN, vol. 3.

65. Albert Gallatin to George Hoffman, April 9, 1807, in Blume, ed., *Transactions of the Supreme Court of the Territory of Michigan,* 2:55; Gabriel Duvall to Albert Gallatin, April 7, 1807, in ibid., 2:55.

66. Alexander Henry to John Askin, January 18, 1800, in *PJA,* 2:275.

67. Alexander Henry to John Askin, March 24, 1807, in ibid., 2:543.

68. Bradford Perkins, *Prologue to War: England and the United States, 1805–1812* (Berkeley: University of California Press, 1967), 102–6, 121.

69. "Thursday, September 4," Diary of Negotiations, Admiralty Papers, 80/117, National Archives of the United Kingdom, Kew.

70. Canada Merchants to Lord Holland and Lord Auckland, September 16, 1806, Admiralty Papers, 80/117.

71. Ibid.

72. Ibid.

73. "Monday, September 22," Diary of Negotiations, Admiralty Papers, 80/117.

74. "Mr. Madison, Secretary of State, to Messrs. Monroe and Pinkney, Ministers Extraordinary and Plenipotentiary of the United States in London, May 30, 1806," in *ASPFR,* 3:126.

75. "Monday, September 22," Diary of Negotiations, Admiralty Papers, 80/117.

76. "Monday, October 6," Diary of Negotiations, Admiralty Papers, 80/117; "Extra Official Communication with Regard to the Canada Trade," n.d., in *ASPFR,* 3:152–53; Perkins, *Prologue to War,* 123.

77. Lord Holland and Lord Auckland to Lord Howick, October 20, 1806, FO 5/51/176–77, 186.

78. "Saturday, December 6," Diary of Negotiations, Admiralty Papers, 80/117.

79. Lord Holland and Lord Auckland to James Monroe and William Pinkney, December 27, 1806, Admiralty Papers, 80/117.

80. James McGill to John Brickwood, January 2, 1807, MS 435, James McGill Collection, folder 7, McGill University Special Collections.

81. James McGill to Isaac Todd, October 23, 1806, James McGill Collection, folder 3; "Agreement between the North West Company and the Michilimackinac Company," December 31, 1806, North West Company Fonds, MG 19, B 1, 2:61, LAC; John Jacob Astor to DeWitt Clinton, January 25, 1808, DeWitt Clinton Papers, vol. 4, Butler Rare Book and Manuscript Library, Columbia University, New York.

82. Lord Howick to David Erskine, January 8, 1807, FO 5/52/25.

83. James Monroe and William Pinkney to James Madison, January 3, 1807, in *ASPFR*, 3:147.

84. "Additional and Explanatory Articles... Signed at London, the 31st Day of December 1806," in ibid., 3:165.

85. Hickey, "The Monroe-Pinkney Treaty of 1806," 65–88; Perkins, *Prologue to War*, 101–39; James Madison to James Monroe and William Pinkney, May 20, 1807, in *ASPFR*, 3:166.

86. James Madison to James Monroe and William Pinkney, July 30, 1807, in *ASPFR*, 3:185–86.

87. David Erskine to Thomas Dunn, March 18, 1807, Governor-General's Office Fonds, RG 7, G 15b, 1:100, 102.

88. Perkins, *Prologue to War*, 140–42; Taylor, *Civil War of 1812*, 101.

89. Perkins, *Prologue to War*, 142–43.

90. Hickey, "The Monroe-Pinkney Treaty of 1806," 87–88.

91. Robert Hamilton and Thomas Dickson to Francis Gore, May 25, 1808, Upper Canada Sundries, RG 5, A-1, 7:3107–3108.

92. "Memorial of the Merchants of Montreal," October 20, 1808, in *MPHC*, 25:255. The Michilimackinac Company reported its annual outfit to be worth £80,000.

93. Robert Hamilton to Capt. Nathaniel Leonard, May 23, 1808, and Leonard to Hamilton, May 24, 1808, both Upper Canada Sundries, RG 5, A-1, 7:3119–20, 3129–30; Act of April 25, 1808, ch. 66, 2 *Stat.* 502.

94. Robert Hamilton and Thomas Dickson to Francis Gore, May 25, 1808, Upper Canada Sundries, RG 5, A-1, 7:3107–3111; Sir James Craig to David Erskine, June 21, 1808, in *MPHC*, 25:248.

95. David Erskine to James Madison, June 21, 1808, BLN, vol. 3.

96. James Madison to David Erskine, June 29, 1808, Upper Canada Sundries, RG 5, A-1, 8:3193.

97. Ibid.; Albert Gallatin to John Lees, June 24, 1808, Governor-General's Office Fonds, RG 7, G 15B, 1:88–93; David Erskine to James Madison, July 2, 1808, BLN, vol. 3.

98. "Memorial of the Merchants of Montreal," October 20, 1808, in *MPHC*, 25:255–56.

99. Ibid., 25:254.

5. "WE OUGHT TO HAVE THE TRADE WITHIN OUR AWEN COUNTRY"

1. John Jacob Astor to Albert Gallatin, September 24, 1808, PAG, 3:129.

2. Nathaniel Atcheson, *American Encroachments on British Rights* (London, 1808), 18.

3. James P. Ronda explores the imperial dimensions of Astor's commercial aspirations in his excellent *Astoria and Empire* (Lincoln: University of Nebraska Press, 1990).

4. Jortner, *Gods of Prophetstown*, 143–53.

5. John Jacob Astor to DeWitt Clinton, July 25, 1811, DeWitt Clinton Papers, vol. 4.

6. Allen, *His Majesty's Indian Allies*, 108–22.

7. Atcheson, *American Encroachments on British Rights*, 19–21.

8. For the failure of the Embargo and Nonintercourse Acts as tools of peaceable coercion and the problems of enforcement born of their unpopularity among the American people, see Perkins, *Prologue to War*, 165; Israel Ira Rubin, "New York State and the Long Embargo" (Ph.D. diss., New York University, 1962), 249–52; Burton Spivak, *Jefferson's English Crisis: Commerce, Embargo, and the Republican Revolution* (Charlottesville: University Press of Virginia, 1988), 198–200; Tucker and Hendrickson, *Empire of Liberty*, 164–66; and Ben-Atar, *Origins of Jeffersonian Commercial Policy*, 166. James P. Ronda is an exception, noting that the uncertainty created by shifting Republican commercial policy shaped how Montreal merchants responded to Astor's advances between 1808 and 1811. Ronda, *Astoria and Empire*, 47–49.

9. John Jacob Astor to DeWitt Clinton, January 25, 1808, DeWitt Clinton Papers, vol. 4.

10. John Jacob Astor to DeWitt Clinton, January 25, 1808, DeWitt Clinton Papers, vol. 4.

11. John Jacob Astor to Thomas Jefferson, February 27, 1808, Thomas Jefferson Papers, Library of Congress, Washington, D.C., https://www.loc.gov/resource/mtj1.040_1210_1213/. James P. Ronda points out that Astor's "approbation" could have meant anything "from mere knowledge and general assent to a full partnership." Ronda, *Astoria and Empire*, 39.

12. Henry Dearborn to Thomas Jefferson, April 8, 1808, Thomas Jefferson Papers, https://www.loc.gov/resource/mtj1.041_0301_0302/.

13. Ronda, *Astoria and Empire*, 40–41.

14. Thomas Jefferson to John Jacob Astor, April 13, 1808, Thomas Jefferson Papers, https://www.loc.gov/resource/mtj1.041_0334_0334/.

15. Thomas Jefferson to Meriwether Lewis, July 17, 1808, Thomas Jefferson Papers, https://www.loc.gov/resource/mtj1.041_1105_1106/.

16. Act of April 25, 1808, ch. 66, 2 *Stat.* 502.//
17. Perkins, *Prologue to War*, 210–11.
18. Frederick Bates to George Hoffman, February 23, 1808, in Thomas Maitland Marshall, ed., *The Life and Papers of Frederick Bates* (St. Louis: Missouri Historical Society, 1926): 1:297.
19. George Hoffman to Frederick Bates, October 21, 1808, in ibid., 1:38.
20. George Hoffman to Frederick Bates, August 23, 1808, in ibid., 1:17–18.
21. "Abstract of Goods, Wares, & Merchandize of the Growth & Manufacture of the United States, Exported from the District of Michilimackinac, Commencing the 1st of July and Ending the 31st of September 1808," October 1, 1808, Solomon Sibly Papers, BHC.
22. Impost Book, U.S. Customs District of Michilimackinac Records.
23. George Hoffman to Albert Gallatin, October 12, 1808, Solomon Sibly Papers.
24. Ronda, *Astoria and Empire*, 49.
25. David Erskine to Forsyth, Richardson & Co. and McTavish, McGillivrays & Co., January 20, 1809, FO 5/7/108–9.
26. Lavender, *Fist in the Wilderness*, 108.
27. Perkins, *Prologue to War*, 211–12, 219.
28. Ibid., 212–19.
29. Lavender, *Fist in the Wilderness*, 103.
30. John Jacob Astor to Albert Gallatin, February 8, 1809, PAG, 6:10.
31. Ibid.
32. Frederick Bates to Meriwether Lewis, November 7, 1807, in Marshall, ed., *Life and Papers of Frederick Bates*, 1:231–32.
33. John Jacob Astor to Albert Gallatin, February 8, 1809, PAG, 6:10.
34. Meriwether Lewis to the Secretary of War, July 1, 1808; Meriwether Lewis to Henry Dearborn, August 2, 1808, in *TPUS*, 14:200–201, 213.
35. William Clark to Henry Dearborn, April 30, 1809, in ibid., 14:271.
36. Frederick Bates to Jacques Porlier and John Bleakley, November 3, 1809, in Marshall, ed., *Life and Papers of Frederick Bates*, 2:105–6.
37. Bernard W. Sheehan, *Seeds of Extinction: Jeffersonian Philanthropy and the American Indian* (Chapel Hill: University of North Carolina Press, 1973).
38. Jortner, *Gods of Prophetstown*, 147.
39. Ibid., 164–65.
40. William Clark to Henry Dearborn, April 30, 1809, in *TPUS* 14:271.
41. John Jacob Astor to Albert Gallatin, May 16, 1809, PAG, 6:25.
42. Lavender, *Fist in the Wilderness*, 102–3.
43. "Protest Relative to the Appointment of Robert Dickson as Indian Agent," September 15, 1808, in *MPHC*, 40:263–66. Despite George Hoffman's hope of securing the appointment, the Jefferson administration appointed Nicholas Boilvin as an

Indian sub-agent at Prairie du Chien as a cost-cutting measure. George Hoffman to Frederick Bates, November 15, 1808, in Marshall, ed., *Life and Papers of Frederick Bates*, 2:40.

44. John Jacob Astor to Albert Gallatin, September 1809, PAG, 6:57.

45. "Memoranda of the Committee of Trade at Montreal," September 30, 1809, in *MPHC*, 25:262.

46. Ibid.

47. Ibid., 25:264.

48. Ibid., 25:263.

49. Perkins, *Prologue to War,* 220–21, 236–37, 274.

50. John Richardson to Thomas Forsyth, February 17, 1810, in *MPHC*, 25:268.

51. Taylor, *Civil War of 1812,* 89–91.

52. John Richardson to Thomas Forsyth, February 17, 1810, in *MPHC*, 25:268.

53. Ibid.

54. Alexander Henry to John Askin, May 16, 1809, in *PJA*, 2:625.

55. Manuel Lisa to Auguste Chouteau, February 14, 1810, Chouteau Family Papers, box 11.

56. John Askin, Jr., to John Askin, October 12, 1809, in *PJA*, 2:645.

57. John Richardson to Thomas Forsyth, February 17, 1810, in *MPHC*, 25:268.

58. Ronda, *Astoria and Empire,* 57–58.

59. Alexander Henry to John Askin, February 26, 1810, in *PJA*, 2:653.

60. John Jacob Astor to Albert Gallatin, April 2, 1810, PAG, 7:9.

61. Ronda, *Astoria and Empire,* 58–59.

62. Perkins, *Prologue to War,* 239–41.

63. "Copy of a Letter from Mr. Atcheson to the Marquis Wellesley," April 2, 1810, FO 115/20/193–95.

64. Forsyth, Richardson & Co. to Jacques Porlier, June 8, 1810, in *WHC,* 19:337–38; Lavender, *Fist in the Wilderness,* 126; Perkins, *Prologue to War,* 244. The firm of McTavish, Frobisher & Company was reorganized as McTavish, McGillivrays & Company in 1806. Simon McTavish had died in 1804 and his partner, Joseph Frobisher, had retired. Campbell, *The North West Company,* 158.

65. Perkins, *Prologue to War,* 246–50.

66. "Memorial of the North West Co. Respecting Indian Traders," November 5, 1810, in *MPHC,* 25:273–74.

67. "Memorandum on Trade and Commerce by Robert Hamilton," September 24, 1798, in *PPR,* 2:266.

68. Rubin, "New York State and the Long Embargo," 107–3; Richard J. Mannix, "The Embargo: Its Administration, Impact, and Enforcement" (Ph.D. diss., New York University, 1975), 155–228.

69. "Articles of Agreement for the South West Fur Company," January 28, 1811, in Porter, *John Jacob Astor*, 1:462–69.

70. Ibid.

71. Ronda, *Astoria and Empire*, 101–15, 125–28, 196, 86.

72. Ibid., 245–47.

73. Atcheson, *On the Origins and Progress of the North-West Company*, 3–4.

74. Ibid., 17.

75. Ibid., 36–37, 22–23, 31–32.

76. John Jacob Astor to Thomas Jefferson, March 14, 1812, in J. Jefferson Looney et al., eds., *The Papers of Thomas Jefferson: Retirement Series* (Princeton, N.J.: Princeton University Press, 2004–), 4:552.

77. Henry Brevoort to Washington Irving, June 28, 1811, in George S. Hellman, ed., *Letters of Henry Brevoort to Washington Irving* (New York: G. P. Putnam's Sons, 1918), 27–28.

78. Henry Brevoort to Washington Irving, July 14, 1811, in ibid., 37.

79. John Askin to John Askin, Jr., August 25, 1811, in *PJA*, 2:694.

80. Ibid.; John Askin, Jr., to Charles Askin, September 18, 1811, in ibid., 2:696.

81. Lavender, *Fist in the Wilderness*, 180.

82. John Jacob Astor to Thomas Jefferson, March 14, 1812; Thomas Jefferson to John Jacob Astor, March 28, 1812, in Looney et al., eds., *Papers of Thomas Jefferson: Retirement Series*, 4:553, 74–75.

83. "Monday, March 30, 1812," U.S. Government, *Journal of the United States House of Representatives*, 12th Cong., 1st sess., 269. For Republican opposition to granting exemptions to the Nonintercourse Act, see Gales et al., eds., *Debates and Proceedings*, 12th Cong., 1st sess., 1241–42.

84. Perkins, *Prologue to War*, 279–82.

85. Benjamin F. Stickney to William Hull, May 25, 1812, Fort Wayne Indian Agency Letter Book, 82–83, WLC.

86. John Jacob Astor to Albert Gallatin, May 13, 1812, PAG, 7:55.

87. Albert Gallatin to the Collector of Customs for the District of Detroit or Michilimackinac, June 16, 1812, PAG, 7:77.

88. Forsyth, Richardson & Co. to John Jacob Astor, June 16, 1812, PAG, 7:77.

89. Porter, *John Jacob Astor*, 1:258.

90. Taylor, *Civil War of 1812*, 147–48.

91. Ibid.

92. John Jacob Astor to Albert Gallatin, June 30, 1812, Papers of Albert Gallatin, New York University and National Historical Publications Commission, New York, reel 24, 89.

93. Taylor, *Civil War of 1812*, 135.

6. "WHEN THE AMERICAN STRIPES ALONE PROTECT THE WESTERN HEMISPHERE"

1. "Our Treaty with the United States," *Morning Chronicle,* October 4, 1815.
2. "Our Announced Commercial Treaty with the United States," *Morning Chronicle,* November 4, 1815.
3. "Our Announced Commercial Treaty with the United States," *Morning Chronicle,* December 27, 1815.
4. "English Policy," *Aurora General Advertiser,* December 15, 1815. The *Aurora General Advertiser* reprinted excerpts of the *Morning Chronicle*'s commentary on the commercial convention in its edition of December 7, 1815.
5. "English Policy," *Aurora General Advertiser,* December 15, 1815.
6. Taylor, *Civil War of 1812,* 4, 170–72, 230.
7. "English Policy," *Aurora General Advertiser,* December 15, 1815.
8. John Askin, Jr., to John Askin, July 19, 1812, in *MPHC,* 32:482.
9. Taylor, *Civil War of 1812,* 158–63.
10. "Charles Askin's Journal of the Detroit Campaign, July 24–September 12, 1812," in *PJA,* 2:717; John Askin to James McGill, September 4, 1812, in *MPHC,* 32:484.
11. Taylor, *Civil War of 1812,* 164–65, 203.
12. "Charles Askin's Journal of the Detroit Campaign, July 24–September 12, 1812," in *PJA,* 2:719–20.
13. Charles Askin to John Askin, October 16, 1812, in *MPHC,* 32:485.
14. John Askin to James McGill, September 4, 1812, in ibid., 32:484.
15. Taylor, *Civil War of 1812,* 159–60, 163.
16. John Jacob Astor to Albert Gallatin, October 5, 1812, Papers of Albert Gallatin, reel 25, 299.
17. John Askin to James McGill, September 4, 1812, in *MPHC,* 32:484.
18. Taylor, *Civil War of 1812,* 257.
19. Ibid., 203–5.
20. Richard Cartwright to Desrivieres, Blackwood & Co., November 23, 1813, Richard Cartwright Papers, Queen's University Archives, Kingston, Ontario, 7:144; Richard Cartwright to Desrivieres, Blackwood & Co., December 23, 1813, Richard Cartwright Papers, 7:147.
21. Ramsey Crooks to John Jacob Astor, August 21, 1814, in *WHC,* 19:361.
22. "Memorial," n.d., in *MPHC,* 16:63–64.
23. John Jacob Astor to Albert Gallatin, June 20, 1812, Papers of Albert Gallatin, reel 25, 89; John Jacob Astor to Peter Sailly, September 30, 1813, John Jacob Astor Business Papers, Baker Library, Harvard University, Cambridge, Mass., 16:59.
24. Taylor, *Civil War of 1812,* 241–46.
25. "Memorial of the Agents of the North West Company," November 8, 1813, in *MPHC,* 25:543–44.

26. John Jacob Astor to John Day, October 19, 1813; John Jacob Astor to John Day, October 26, 1813; John Jacob Astor to George Astor, October 26, 1813, all John Jacob Astor Business Papers, 16:79, 84, 85.

27. John Jacob Astor to Ramsey Crooks, October 8, 1813, John Jacob Astor Business Papers, 16:67.

28. Ramsey Crooks to John Jacob Astor, October 31, 1813, John Jacob Astor Papers, New-York Historical Society, vol. 1.

29. John Jacob Astor to Ramsey Crooks, November 15, 1813, John Jacob Astor Business Papers, 16:107.

30. Taylor, *Civil War of 1812*, 283–87.

31. Ronda, *Astoria and Empire*, 264–65, 277–96.

32. "To His Excellency Sir George Prevost, Bart., Captain General and Governor in Chief, in and over the Provinces of Lower Canada, Upper Canada, &c.," October 14, 1812, FO 5/103/71–73.

33. John Jacob Astor to Ramsey Crooks, February 14, 1814, John Jacob Astor Papers, vol. 1.

34. Frederick Oliver to Louis Grignon, March 29, 1814, in *MPHC*, 25:351.

35. "To His Excellency Sir George Prevost, Bart., Captain General and Governor in Chief, in and over the Provinces of Lower Canada, Upper Canada, &c.," October 14, 1812, FO 5/103/71. Nathaniel Atcheson repeated the Oswald story in *A Compressed View of the Points to Be Discussed in Treating with the United States* (London, 1814), 5.

36. John Inglis and John Bainbridge to the Earl of Liverpool, February 7, 1814, FO 5/103/68–69.

37. Atcheson, *A Compressed View*, 2–3, 4.

38. Ibid., 6, 12–14.

39. "Canada Merchants Memorial to Lord Bathurst," May 7, 1814, FO 5/103/188.

40. Ibid., 189–90.

41. Ibid., 190–91.

42. Lord Castlereagh to the British Commissioners, July 28, 1814, Henry Goulburn Papers, WLC, box 1.

43. "Memm Respecting Indian Boundary," n.d., Henry Goulburn Papers, box 2.

44. "Mr. Monroe, Secretary of State, to the Plenipotentiaries of the United States for Treating of Peace with Great Britain," April 15, 1813; "Extract of a Letter from the Secretary of State to the Commissioners of the United States for Treating of Peace with Great Britain," June 23, 1813, in *ASPFR*, 3:695, 701.

45. "Protocol of Conferences," in British Commissioners to Lord Castlereagh, August 8–9, 1814, Henry Goulburn Papers, box 1.

46. "From the Commissioners Extraordinary and Plenipotentiary of the United States for Treating of Peace with Great Britain, to the Secretary of State," August 12, 1814, in *ASPFR*, 3:706.

47. Ibid., 3:706–7.

48. Lord Castlereagh to British Commissioners, August 14, 1814, Henry Goulburn Papers, box 1; "Messrs Adams, Bayard, Clay, Russell, and Gallatin to Mr. Monroe, Secretary of State," August 19, 1814, in *ASPFR,* 3:708.

49. Lord Castlereagh to British Commissioners, August 14, 1814, Henry Goulburn Papers, box 1; "Messrs Adams, Bayard, Clay, Russell, and Gallatin to Mr. Monroe, Secretary of State," August 19, 1814, in *ASPFR,* 3:708.

50. "Messrs Adams, Bayard, Clay, Russell, and Gallatin to Mr. Monroe, Secretary of State," August 19, 1814, in *ASPFR,* 3:708–9.

51. "The American to the British Ministers," August 24, 1814, in ibid., 3:711–13, 713 (quotation).

52. Henry Goulburn to Lord Castlereagh, August 26, 1814, Henry Goulburn Papers, box 1.

53. British Commissioners to Lord Castlereagh, September 4, 1814, Henry Goulburn Papers, box 2.

54. "From the American to the British Ministers," September 9, 1814, in *ASPFR,* 3:715–16.

55. Lord Bathurst to Henry Goulburn, September 12, 1814; Lord Bathurst to Henry Goulburn, September 16, 1814, both Henry Goulburn Papers, box 2.

56. Lord Liverpool to Henry Goulburn, September 17, 1814, Henry Goulburn Papers, box 2.

57. "From the American to the British Ministers," September 26, 1814, in *ASPFR,* 3:720.

58. Ibid.

59. Lord Bathurst to Henry Goulburn, October 4, 1814, Henry Goulburn Papers, box 2.

60. "From the British to the American Ministers," October 8, 1814; "From the American to the British Ministers," October 14, 1814, in *ASPFR,* 3:721–23, 723–24.

61. Lord Bathurst to Henry Goulburn, No. 7, October 18, 1814; Lord Bathurst to British Commissioners, October 18, 1814; and Lord Bathurst to British Commissioners, October 20, 1814, all Henry Goulburn Papers, box 2.

62. "From the American to the British Ministers," October 24, 1814; "The Secretary of State to the American Plenipotentiaries," March 22, 1814, in *ASPFR,* 3:725, 731.

63. Lord Liverpool to Henry Goulburn, October 21, 1814, Henry Goulburn Papers, box 2.

64. Lord Bathurst to British Commissioners, November 15, 1814, Henry Goulburn Papers, box 2; "The American to the British Plenipotentiaries," November 10, 1814, in *ASPFR,* 3:733.

65. Lord Bathurst to British Commissioners, November 20, 1814, Henry Goulburn Papers, box 2.

66. "Treaty of Peace and Amity between His Britannic Majesty and the United States," December 24, 1814, in *ASPFR*, 3:745–48.

67. Bradford Perkins, *Castlereagh and Adams: England and the United States, 1812–1823* (Berkeley: University of California Press, 1964), 131, 156; Fred L. Engelman, *The Peace of Christmas Eve* (London: Rupert Hart-Davis, 1962), 283.

68. "The British Ministers to the American Ministers," September 4, 1814, in *ASPFR*, 3:715.

69. "Memorial of Mr. Richardson and Mr. McGillivray," April 20, 1815, in *MPHC*, 16:77–80.

70. Lt.-Col. John Harvey to John Richardson and William McGillivray, April 24, 1815, in ibid., 16:80–81.

71. Sir Gordon Drummond to Lord Bathurst, April 25, 1815, CO 42/162/21–22.

72. James Monroe to Anthony St. John Baker, May 6, 1815, June 3, 1815, in *MPHC*, 16:94–95, 126–27.

73. Sir Gordon Drummond to Lord Bathurst, May 20, 1815, CO 42/162/78–79.

74. "Projet of a Commercial Treaty," December 26, 1814, Henry Goulburn Papers, box 2.

75. British Commissioners to U.S. Commissioners, December 30, 1814, Henry Goulburn Papers, box 2.

76. "Extract of a Minute of a Conversation Which Took Place at Lord Castlereagh's, between His Lordship and Messrs. Clay and Gallatin," April 16, 1815, in *ASPFR*, 4:11.

77. "Extract of a Letter from the American Commissioners, Messr. Clay and Gallatin, to the Secretary of State," May 18, 1815, in ibid., 4:8.

78. Ibid., 4:9, 10.

79. "Memoranda," March 28, 1815, in *MPHC*, 16:67–68.

80. Edward Ellice to Henry Goulburn, June 9, 1815, CO 42/165/218; "Extract of a Letter from Montreal," April 26, 1815, CO 42/165/219.

81. "Extract of a Letter from the American Commissioners, Messr. Clay and Gallatin, to the Secretary of State," May 18, 1815, in *ASPFR*, 4:10.

82. British Commissioners to Lord Castlereagh, June 7, 1815, FO 5/109/9–10; British Commissioners to American Commissioners, June 16, 1815, FO 5/109/17–18.

83. "A Convention to Regulate the Commerce between the Territories of the United States and His Britannic Majesty," July 3, 1815, in *ASPFR*, 4:7–8.

84. Albert Gallatin to James Monroe, December 25, 1814, Records of Negotiations Connected with the Treaty of Ghent, 1813–15, Despatches from the American Commissioners, August 29, 1813–July 3, 1815, RG 59, M35, Department of State, National Archives of the United States, Washington, D.C., reel 1.

85. Anthony Baker to Lord Bathurst, February 19, 1815, FO 5/106/4.

86. Sadosky, *Revolutionary Negotiations*, 200–201.

7. "BRITISH SUBJECTS ARE ALWAYS BLACK SHEEP"

1. John Lawe to Thomas Anderson, November 13, 1818, in *WHC*, 20:90–91.
2. Louis Grignon to Robert Dickson, February 6, 1819, in ibid., 20:102–3.
3. "Copy of a Speech by Prevost to Indian Allies, Enclosure in Sir George Prevost to Lord Bathurst," March 13, 1815, CO 42/161/76.
4. William Caldwell to William Claus, June 15, 1815, in *MPHC*, 16:134.
5. Anthony Baker to Lord Bathurst, June 21, 1815, FO 5/107/1; James Monroe to Anthony Baker, July 10, 1815, FO 5/107/70.
6. Anthony Baker to Lord Castlereagh, August 16, 1815, FO 5/107/191–92; Sir Gordon Drummond to Lord Bathurst, August 27, 1815, CO 42/163/73.
7. "Speech of Black Hawk, Head War Chief of the Sauk Nation," August 3, 1815, in *MPHC*, 16:197.
8. Lt.-Col. James McDonnell to Sir George Murray, May 17, 1815; Lt.-Col. James McDonnell to John Augustus Foster, May 15, 1815, in ibid., 16:109, 104.
9. Inglis, Ellices & Co. to Henry Goulburn, July 25, 1815, CO 42/164/497.
10. Jean Baptiste Berthelot to Louis Grignon, March 22, 1816, in *WHC*, 19:404.
11. Forsyth, Richardson & Co. to Jacques Porlier, May 15, 1816, in ibid., 19:414.
12. Benjamin F. Stickney to James Monroe, April 30, 1815, Fort Wayne Indian Agency Letter Book, 165–66.
13. Lewis Cass to Alexander James Dallas, June 20, 1815, in *WHC*, 19:376–77.
14. Benjamin F. Stickney to Lewis Cass, October 6, 1815, Lewis Cass Papers, Bentley Historical Library, 32:133.
15. "Indian Council," June 29, 1816, in *MPHC*, 16:480–81.
16. William H. Puthuff to Lewis Cass, May 14, 1816, in *WHC*, 19:408–9, 411–12.
17. Lavender, *Fist in the Wilderness*, 241–42.
18. Lt.-Col. James McDonnell to Maj.-Gen. Frederick Robinson, September 24, 1815, in *MPHC*, 16:289.
19. Lt.-Col. James McDonnell to John Augustus Foster, October 26, 1815, in ibid., 16:369.
20. Act of April 29, 1816, ch. 165, 3 *Stat.* 332–33.
21. William H. Puthuff to Lewis Cass, June 6, 1816, in *WHC*, 19:415.
22. William H. Puthuff to Lewis Cass, June 20, 1816, in ibid., 19:420.
23. Pierre Rocheblave to Jacques Porlier, June 20, 1816; Rocheblave to Louis Grignon, June 20, 1816, in ibid., 19:415–16, 416–17.
24. Ramsey Crooks and Robert Stuart to John Jacob Astor, January 24, 1818, in ibid., 20:19, 18.
25. Lewis Cass to William H. Puthuff, July 20, 1816, in ibid., 19:427.
26. Jacques Porlier to Pierre Rocheblave, c. winter 1816–17, in ibid., 19:445–46.
27. John Jacob Astor to Ramsey Crooks, March 17, 1817, in ibid., 19:451.

28. John C. Calhoun to Lewis Cass, March 25, 1818, in *TPUS*, 10:738–39; Cass to the Agents at Mackinac, Green Bay, and Chicago, April 23, 1818, in *WHC*, 20:43.

29. Indian Trade License Issued by Henry Puthuff to Robert Stuart and William H. Wallace, August 27, 1818, Michigan Collection, box 2, WLC.

30. William H. Puthuff to Lewis Cass, March 4, 1818, in *WHC*, 20:32.

31. John Bowyer to Lewis Cass, May 16, 1818, in ibid., 20:56–57.

32. Ninian Edwards to James Monroe, March 3, 1816, in ibid., 19:401.

33. Louis Grignon to Lewis Cass, July 17, 1819; Adam D. Stewart to John Bowyer, September 2, 1819, in ibid., 20:120–21.

34. William H. Puthuff to Lewis Cass, August 24, 1818, William Woodbridge Papers, box 15.

35. William Woodbridge to John Bowyer, September 8, 1818, William Woodbridge Papers, box 15.

36. William Wirt to John C. Calhoun, September 3, 1819, in *WHC*, 20:121–22.

37. John C. Calhoun to Lewis Cass, September 6, 1819, in ibid., 20:123.

38. Lewis Cass to Agents at Michilimackinac, Green Bay, Chicago, Fort Wayne, and Piqua, October 11, 1819, in ibid., 20:127.

39. Robert Stuart to Bernard Grignon, October 28, 1819, in ibid., 20:128.

40. Robert Stuart to Lewis Cass, November 13, 1819, in ibid., 20:135; Robert Stuart to Lewis Cass, November 21, 1819, Lewis Cass Papers, Bentley Historical Library, 32:424–25.

41. Lewis Cass to Robert Stuart, February 28, 1820, Lewis Cass Papers, box 1, WLC; Act of April 14, 1802, ch. 28, 2 *Stat.* 154.

42. Robert Stuart to Jacques Porlier, May 20, 1820, in *WHC*, 20:171–72.

43. Lewis Cass appointed Jacques Porlier as the chief justice of Brown County on September 7, 1820, meaning that he must have become a naturalized U.S. citizen by this date. "Executive Proceedings of Michigan Territory," September 7, 1820, in *TPUS*, 11:80.

44. Act of April 14, 1802, ch. 28, 2 *Stat.* 154.

EPILOGUE

1. "Land Titles in Oregon," December 26, 1850, in U.S. Government, *Congressional Globe*, Appendix, 31st Cong., 2nd sess., 37–38. I am indebted to Bill Rowley and Jacki Hedlund Tyler for discovering the case of John McLoughlin.

2. Frederick V. Holman, *Dr. John McLoughlin, the Father of Oregon* (Cleveland: Arthur H. Clark, 1907), 22–27, 31 (quotation).

3. "Land Titles in Oregon," December 26, 1850, in U.S. Government, *Congressional Globe*, Appendix, 31st Cong., 2nd sess., 37.

4. Weeks, *Dimensions of the Early American Empire*, 186–87.

5. "The Oregon Treaty," June 15, 1846, in Miller, ed., *Treaties*, 5:3–4.

6. "Report of Legislative Committee, upon the Judiciary," July 5, 1843, in La Fayette Grover, ed., *The Oregon Archives: Including the Journals, Governors' Messages and Public Papers of Oregon* (Salem, Ore., 1853), 29; "To the Governor, Deputy Governor & Committee of the Hudson's Bay Company," August 12, 1844, in E. E. Rich, ed., *The Letters of John McLoughlin from Fort Vancouver to the Governor and Committee* (Toronto: The Champlain Society, 1941–44), 3:4; "To the Governor, Deputy Governor & Committee of the Hudson's Bay Company," in ibid., 32; "Organic Law of the Provisional Government of Oregon," July 5, 1845, in Matthew P. Deady and Lafayette Lane, eds., *The Organic and Other General Laws of Oregon: Together with the National Constitution, and Other Public Acts and Statutes of the United States, 1843–1872* (Portland, Ore., 1874), 50.

7. "Letter to the Editor," *Oregon Spectator*, September 12, 1850.

8. "Land Titles in Oregon," December 26, 1850, in U.S. Government, *Congressional Globe*, Appendix, 31st Cong., 2nd sess., 41.

9. "Communications," *Oregon Spectator*, May 1, 1851.

10. Robert C. Johnson, *John McLoughlin: Patriarch of the Northwest* (Portland, Ore.: Metropolitan Press, 1935), 275, 296.

11. "Treaty for the Final Settlement of Claims of the Hudson's Bay Company and Puget's Sound Agricultural Company," July 1, 1863, in Miller, ed., *Treaties*, 8:949–1065.

12. Keith Murray, *The Pig War* (Tacoma: Washington State Historical Society, 1968); "Tuna Treaty: Canada, U.S. Fishing Dispute Heats up Ahead of Talks," *The Huffington Post Canada,* May 20, 2015, http://www.huffingtonpost.ca/2012/05/20/canada-us-tuna-treaty-_n_1530591.html; "The Tiny Islands Where Canada and America Are at War," *Maclean's,* July 22, 2015, http://www.macleans.ca/news/canada/the-tiny-islands-where-canada-and-america-are-at-war/.

SELECTED BIBLIOGRAPHY

MANUSCRIPT COLLECTIONS

Baker Library, Harvard University, Cambridge, Mass.
    John Jacob Astor Business Papers

Bentley Historical Library, University of Michigan, Ann Arbor
    Lewis Cass Papers
    Michigan Supreme Court Records
    U.S. Customs District of Michilimackinac Records

Burton Historical Collection, Detroit Public Library
    John Askin Papers
    Solomon Sibly Papers
    Wayne County, Northwest Territory Papers
    Hershel Whitaker Papers
    William Woodbridge Papers

Butler Rare Book and Manuscript Library, Columbia University, New York
    DeWitt Clinton Papers

Library and Archives of Canada, Ottawa
    Askin Family Fonds
    Civil and Provincial Secretaries Fonds
    Colonial Office Papers "Q" Series
    Department of National Revenue Fonds
    Executive Council Fonds
    Governor-General's Office Fonds
    Angus Mackintosh Fonds
    North West Company Fonds
    Upper Canada Sundries

Library of Congress, Washington, D.C.
    Thomas Jefferson Papers (online)

Massachusetts Historical Society, Boston
    Winthrop Sargent Papers (microfilm)

McCord Museum, Montreal
    Beaver Club Minute Book

McGill University Archives, Montreal
    James McGill Papers

McGill University Special Collections, Montreal
    Thomas Blackwood Papers
    James McGill Collection

Missouri History Museum Archives, St. Louis
  Chouteau Family Papers
National Archives of the United Kingdom, Kew
  Admiralty Papers
  Colonial Office Papers
  Foreign Office Papers
National Archives of the United States, Washington, D.C. (Record Group 59, General Records of the Department of State)
  Notes from Foreign Legations, Great Britain (microfilm)
  Records of Negotiations Connected with the Treaty of Ghent (microfilm)
New-York Historical Society, New York
  John Jacob Astor Papers
  Albert Gallatin Papers
New York University and National Historical Publications Commission, New York
  Papers of Albert Gallatin (microfilm)
Provincial Archives of Manitoba, Winnipeg (Hudson Bay Company Archives)
  North West Company Papers (microfilm)
Queen's University Archives, Kingston, Ontario
  Richard Cartwright Papers
William L. Clements Library, University of Michigan, Ann Arbor
  Lewis Cass Papers
  Fort Wayne Indian Agency Papers
  Henry Goulburn Papers
  James McHenry Papers
  Michigan Collection
  Shelburne Papers
  Wilkinson-Burbeck Papers

NEWSPAPERS AND PERIODICALS

Aurora General Advertiser (Philadelphia)
Morning Chronicle (London)
Morning Herald, and Daily Advertiser (London)
Oregon Spectator (Oregon City)

PUBLISHED PRIMARY SOURCES

Atcheson, Nathaniel. *American Encroachments on British Rights.* London, 1808.
———. *A Compressed View of the Points to Be Discussed in Treating with the United States.* London, 1814.
———. *On the Origins and Progress of the North-West Company of Canada.* London, 1811.

Baker-Holroyd, John (Lord Sheffield). *Observations on the Commerce of the United States*. 2nd edition. Dublin, 1784.

Blume, William Wirt, ed. *Transactions of the Supreme Court of the Territory of Michigan, 1805–1814*. 2 vols. Ann Arbor: University of Michigan Press, 1935.

Brymner, Douglas, ed. *Report on Canadian Archives, 1890*. Ottawa, 1891.

Carter, Clarence Edwin, ed. *Territorial Papers of the United States*. 26 vols. Washington, D.C.: U.S. Printing Office, 1934–62.

Chalmers, George, ed. *A Collection of Treaties between Great Britain and Other Powers*. 2 vols. London, 1790.

Cruikshank, E. A., ed. *The Correspondence of Lieut. Governor John Graves Simcoe, with Allied Documents Relating to His Administration of the Government of Upper Canada*. 5 vols. Toronto: Ontario Historical Society, 1923–31.

Cruikshank, E. A., and A. F. Hunter, eds. *The Correspondence of the Honourable Peter Russell, with Allied Documents Relating to His Administration of the Government of Upper Canada during the Official Term of Lieut.-Governor J. G. Simcoe, While on Leave of Absence*. 3 vols. Toronto: Ontario Historical Society, 1932.

Deady, Matthew P., and Lafayette Lane, eds. *The Organic and Other General Laws of Oregon: Together with the National Constitution, and Other Public Acts and Statutes of the United States, 1843–1872*. Portland, 1874.

Doughty, Arthur G., ed. *Report of the Work of the Public Archives for the Years 1914 and 1915*. Ottawa: King's Printer, 1916.

Easrey, Logan., ed. *Messages and Letters of William Henry Harrison*. 2 vols. Indianapolis: Indiana Historical Commission, 1922.

Fitzpatrick, John C., ed. *The Writings of George Washington*. 39 vols. Washington, D.C.: Government Printing Office, 1931–44.

Gales, Joseph, et al., eds. *The Debates and Proceedings in the Congress of the United States: With an Appendix Containing Important State Papers and Public Documents*. 42 vols. Washington, D.C., 1834–56.

Giunta, Mary A., et al., eds. *The Emerging Nation: A Documentary History of the Foreign Relations of the United States under the Articles of Confederation, 1780–1789*. 3 vols. Washington, D.C.: National Historical Publications and Records Commission, 1996.

Grotius, Hugo. *The Freedom of the Seas; or, The Right Which Belongs to the Dutch to Take Part in the East Indian Trade*. Translated by Ralph Van Deman Magoffin. Oxford: Oxford University Press, 1916.

Grover, La Fayette, ed. *The Oregon Archives: Including the Journals, Governors' Messages and Public Papers of Oregon*. Salem, Ore., 1853.

Hadfield, Joseph. *An Englishman in America, 1785*. Edited by Douglas S. Robertson. Toronto: Hunter-Rose, 1933.

Hellman, George S., ed. *Letters of Henry Brevoort to Washington Irving.* New York: G. P. Putnam's Sons, 1918.

Historical Collections of the Michigan Pioneer and Historical Society. 40 vols. Lansing, Mich., 1874–1929.

Journal of the House of Representatives of the Territory of the United States, North West of the Ohio, at the First Session of the Second General Assembly, A.D. 1801. Chillicothe, 1801.

Kappler, Charles J., ed. *Indian Affairs: Laws and Treaties.* 7 vols. Washington, D.C.: Government Printing Office, 1903–.

Labaree, Leonard Woods, et al., eds. *The Papers of Benjamin Franklin.* 41 vols. New Haven, Conn.: Yale University Press, 1959–.

Looney, J. Jefferson, et al., eds. *The Papers of Thomas Jefferson: Retirement Series.* 11 vols. Princeton, N.J.: Princeton University Press, 2004–.

Lowrie, Walter, et al., eds. *American State Papers: Documents, Legislative and Executive, of the Congress of the United States, Foreign Relations Series.* 38 vols. Washington, D.C., 1832–61.

Marshall, Thomas Maitland., ed. *The Life and Papers of Frederick Bates.* 2 vols. St. Louis: Missouri Historical Society, 1926.

Mayo, Bernard., ed. *Instructions to the British Ministers to the United States, 1791–1812.* New York: Da Capo Press, 1971.

Miller, Hunter, ed. *Treaties and Other International Acts of the United States of America.* 8 vols. Washington, D.C.: Government Printing Office, 1931–48.

Quaife, Milo M., ed. *The John Askin Papers.* 2 vols. Detroit: Detroit Library Commission, 1928–31.

Rich, E. E., ed. *The Letters of John McLoughlin from Fort Vancouver to the Governor and Committee.* 3 vols. Toronto: The Champlain Society, 1941–44.

Russell, Donna Valley, ed. *Michigan Censuses, 1710–1830, under the French, British, and Americans.* Detroit: Detroit Society for Genealogical Research, 1982.

Smith, William Henry, ed. *The St. Clair Papers: The Life and Public Services of Arthur St. Clair, Soldier of the Revolutionary War; President of the Continental Congress; and Governor of the North-Western Territory, with His Correspondence and Other Papers.* 2 vols. Cincinnati, 1882.

Syrett, Harold C., et al., eds. *The Papers of Alexander Hamilton.* 27 vols. New York: Columbia University Press, 1961–87.

Thwaites, Reuben Gold, et al., eds. *Collections of the State Historical Society of Wisconsin.* 20 vols. Madison, Wis., 1888–1931.

U.S. Government. *American State Papers, Documents, Legislative and Executive, of the Congress of the United States, Indian Affairs Series.* 2 vols. Washington, D.C., 1832–34.

———. *Congressional Globe*. 46 vols. Washington, D.C., 1834–73.
———. *Journal of the United States House of Representatives*. Washington, D.C., 1826–.
———. *The Public Statutes at Large of the United States of America: from the Organization of the Government in 1789 to March 3, 1845*. 4 vols. Boston, 1845–46.
Upper Canada. *The Provincial Statutes of Upper-Canada, Revised, Corrected, and Republished by Authority*. York, Ont., 1818.
Vattel, Emer de. *The Law of Nations; or, The Principles of Natural Law Applied to the Conduct and Affairs of Nations and Sovereigns*. Philadelphia, 1829.
Weld, Isaac. *Travels through the States of North America and the Provinces of Upper and Lower Canada during the Years 1795, 1796 and 1797*. 4th edition. London, 1800.

SECONDARY SOURCES

Adelman, Jeremy, and Stephen Aron. "From Borderlands to Borders: Empires, Nation-States, and the Peoples in between in North American History." *American Historical Review*, 104 (June 1999): 814–41.
Allen, Robert S. *His Majesty's Indian Allies: British-Indian Policy in the Defence of Canada, 1774–1815*. Toronto: Dundurn Press, 1992.
Anderson, Benedict. *Imagined Communities: Reflections on the Origins and Spread of Nationalism*. New York: Verso, 1983.
Aron, Stephen. *American Confluence: The Missouri Frontier from Borderland to Border State*. Bloomington: Indiana University Press, 2006.
Balogh, Brian. *A Government out of Sight: The Mystery of National Authority in Nineteenth-Century America*. Cambridge: Cambridge University Press, 2009.
Barker, Rodney. *Political Legitimacy and the State*. Oxford: Clarendon Press, 1990.
Beetham, David. *The Legitimation of Power*. Atlantic Highlands, N.J.: Humanities Press International, 1991.
Bemis, Samuel Flagg. *The Diplomacy of the American Revolution*. Bloomington: Indiana University Press, 1935.
———. *Jay's Treaty: A Study in Commerce and Diplomacy*. New Haven, Conn.: Yale University Press, 1962.
Ben-Atar, Doron. *The Origins of Jeffersonian Commercial Policy and Diplomacy*. New York: St. Martin's Press, 1993.
Bergmann, William. *The American National State and the Early West*. Cambridge: Cambridge University Press, 2012.
Bradburn, Douglas. *The Citizenship Revolution: Politics and the Creation of the American Union, 1774–1804*. Charlottesville: University of Virginia Press, 2009.

Brooks, George E., Jr. *Eurafricans in Western Africa: Commerce, Social Status, Gender, and Religious Observance from the Sixteenth to the Eighteenth Century*. Athens: Ohio University Press, 2003.

Brunsman, Denver. *The Evil Necessity: British Naval Impressment in the Eighteenth-Century Atlantic World*. Charlottesville: University of Virginia Press, 2013.

Burt, Alfred Leroy. *The United States, Great Britain and British North America: From the Revolution to the Establishment of Peace after the War of 1812*. New York: Russell and Russell, 1961.

Burton, Clarence M., et al., eds. *The City of Detroit Michigan, 1701–1922*. 5 vols. Detroit and Chicago: S. J. Clarke, 1922.

Calloway, Colin G. *The American Revolution in Indian Country: Crisis and Diversity in Native American Communities*. Cambridge: Cambridge University Press, 1995.

Campbell, Marjorie Wilkins. *McGillivray: Lord of the Northwest*. Toronto: Clarke, Irwin, 1962.

———. *The North West Company*. New York: St. Martin's Press, 1957.

Cangany, Catherine. *Frontier Seaport: Detroit's Transformation into an Atlantic Entrepôt*. Chicago: University of Chicago Press, 2014.

Cayton, Andrew R. L. "'Separate Interest' and the Nation-State: The Washington Administration and the Origins of Regionalism in the Trans-Appalachian West." *Journal of American History*, 79 (June 1992): 39–67.

Chaudhuri, K. N. *The Trading World of Asia and the English East India Company, 1660–1760*. Cambridge: Cambridge University Press, 1978.

Chaudhuri, Susil. *Trade and Commercial Organization in Bengal, 1650–1720*. Calcutta: Firma K. L. Mukhopadhyay, 1975.

Chew, Richard S. "Certain Victims of an International Contagion: The Panic of 1797 and Hard Times of the Late 1790s in Baltimore." *Journal of the Early Republic*, 25 (Winter 2005): 567–613.

Chittenden, Hiram Martin. *The American Fur Trade of the Far West*. New York: Press of the Pioneers, 1935.

Clarfield, Gerald H. *Timothy Pickering and American Diplomacy, 1795–1800*. Columbia: University of Missouri Press, 1969.

Clarke, John. *Land, Power, and Economics on the Frontier of Upper Canada*. Montreal and Kingston: McGill–Queen's University Press, 2001.

Cogliano, Francis D. *Emperor of Liberty: Thomas Jefferson's Foreign Policy*. New Haven, Conn.: Yale University Press, 2014.

Cohen, Elizabeth F. *Semi-Citizenship in Democratic Politics*. Cambridge: Cambridge University Press, 2009.

Combs, Jerald A. *The Jay Treaty: Political Battleground of the Founding Fathers*. Berkeley: University of California Press, 1970.

Cooper, John. *James McGill of Montreal: Citizen of the Atlantic World*. Ottawa: Borealis Press, 2003.
Creighton, Donald. *The Empire of the St. Lawrence*. Toronto: Macmillan, 1956.
Cruzat, Heloise Hulse. "General Collot's Reconnoitering Trip down the Mississippi and His Arrest in New Orleans, by Order of the Baron de Carondelet, Governor of Louisiana." *Louisiana Historical Quarterly*, 1 (April 1918): 303–26.
Curtin, Philip D. *Cross-Cultural Trade in World History*. Cambridge: Cambridge University Press, 1984.
Davidson, Gordon Charles. *The North West Company*. Berkeley: University of California Press, 1918.
Devine, Heather. *People Who Own Themselves: Aboriginal Ethnogenesis in a Canadian Family, 1660–1900*. Calgary: University of Calgary Press, 2004.
Dowd, Gregory Evans. *A Spirited Resistance: The North American Indian Struggle for Unity, 1745–1815*. Baltimore: Johns Hopkins University Press, 1993.
———. *War under Heaven: Pontiac, the Indian Nations and the British Empire*. Baltimore: Johns Hopkins University Press, 2004.
Downes, Randolph C. *Council Fires on the Upper Ohio*. Pittsburgh: University of Pittsburgh Press, 1969.
Doyle, William. *The Oxford History of the French Revolution*. Oxford: Oxford University Press, 2002.
Edling, Max M. *A Revolution in Favor of Government: Origins of the U.S. Constitution and the Making of the American State*. Oxford: Oxford University Press, 2003.
Eldem, Edhem. "Capitulations and Western Trade." In Suraiya N. Faroqhi, ed., *The Cambridge History of Turkey*, vol. 3, *The Later Ottoman Empire, 1603–1839*. Cambridge: Cambridge University Press, 2006. 283–325.
Eldem, Edhem, Daniel Goffman, and Bruce Masters, eds. *The Ottoman City between East and West: Aleppo, Izmir, and Istanbul*. Cambridge: Cambridge University Press, 1999.
Elkins, Stanley, and Eric McKitrick. *The Age of Federalism: The Early Republic, 1788–1800*. Oxford: Oxford University Press, 1993.
Engelman, Fred L. *The Peace of Christmas Eve*. London: Rupert Hart-Davis, 1962.
Englebert, Robert. "Merchant Representatives and the French River World, 1763–1803." *Michigan Historical Review*, 34 (Spring 2008): 63–82.
Estes, Todd. *The Jay Treaty Debate, Public Opinion, and the Evolution of Early American Political Culture*. Amherst: University of Massachusetts Press, 2006.
Faragher, John Mack. *Daniel Boone: The Life and Legend of an American Pioneer*. New York: Henry Holt, 1992.
Fleming, R. H. "Phyn, Ellice and Company of Schenectady." *Contributions to Canadian Economics*, 4 (1932): 7–41.

Fisher, H. E. S. "Lisbon, Its English Merchant Community, and the Mediterranean in the Eighteenth Century." In P. L. Cottrell and D. H. Aldcroft, eds., *Shipping, Trade and Commerce: Essays in Memory of Ralph David.* Leicester: Leicester University Press, 1981. 23–44.

Foley, William E., and C. David Rice. *The First Chouteaus: River Barons of Early St. Louis.* Urbana: University of Illinois Press, 1982.

Furstenburg, François. "The Significance of the Trans-Appalachian West in Atlantic History." *American Historical Review,* 113 (June 2008): 647–77.

Gates, Lillian F. *Land Policies of Upper Canada.* Toronto: University of Toronto Press, 1968.

Gautham, Rao. *National Duties: Custom Houses and the Making of the American State.* Chicago: University of Chicago Press, 2016.

Gitlin, Jay. *The Bourgeois Frontier: French Towns, French Traders and American Expansion.* New Haven, Conn.: Yale University Press, 2010.

Gould, Eliga H. *Among the Powers of the Earth: The American Revolution and the Making of a New World Empire.* Cambridge, Mass.: Harvard University Press, 2012.

Greenwood, Murray F. *Legacies of Fear: Law and Politics in Quebec in the Era of the French Revolution.* Toronto: University of Toronto Press, 1993.

Griffin, Patrick. *American Leviathan: Empire, Nation, and Revolutionary Frontier.* New York: Hill and Wang, 2007.

Gupta, Ashin Das. *India and the Indian Ocean World: Trade and Politics.* Oxford: Oxford University Press, 2004.

Hämäläinen, Pekka. *The Comanche Empire.* New Haven, Conn.: Yale University Press, 2008.

Hämäläinen, Pekka, and Samuel Truett. "On Borderlands." *Journal of American History,* 98 (September 2011): 338–61.

Hammond, John Craig. *Slavery, Freedom and Expansion in the Early American West.* Charlottesville: University of Virginia Press, 2007.

Harlow, Vincent T. *The Founding of the Second British Empire, 1763–1793.* 2 vols. New York: Longmans, Green, 1952.

Hatter, Lawrence B. A. "The Jay Charter: Rethinking the American National State in the West, 1796–1819." *Diplomatic History,* 37 (September 2013): 693–726.

Hendrickson, David C. *Peace Pact: The Lost World of the American Founding.* Lawrence: University Press of Kansas, 2003.

Herring, George. *From Colony to Superpower: U.S. Foreign Relations since 1776.* Oxford: Oxford University Press, 2008.

Hickey, Donald R. "The Monroe-Pinkney Treaty of 1806: A Reappraisal." *William and Mary Quarterly,* 3rd series, 44 (January 1987): 65–88.

———. *The War of 1812: A Forgotten Conflict*. Urbana: University of Illinois Press, 1989.

Hinderaker, Eric, and Peter C. Mancall. *At the Edge of Empire: The Backcountry in British North America*. Baltimore: Johns Hopkins University Press, 2003.

Hinderaker, Eric. *Elusive Empires: Constructing Colonialism in the Ohio Valley, 1673–1800*. Cambridge: Cambridge University Press, 1999.

Holman, Frederick V. *Dr. John McLoughlin, the Father of Oregon*. Cleveland: Arthur H. Clark, 1907.

Horsman, Reginald. *Expansion and American Indian Policy, 1783–1812*. Norman: University of Oklahoma Press, 1967.

Jasanoff, Maya. *Liberty's Exiles: American Loyalists in the Revolutionary World*. New York: Vintage Books, 2012.

Jennings, Francis. *The Invasion of America: Indians, Colonialism, and the Cant of Conquest*. New York: Norton, 1976.

Johnson, Robert C. *John McLoughlin: Patriarch of the Northwest*. Portland, Ore.: Metropolitan Press, 1935.

Jortner, Adam. *The Gods of Prophetstown: The Battle of Tippecanoe and the Holy War for the American Frontier*. Oxford: Oxford University Press, 2012.

Kastor, Peter J. *The Nation's Crucible: The Louisiana Purchase and the Creation of America*. New Haven, Conn.: Yale University Press, 2004.

Kea, Ray A. *Settlements, Trade, and Polities in the Seventeenth-Century Gold Coast*. Baltimore: Johns Hopkins University Press, 1982.

Kelsay, Isabel Thompson. *Joseph Brant, 1743–1807: Man of Two Worlds*. Syracuse, N.Y.: Syracuse University Press, 1984.

Kettner, James H. *The Development of American Citizenship, 1608–1870*. Chapel Hill: University of North Carolina Press, 1978.

Lavender, David. *The Fist in the Wilderness*. New York: Doubleday, 1964.

Lewis, James E., Jr. *The American Union and the Problem of Neighborhood: The United States and the Collapse of the Spanish Empire, 1783–1829*. Chapel Hill: University of North Carolina Press, 1998.

Mancke, Elizabeth. "Polity Formation and Atlantic Political Narratives." In Nicholas Canny and Philip Morgan, eds. *The Oxford Handbook of the Atlantic World, c. 1450–c. 1850*. Oxford: Oxford University Press, 2011. 382–99.

Mannix, Richard J. "The Embargo: Its Administration, Impact, and Enforcement." Ph.D. diss., New York University, 1975.

Marrero, Karen. "On the Edge of the West: The Roots and Routes of Detroit's Urban Eighteenth Century." In Jay Gitlin, Barbara Berglund, and Adam Arenson, eds. *Frontier Cities: Encounters at the Crossroads of Empire*. Philadelphia: University of Pennsylvania Press, 2013. 67–86.

Masters, Bruce. *The Origins of Western Economic Dominance in the Middle East: Mercantilism and the Islamic Economy in Aleppo, 1600–1750*. New York: New York University Press, 1988.

Mather, James. *Pashas: Traders and Travellers in the Islamic World*. New Haven, Conn.: Yale University Press, 2009.

McCoy, Drew R. *The Elusive Republic: Political Economy in Jeffersonian America*. Chapel Hill: University of North Carolina Press, 1980.

McCusker, John J., and Russell R. Menard. *The Economy of British America, 1607–1789*. Chapel Hill: University of North Carolina Press, 1985.

Morrissey, Robert Michael. *Empire by Collaboration: Indians, Colonists, and Governments in Colonial Illinois Country*. Philadelphia: University of Pennsylvania Press, 2015.

Morrison, Andrew. *The Industries of Cincinnati: Her Relations as a Center of Trade; Manufacturing Establishments and Business Houses*. Cincinnati, 1886.

Murray, Keith. *The Pig War*. Tacoma: Washington State Historical Society, 1968.

Nelson, Larry L. *A Man of Distinction among Them: Alexander McKee and the Ohio Country Frontier, 1754–1799*. Kent, Ohio: Kent State University Press, 1999.

Nelson, Paul David. *General Sir Guy Carleton, Lord Dorchester: Soldier-Statesman of Early British Canada*. London: Associated University Presses, 2000.

Novak, William J. *The People's Welfare: Law and Regulation in Nineteenth-Century America*. Chapel Hill: University of North Carolina Press, 1996.

———. "The Myth of the 'Weak' American State." *American Historical Review*, 113 (June 2008): 752–72.

Onuf, Peter S. "The Expanding Union." In David Thomas Konig, ed. *Devising Liberty: Preserving and Creating Freedom in the New American Republic*. Stanford, Cal.: Stanford University Press, 1995. 50–80.

———. *Jefferson's Empire: The Language of American Nationhood*. Charlottesville: University Press of Virginia, 2000.

———. *The Mind of Thomas Jefferson*. Charlottesville: University of Virginia Press, 2007.

———. *Statehood and Union: A History of the Northwest Ordinance*. Bloomington: Indiana University Press, 1987.

Onuf, Peter, and Nicholas Onuf. *Federal Union, Modern World: The Law of Nations in an Age of Revolutions, 1776–1814*. Madison, Wis.: Madison House, 1993.

O'Shaughnessy, Andrew Jackson. *An Empire Divided: The American Revolution and the British Caribbean*. Philadelphia: University of Pennsylvania Press, 2000.

Ouellet, Fernand. *Economic and Social History of Quebec, 1760–1850*. Ottawa: Institute of Canadian Studies, Carleton University, 1967.

Pasley, Jeffrey L. *The First Presidential Contest: 1796 and the Founding of American Democracy*. Lawrence: University Press of Kansas, 2013.

Pearce, Adrian J. *British Trade with Spanish America, 1763–1808*. Liverpool: Liverpool University Press, 2007.

Perkins, Bradford. *Castlereagh and Adams: England and the United States, 1812–1823*. Berkeley: University of California Press, 1964.

———. *The Creation of a Republican Empire, 1776–1865*. Cambridge: Cambridge University Press, 1993.

———. *The First Rapprochement: England and the United States, 1795–1805*. Berkeley: University of California Press, 1967.

———. *Prologue to War: England and the United States, 1805–1812*. Berkeley: University of California Press, 1967.

Pocock, J. G. A. "States, Republics, and Empires: The American Founding in Early Modern Perspective." In Terence Ball and J. G. A. Pocock, eds. *Conceptual Change and the Constitution*. Lawrence: University Press of Kansas, 1988. 55–77.

Podruchny, Carolyn. *Making the Voyageur World: Travelers and Traders in the North American Fur Trade*. Lincoln: University of Nebraska Press, 2006.

Porter, Kenneth Wiggins. *John Jacob Astor: Business Man*. 2 vols. Cambridge, Mass.: Harvard University Press, 1931.

Richter, Daniel K. *The Ordeal of the Longhouse: The Peoples of the Iroquois League in the Era of European Colonization*. Chapel Hill: University of North Carolina Press, 1992.

Risjord, Norman K. "1812: Conservatives, War Hawks and the Nation's Honor." *William and Mary Quarterly*, 3rd series, 18 (April 1961): 196–210.

Ritcheson, Charles R. *Aftermath of Revolution: British Policy towards the United States, 1783–1795*. Dallas: Southern Methodist University Press, 1969.

———. "The Earl of Shelburne and Peace with America, 1782–1783: Vision and Reality." *International History Review*, 5 (August 1983): 322–45.

Rockwell, Stephen J. *Indian Affairs and the Administrative State in the Nineteenth Century*. Cambridge: Cambridge University Press, 2010.

Rohrbough, Malcolm J. *The Land Office Business: The Settlement and Administration of American Public Lands, 1789–1837*. Oxford: Oxford University Press, 1968.

———. *Trans-Appalachian Frontier: People, Societies, and Institutions, 1775–1850*. Bloomington: Indiana University Press, 2008.

Ronda, James P. *Astoria and Empire*. Lincoln: University of Nebraska Press, 1990.

Rubin, Israel Ira. "New York State and the Long Embargo." Ph.D. diss., New York University, 1962.

Sadosky, Leonard J. *Revolutionary Negotiations: Indians, Empires, and Diplomats in the Founding of America*. Charlottesville: University of Virginia Press, 2009.

Sahlins, Peter. *The Making of France and Spain in the Pyrenees*. Berkeley: University of California Press, 1989.

Saler, Bethel. *The Settlers' Empire: Colonialism and State Formation in America's Old Northwest.* Philadelphia: University of Pennsylvania Press, 2015.

Scully, Eileen P. *Bargaining with the State from Afar: American Citizenship in Treaty Port China, 1844–1942.* New York: Columbia University Press, 2001.

Sexton, Jay. *The Monroe Doctrine: Empire and Nation in Nineteenth-Century America.* New York: Hill and Wang, 2001.

Shaw, L. M. E. *Trade, Inquisition and the English Nation in Portugal, 1650–1690.* Aldershot, Eng.: Carcarnet Press, 1989.

Sheehan, Bernard W. *Seeds of Extinction: Jeffersonian Philanthropy and the American Indian.* Chapel Hill: University of North Carolina Press, 1973.

Sleeper-Smith, Susan. *Indian Women and French Men: Rethinking Cultural Encounter on the Great Lakes.* Amherst: University of Massachusetts Press, 2001.

Smith, Rogers M. *Civic Ideals: Conflicting Visions of Citizenship in U.S. History.* New Haven, Conn.: Yale University Press, 1997.

Spivak, Burton. *Jefferson's English Crisis: Commerce, Embargo, and the Republican Revolution.* Charlottesville: University Press of Virginia, 1988.

Stagg, J. C. A. *Mr. Madison's War: Politics, Diplomacy, and Warfare in the Early American Republic, 1783–1830.* Princeton, N.J.: Princeton University Press, 1983.

Sugden, John. *Blue Jacket: Warrior of the Shawnees.* Lincoln: University of Nebraska Press, 2000.

Tanner, Helen Hornbeck, ed. *Atlas of Great Lakes Indian History.* Norman: University of Oklahoma Press, 1987.

Taylor, Alan. *The Civil War of 1812: American Citizens, British Subjects, Irish Rebels and Indian Allies.* New York: Vintage Books, 2010.

———. *The Divided Ground: Indians, Settlers, and the Northern Borderland of the American Revolution.* New York: Knopf, 2006.

Tohill, Louis Arthur. "Robert Dickson, British Fur Traders on the Upper Mississippi: A Story of Trade, War, and Diplomacy." Ph.D. diss., University of Minnesota, 1926.

Torpey, John. *The Invention of the Passport: Surveillance, Citizenship, and the State.* Cambridge: Cambridge University Press, 2000.

Tucker, Robert W., and David C. Hendrickson. *Empire of Liberty: The Statecraft of Thomas Jefferson.* Oxford: Oxford University Press, 1990.

Updyke, Frank A. *The Diplomacy of the War of 1812.* Baltimore: Johns Hopkins University Press, 1965.

Van Den Boogert, Maurits H. *The Capitulations and the Ottoman Legal System: Qadis, Consuls and Berathes in the 18th Century.* Leiden: Brill, 2005.

Wallace, Anthony F. C. *Jefferson and the Indians: The Tragic Fate of the First Americans.* Cambridge, Mass.: Belknap Press of Harvard University Press, 1999.

Weeks, William Earl. *The New Cambridge History of American Foreign Relations*, vol. 1, *Dimensions of the Early American Empire, 1754–1865*. Cambridge: Cambridge University Press, 2013.

White, Richard. *The Middle Ground: Indians, Empires, and Republics in the Great Lakes Region, 1650–1815*. Cambridge: Cambridge University Press, 1991.

Widder, Keith R. "After the Conquest: Michilimackinac, a Borderlands in Transition, 1760–63." *Michigan Historical Review*, 34 (Spring 2008): 43–61.

Willmott, Cory. "From Stroud to Strouds: The Hidden History of a British Fur Trade Textile." *Textile History*, 36 (November 2005): 196–234.

Wilson, Bruce G. *The Enterprises of Robert Hamilton: A Study in Wealth and Influence in Early Upper Canada, 1776–1812*. Ottawa: Carleton Press, 1983.

Wood, Gordon S. *Empire of Liberty: A History of the Early American Republic, 1789–1815*. Oxford: Oxford University Press, 2009.

Wright, J. Leitch. *Britain and the American Frontier, 1783–1815*. Athens: Georgia University Press, 1975.

Zornow, William Frank. "The Tariff Policies of Virginia, 1775–1789." *Virginia Magazine of History and Biography*, 62 (July 1954): 306–19.

INDEX

Page numbers in italics refer to illustrations.

Abbott, James, 83
Abbott, Samuel, 158–59
Adams, John, 32, 35–38, 187
Adams, John Quincy, 179
Adams, William, 178, 187–88
Adet, Pierre, 93
Aird, James, 118–19, 141–42, 146, 157, 202
American Fur Company, 135, 137, 138–40, 143–47, 152, 155, 159, 161, 198, 201
American imperialism, 9–10, 29, 42–44, 49–50, 53–54, 58, 59, 65, 78–79, 91–92, 163–64, 181; Astor and, 137, 146; resistance to, 121–22, 134, 137, 145, 178; Treaty of Ghent and, 176–78, 185, 191, 202; after War of 1812, 192
American Indians, 1, 4, 10, 13, 15, 17–18, 29; Astor and, 137; dispossession of, 42–44, 54, 58, 117, 121, 176; fear and hatred of, 165, 167, 169; gift exchange obligations, 28–29, 54; Indian state proposals, 13, 48–49, 57, 58–59, 164, 175–82; raids and battles, 43–44, 47–49, 53–55, 64–66, 160, 166–67; Treaty of Ghent aftermath, 185, 191, 193–96; Treaty of Greenville and, 92; Treaty of Paris and, 39–42; U.S. Indian factory system, 91–92, 118, 120, 139
American nationhood, 2, 17, 18, 32, 37–38, 46, 50, 65, 72, 74, 81–82, 99, 138, 162, 165, 180, 189
American West, concerns for, 5, 7, 8, 10, 12, 42, 53, 134
Anderson, John, 95

Anderson, Thomas, 192
Armstrong, John, Jr., 153
Askin, Charles, 159, 166–67
Askin, John, 26, 27–28, 57, 67, *80*, 82–83, 89, 95–96, 100, 102, 109, 123–24, 150–51, 168–69
Askin, John, Jr., 26, 64, 150–51, 158–59, 166
Astor, George, 171
Astor, John Jacob, 98, 135–62, *136*, 165, 168, 170–72, 174, 197–98
Atcheson, Nathaniel, 135–36, 137–38, 147, 153, 157–58, 175–77
Auckland, Baron of (William Eden), 33, 124–28
Audrain, Peter, 82–83, 87–89, 90, 95, 100, 102, 111
Aurora General Advertiser, 164–66

Bainbridge, John, 175
Baker, Anthony St. John, 186, 190, 193
Barron, James, 130
Barthe, Jean Baptiste, 26
Barthe, Marie Archange, 26
Bates, Frederick, 144
Bathurst, Henry, 176–77, 181–84, 186
Battle of Fallen Timbers, 49, 50, 65, 68, 76–77
Battle of Lake Erie, 171
Battle of Moraviantown, 171
Battle of New Orleans, 190
Battle of Plattsburgh, 184
Battle of Queenston Heights, 167–68, 170

Battle of the Wabash, 47, 59
Battle of Tippecanoe, 160
Battle of Trafalgar, 121
Bayard, Jonathan, 179
Beaufait, Louis, 88
Beaver Club, 19–20, 143; membership medal, 19, *20*
Beckwith, George, 56
Belangé, Philip, 89
Bentzon, Adrian, 157
Berczy, William, *23*
Berkeley, George, 130
Berthelot, Jean Baptiste, 159, 194
Black, William, 172–73
Black Hawk, 193–94
Bleakley, John, 145
Blount, William, 85–86
Blue Jacket, 47, 54–55, 59–61, 92
Boilvin, Nicholas, 144, 235n43
Bond, Phineas, 76, 91, 108, 112
Boudinot, Elias, 37
Bowyer, John, 199–201
Brant, Joseph (Thayendanega), 18, 41–43, 48, 59–62, 92–93
Breckinridge, John, 122
Brevoort, Henry, 158
Brickwood, John, 96, 127
British-American commercial convention (1815), 11, 13, 163, 187–90, 192
British imperialism, 48–52, 55–64, 66, 75–77, 163–64, 177
British West Indies, 17, 18, 21, 35, 37, 49, 50, 52, 66, 72, 111, 124, 175, 188, 189
Brock, Isaac, 161, 167–69
Brush, Elijah, 168–69
Buchanan, James, 204
Buckongahelas, 47, 62
Butler, Anthony, 193
Butler, John, 61

Cadillac, Antoine de La Mothe, 26, 78
Caldwell, Fraser & Company, 110
Caldwell, William, 193
Calhoun, John C., 200–201
Campbell, John, 146
Campbell, William, 64–65
Canning, George, 131, 141, 143, 149
Carp, Mr. (agent of Astor), 161
Cartwright, Richard, 25, 96
Cass, Lewis, 194–95, 197, 200–201
Castlereagh, Viscount (Robert Stewart), 178, 180–81, 187, 193
Cavendish-Bentinck, William, 34
Chaboillez, Charles, 19, 23
Chalbert Joncaire, Philippe-Thomas, 84–85, 99
Chambers, Talbott, 195–96
Chapoton, Angélique, 26
Chisholm, John, 86
Chouteau, Auguste, 114, 116, 150
Chouteau, Pierre, 116
Cissne, Joseph, 99
citizenship, 4, 10, 50, 69–71, 99–103, 118–19, 210n12; in Oregon, 205–6; after War of 1812, 199–202
citizens of convenience status, 4, 10, 11–12, 50, 79, 102, 103, 106, 114, 118, 169; after War of 1812, 199, 202, 206
Clark, George Rogers, 43
Clark, Thomas, 161
Clark, William, 144, 146
Clay, Henry, 179, 187–88
Clinton, DeWitt, 138–39
Clinton, George, 15, 139–40
Cohen, Elizabeth F., 10, 71, 223n6
Columbia River, 137–39, 146, 148, 156–58, 172, 187, 204–5
Congress of Vienna, 163, 180, 184, 190
Connor, John, 96
Constitution, U.S., 47, 52–54, 89

Cooper, William, 75
Cornplanter, 43
Craig, Francis, 132–33
Craig, James, 151, 160
"creole corridor," 8, 115
Crooks, Ramsey, 170–72, 174, 197
Curry, George L., 206
Curry, Peter, 87–88
Customs Act, 104, 108–11
customs agents, 108, 110–12, 114, 120, 122–25, 130, 149, 154–55, 159, 173, 177; Lees's seizure, 131–33, 175; War of 1812, actions after, 192, 195–97

Dallas, James, 195
Day, John, 171
Dearborn, Henry, 117, 119, 140
Declaration of Independence, 3, 72
Deer, The, 55
Desrivières, François-Amable, 22
Desrivières, Marie-Charlotte, 22
Detroit, 26–29, 82–89, 93–95, 101–3, 109, 224n12; occupation of, 78–82, *80*, 85–87, 102; War of 1812 and, 166–68, 170–71
diasporic communities, 6, 79, 211n20; commercial privileges of, 5–6, 11, 35, 70–71, 79
Dickson, Robert, 101, 118–19, 143–44, 146–47, 159, 164–65, 168, 192–93, 202
Dickson, Thomas, 132, 170
Dolson, Mathew, 83–84
Donation Land Claim Act, 203, 206
Dorchester, Lord (Guy Carleton), 51–52, 55–57, 63–64, 66, 75–77, 91
Drummond, Gordon, 185–87, 193
Drummond Island, 195, 196
Duane, William, 164–65
Duncan, David, 104–5, 111–14, 120, 122–23, 165, 207

Dundas, Henry, 57, 64
Dunn, Thomas, 119, 130

Edling, Max, 53
Edwards, Ninian, 199
Ellice, Alexander, 21
Ellice, Edward, 176–77, 188
Ellice, Robert, 21
Elliott, Matthew, 42, 62, 160, 164–65
Embargo Acts, 12, 108, 131, 135, 138, 141–43, 147, 154–55
England, Richard, 82
English fur trade, 21, 75
Equshaway, 59
Ermatinger, Charles Oakes, 151
Ernest, Matthew, 101, 111–12, 122
Erskine, David, 128–29, 132–33, 141–43
Essex decision, 121, 124, 129
European Republic, 4–5

Fearson, John, 83
Forsyth, John, 21
Forsyth, Richardson & Company, 21, 96, 104, 108, 112, 128, 153, 156, 194, 197
Fort Erie, 25
Fort Niagara, 15, 17, 18, 25, 131, 161, 183
Fort Oswego, 15–16, 25
Fort St. Joseph. *See* St. Joseph's Island
Fort William, 104, 113, 123, 151, 154, 228n3
Foster, John Augustus, 160
Fox, Charles James, 34–35, 36–37, 124, 127
Franco-American Treaty, 174
Franklin, Benjamin, 34, 35–38, 187
Fraser, John, 23–24
French Revolution and Jacobinism, 27, 49, 65, 67, 73, 74
Frobisher, Benjamin, 45

Frobisher, Joseph, 51, 56
Furstenburg, François, 10

Gallatin, Albert, 74, 101, 105, 109–12, 120, 123, 133; Astor and, 135, 138, 142, 143–44, 152, 160–61, 165; peace negotiations and, 179, 187–88, 190
Gambier, James, 178
Genet, Edmond, 66
George III, 1, 19, 34, 42
Gillespie, George, 116, 119–20, 159, 231n42
Glaize, the, 28, 59, 60, 220n41
Goodhue, Benjamin, 74–75
Gore, Francis, 132, 154
Gouin, Thérèse, 26
Goulburn, Henry, 178, 181–83, 187–88, 194
Gould, Eliga H., 10
Grand Portage, 30, 45, 96, 104, 110, 230n30
Green Bay, 30, 101, 159, 192–94, 199–201
Grenville, William, 49, 56, 67–72, 86, 124, 129
Grignon, Louis, and family, 192, 197, 199–200, 201
Grotius, Hugo, 6

Haldimand, Frederick, 15, 17, 38–39, 41, 46, 186
Hallowell, William, 98
Hamilton, Alexander, 58, 68
Hamilton, Robert, 25, 48, 96–98, 131–32, 154
Hammond, George, 57–58, 68
Hamtramck, John Francis, 82, 92
Hanks, Porter, 166
Harmar, Josiah, 47, 48, 55–56
Harrison, William Henry, 101, 116, 120–21, 137, 145, 146, 160, 171

Hartley, David, 34–38
Henry, Alexander, 97, 123–24, 150, 151–52
Heward, Hugh, 101
Hill, Aaron, 39–40, 43
Hill, Donald, *16*
Hoffman, George, 123, 141–42, 146
Holland, Baron (Henry Vassal-Fox), 124–28
Holman, Frederick V., 203–4
Holmes, Andrew, 170
Hopkins, Frances Anne, *132*
Howick, Viscount (Charles Grey), 127–28
Hudson's Bay Company, 30, 129–30, *132*, 149, 171, 203–4, 206
Hull, William, 137, 167–69
Humphreys, Salusbury, 130, 134
Hunot, Gabriel, 28, 83
Hunt, William Price, 156–57
Hunter, Peter, 104, 110
Huntington, Benjamin, 99

immigration and naturalization laws, 73, 79, 100, 118–19
impressment of American sailors, 12, 112, 121, 129, 131, 178, 188
Indian Intercourse Act, 91, 106
Inglis, Ellices & Company, 194
Inglis, John, 175, 176–77

Jackson, Andrew, 190, 191
Jackson, Francis James, 147–50
Jacobs, George, 109
James and Andrew McGill & Company, 96, 123, 128
Jasanoff, Maya, 3
Jay, John, 35–38, 49, 65–71, 75, 187
Jay Treaty, 9, 11–13, 49–50, 65–77, 79, 83, 89–90, 92–103, 105–8, 112–15, 118–22,

131, 148–49, 173, 178, 190, 205, 213n34; commercial clauses of, 107, 182; dissolution of, 148, 151, 166, 185, 187; operation as a charter of rights, 12, 87, 90; second article of, 199–201; third article of, 70, 76, 90–91, 105, 108, 110, 126–27, 129, 189; western provisions of, 74–76, 81, 86, 94, 101, 106, 118, 122, 135–37
Jefferson, Thomas, 3, 5, 6–7, 8–9, 66, 72, 101–2, 134, 138, 144, 154–55; Astor and, 139–41, 159; on French Catholics, 115; Indian policies, 91–92, 118, 120, 145; Jay Treaty opposition, 12, 105–6, 129–30
Jenkinson, Robert, 52
Jennings, Francis, 40
Johnny, Captain, 29, 92
Johnson, John, 40, 41, 55–56
Johnson, William, 39, 41, 59
Johnston, John, 101
Jortner, Adam, 145

Kaministiquia. *See* Fort William
Kastor, Peter, 10–11
Knox, Henry, 42, 54, 58, 60
Knox, William, 36–37

Labelle, Joseph, 113
Laclède Liguest, Pierre, 114–15
Lafond, Antoine, 96
Laurens, Henry, 34, 36
Lawe, John, 192, 199–200
Lees, John, 131–33
Le Gris, 55
Leith, James, 90
Leith, Shepherd & Duff, 90
Leonard, Nathaniel, 131–32
Leopard-Chesapeake affair, 130–31, 133–34, 137, 149

Levadoux, Michael, 89
Lewis, Meriwether, 140, 144
Lincoln, Benjamin, 62
liquor trade, 109
Lisa, Manuel, 150
Liston, Robert, 86, 93–95
Little Corbeau, 195
Little Turtle, 47, 55, 145
Liverpool, Earl of (Robert Jenkinson), 157, 175, 181, 183–84
Loch Ness, 30
Logan, Benjamin, 44
Lorimer, Louis, 28
Louisiana Purchase, 106, 116–17, 125, 137
Lower Canada. *See* Quebec, Province of

Mabane, Adam, 45
Mackenzie, Donald, 152, 172
Mackintosh, Angus, 96, 102, 109
Maclean, Allan, 15–17, 39, 46
Maçon, Joseph, 198
Macon's Bill No. 2, 152–53
Madison, James, 5, 6–7, 8–9, 138; Jay Treaty opposition, 12, 74, 105–6, 112, 120–22, 126, 128–30; Michilimackinac Company conflict, 133; as president, 141, 147–53, 155, 158–60; War of 1812 and, 12–13, 167
Mahoney, Cornelius, 87–88
Mancke, Elizabeth, 6
Manette, 26, 166
May, James, 99
McDonald, John, 89–90, 92–93
McDonnell, James, 186, 193–94, 196
McDougal, George, 89–90, 99
McDougall, Duncan, 152, 172
McGill, James, 16, *20*, 22–24, *23*, 51, 56–57, 67, 96, 127–28, 153
McGill & Company, James and Andrew, 96, 123, 128

McGillivray, William, 24, 98, 105, 123; Astor and, 150–51, 153–55, 158, 188; Treaty of Ghent defiance, 185–86; William and Duncan McGillivray & Company, 113, 128, 153
McHenry, James, 93–95
McKay, Alexander, 152
McKay, William, 195
McKee, Alexander, 42, 59–61, 63–64, 75
McLoughlin, John, 203–4, 206
McNiff, Patrick, 82, 84, 86–87, 101–2, 109, 111
McTavish, Frobisher & Company, 109–10
McTavish, McGillivrays & Company, 153–54, 156, 197, 236n64
McTavish, Simon, 23–24, 27, 96, 104–5
Meigs, Return Jonathan, 101
Meldrum, George, 26, 28, 89
mercantilism, 33, 211n19
Merry, Anthony, 112–13, 120–24
Miami Company, 28, 29
Michilimackinac, 29–30, 45, 113, 117, 123, 141, 146, 166, 168, 172, 185–87, 195–97; removal of fortifications to Mackinac Island, 29
Michilimackinac Company, 108, 128, 131–32, 142, 175; Astor and, 135, 137, 139, 141, 143–45, 147, 150–53, 156
Milnes, Robert, 119
Mississippi River, 29, 30, 36, 45, 52, 68, 75, 114, 115, 148
Missouri River, 106, 114–20, 122, 129, 144, 149, 151, 157, 173, 197
Mitchell, David, 196
Mitchell, Elizabeth, 196
Mitchell, Samuel L., 159
Monroe, James, 107, 124, 126–29, 131, 193–94, 198; Treaty of Ghent and, 179, 186, 190

Monroe-Pinckney Treaty, 124–31
Montreal, characteristics of, 21–24
Montreal fur trade: border concerns of, 1, 24–25, 29–31, 41, 45, 48, 51, 55, 56–58, 123, 135, 150, 155, 173–77; British market for, 20–21, 24, 139, 142; "Canada merchants" designation, 8; diplomatic activities, 11, 28–29; estimated value of, 24, 96, 111–12, 119, 122, 139, 142, 177, 227n69; European conflicts and, 123–24; importance of, 7–9; Jay Treaty and, 12–13, 95–98, 123–24, 126; lack of American competition, 97–98, 108–9, 115; manpower employed in, 24, 122, 151; map of, 2; merchants delegation to London (1806), 124–30; peltry returns of, 24, 128, 155, 142; trade goods employed in, 27–28; Treaty of Paris and, 20–21; U.S. impediments to, 113–14, 117, 122, 133–34, 138, 150, 154–55, 176, 194; value of trade goods employed in, 24; War of 1812 and, 169–72
Montreal-Michilimackinac Company, 153, 155
Morning Chronicle, 163–64, 166
Mulgrave, Earl of (Henry Phipps), 122

Nanaume, 76–77
Napoleon I, 123–24, 153, 174, 182, 187
nationality: defined, 4, 70, 223n6; movement and, 3, 50, 70, 79, 107. *See also* citizenship
Native Americans. *See* American Indians
Naturalization Acts, 200–202
Navigation Acts, 5, 17, 33, 36, 70
Nelson, Jonathan, 101
New North West Company. *See* XY Company

New Orleans, 8, 9, 22, 49, 86, 114, 115
Niagara River, 43, 96, 108, 113, 131–34, 135, 143, 151, 155, 175, 183
Nonintercourse Acts, 12, 108, 138, 142–43, 147–52, 154–56, 158–60
North, Frederick, 36–37
North West Company, 8, 27, 28, 30, 96, 98, 104–5, 109, 113–14, 120, 122–23, 135, 139, 154, 156–58; during War of 1812 and after, 165, 169–72, 174, 186, 197
Northwest Ordinance, 53–54, 98

Ohio River Valley, 22, 24, 43, 47, 77
Oliver, Frederick, 174
"Oregon Question," 203–6, 205
Orléans, duc d' (Louis Philippe), 86
Osborne, Francis, 38
Oswald, Richard, 1–3, 15, 32–34, 37, 56, 148, 168, 174, 177

Pacific Fur Company, 152, 156
Packenham, Richard, 204
Park, William, 26, 28
Parker, Gerrard, Ogilvy & Company, 104, 128, 153
Patterson, Charles, 21
Pattinson and McGregor, 109
Perceval, Spencer, 143, 157
Perry, Oliver Hazard, 171
Phyn, James, 21
Phyn, Ellice & Inglis Company, 21, 25, 27–28, 96
Pickering, Timothy, 62, 76, 91, 94–95
Pinkney, William, 107, 124, 126–29, 131, 141, 149
Pitt, William, 38, 51, 57, 112, 124
Polk, James K., 204
Pontiac's War, 41
Porlier, Jacques, 145, 194, 197, 199–202, 243n43

Porteous, John, 21
Pothier, Toussaint, 159
Pownall, John, 31, 33
Prairie du Chien, 30, 101, 115, 146, 193
Prevost, George, 170–71, 173, 176, 184, 186, 188, 192–93
Proclamation of Neutrality, 66
Puthuff, William H., 195–200, 207

Quebec Act, 56
Quebec, Province of, 1, 2, 8, 21–22, 25, 43, 52, 56, 180, 203; ethnic divisions in, 22, 27, 30, 63; political division into Upper and Lower Canada, 27, 50
Queenston, 110, 131, 159, 161. *See also* Battle of Queenston Heights

Randolph, Beverly, 62
Reaumé, Alexis Luc, 190
Reaumé, Charles, 101
Red Jacket, 59–60
Red Pole, 59–61, 92
Richardson, John, 21, 51, 56; Astor and, 150–51, 153–55, 158, 160–61; Treaty of Ghent defiance, 185–86
Roberts, Charles, 166
Robertson, William, 57
Robinson, Frederick, 187–89
Rocheblave, Pierre, 120, 197
Rodney, Caesar, 123
Ronda, James P., 234n8, 234n11
Ross, John, 15
Rule of 1756, 143
Russell, Jonathan, 179
Russell, Peter, 93–94, 96
Russian American Company, 157

Sadosky, Leonard J., 10
Sandwich, 102, 109, 154, 167, 169, 193, 229n19

Sargent, Winthrop, 81, 83–84, 88–90, 93, 95, 100
Schieffelin, Jonathan, 99–101
Schuyler, Philip, 15, 40, 42
Selkirk, Earl of (Thomas Douglas), 197
separatist movements, 51–52, 78–79, 85–86
Sharp, George, 82; petition, 82–84, 85–86, 99–101
Shays' Rebellion, 51, 52
Sheffield, Lord (John Baker-Holroyd), 33, 36, 51–52
Shelburne, Lord (William Petty), 1–3, 15, 20, 31–34
Shetoon, 160
Simcoe, John Graves, 48, 50–51, 56–57, 58–63, 82, 175
Smith, Robert, 147–49
Smith, Rogers M., 210n12
South West Company, 138, 155–59, 170–71, 174, 198
Spanish American revolutions, 163
St. Clair, Arthur, 47–48, 54, 56, 115
St. Joseph's Island, 113, 150–51, 158, 160, 161, 166, 170, 172
St. Lawrence River, 7, 19, 24–25, 36, 45, 67, 97, 113, 154, 172
St. Louis, 114–16, 118–19, 144–45, 230n35; occupation of, 106, 116–17
St. Louis Missouri Fur Company, 150
Steele, John, 110
Steuben, Friedrich Wilhelm von, 17
Stevenson, Charles, 57
Stewart, Adam, 200
Stickney, Benjamin, 160, 194–95
Stoddard, Amos, 114
Strong, David, 88
Stuart, Gilbert, *136*
Stuart, Robert, 198, 201–2

Sugden, John, 58
Sydney, Baron (Thomas Townshend), 51
Symmes, John Cleves, 102

Taylor, Alan, 40, 106, 162, 164–65, 169
Tecumseh, 59, 77, 145, 167, 171
Tenskwatawa, 59, 77, 121, 137, 145
The Deer, 55
Thornton, Edward, 104–5
Thurston, Samuel R., 203–4, 206
Todd, Andrew, 116
Todd, Isaac, 15–17, *16*, 21, 22–23, 57, 67, 95
Todd, McGill & Company, 22, 27–28, 96, 116. *See also* James and Andrew McGill & Company
Torpey, John, 3
Townshend, Thomas, 209n1
Treaties of Fort Harmar, 54–55
Treaty of Amity, Commerce, and Navigation (1795). *See* Jay Treaty
Treaty of Amity, Commerce, and Navigation (1806). *See* Monroe-Pinckney Treaty
Treaty of Cession, 115
Treaty of Fort McIntosh, 43
Treaty of Fort Stanwix, 39, 40–42, 44, 61
Treaty of Fort Wayne, 121, 145
Treaty of Ghent, 11, 13, 163, 165–66, 176–92
Treaty of Greenville, 49–50, 65, 75–76, 91–92, 121, 176, 180
Treaty of Paris (1763), 22, 115
Treaty of Paris (1783–84), 1, 11, 16–17, 20–21, 32, 38, 48, 50, 51, 56, 68, 75, 148, 168, 173–75, 194, 209n1
Treaty of San Lorenzo (Pinckney's Treaty), 49

U.S. Constitution, 47, 52–54, 89

Van Resselaer, Stephen, 168
Vattel, Emer de, 71
Vigo, Francis, 28
Vosburgh, James, 161
voyageurs, 24, 30, *132,* 198–99

Wabasha, 195
Wallace, William H., 198
War of 1812, 3, 12–13, 59, 77, 160–73, 190; peace negotiations, 176–85
Washington, George, 42, 49, 52–53, 54, 57–58, 66, 71, 75, 85
Wayne, Anthony, 49, 60, 64–65, 75, 77, 85, 92, 194

Weld, Isaac, 19, 22, 25
Wellesley, Lord (Richard Colley), 149, 157
Wellington, Duke of (Arthur Wellesley), 184
White Hair, 116
Wilkinson, James, 78, 81, 85–87, 89–90, 92–95, 100–101; as governor, 106, 114, 117–22, 141; War of 1812 and, 171–72
William and Duncan McGillivray & Company, 113, 128, 153
Wirt, William, 200–201
Woodbridge, William, 200–201

XY Company, 27, 96, 104–5

EARLY AMERICAN HISTORIES

Douglas Bradburn and John C. Coombs, editors
Early Modern Virginia: Reconsidering the Old Dominion

Denver Brunsman
The Evil Necessity: British Naval Impressment in the Eighteenth-Century Atlantic World

Jack P. Greene
Creating the British Atlantic: Essays on Transplantation, Adaptation, and Continuity

James Corbett David
Dunmore's New World: The Extraordinary Life of a Royal Governor in Revolutionary America—with Jacobites, Counterfeiters, Land Schemes, Shipwrecks, Scalping, Indian Politics, Runaway Slaves, and Two Illegal Royal Weddings

Turk McCleskey
The Road to Black Ned's Forge: A Story of Race, Sex, and Trade on the Colonial American Frontier

Antoinette Sutto
Loyal Protestants and Dangerous Papists: Maryland and the Politics of Religion in the English Atlantic, 1630–1690

Jack P. Greene
Settler Jamaica in the 1750s: A Social Portrait

Warren M. Billings and Brent Tarter, editors
"Esteemed Bookes of Lawe" and the Legal Culture of Early Virginia

Lawrence B. A. Hatter
Citizens of Convenience: The Imperial Origins of American Nationhood on the U.S.-Canadian Border

www.ingramcontent.com/pod-product-compliance
Lightning Source LLC
Chambersburg PA
CBHW021341230426
43666CB00006B/369